WHEN RACE BECOMES REAL

WHEN RACE BECOMES REAL

*Black and
White Writers
Confront
Their Personal
Histories*

Edited by Bernestine Singley
Epilogue by Derrick Bell

Lawrence Hill Books

Library of Congress Cataloging-in-Publication Data

When race becomes real : black and white writers confront their personal histories / edited by Bernestine Singley ; epilogue by Derrick Bell.—1st ed.

    p. cm.

Includes bibliographical references.

ISBN 1-55652-448-X (hard : alk. paper)

1. United States—Race relations—Anecdotes.   2. Racism—United States—Anecdotes.   3. African American authors—Biography—Anecdotes.   4. African Americans—Race identity—Anecdotes.   5. African Americans—Social conditions—Anecdotes.   6. Authors, American—Biography—Anecdotes.   7. Whites—Race identity—United States—Anecdotes.   8. Whites—United States—Social conditions—Anecdotes.   I. Singley, Bernestine.   II. Bell, Derrick A.

E185.615 S566 2002

2002002894

Jacket and interior design: Rattray Design

© 2002 by Bernestine Singley
First edition
Published by Lawrence Hill Books
an imprint of Chicago Review Press, Incorporated
814 North Franklin Street
Chicago, Illinois 60610
1-55652-448-X

Printed in the United States of America
5 4 3 2 1

Odessa Roberts Singley and
Walter O. Weyrauch, this one is for you.

)

CONTENTS

Introduction by Bernestine Singley   xi

I. GENESIS   1

Jim Schutze, *Race Story*   3
Leonard Pitts, Jr., *Crazy Sometimes*   21
Robert Coles, *Experiences and Memories*   29
Les Payne, *The Night I Stopped Being a Negro*   37
John Seigenthaler, Sr., *Son of the South*   51
Kimberly Springer, *Talking White*   71
Natalie Angier, *Central Park Samaritan*   79
Lucy Gibson, *It All Started with My Parents*   87

II. FEAR AND LONGING   99

Julianne Malveaux, *Race, Rage, and the Ace of Spades*   101
David Bradley, *To Make Them Stand in Fear*   111
Theresa M. Towner, *Passing*   139
Robert Jensen, *Black and White*   143
Joycelyn K. Moody, *For Colored Girls Who Have Resisted
    Homogenization When the Rainbow Ain't Enough*   159
Patricia J. Williams, *Anatomy of a Fairy Princess*   173
Kalamu ya Salaam, *A Rambling Response to the Play
    Marie Christine*   183
Shawn E. Rhea, *Black, White, and Seeing Red All Over*   193
Ira J. Hadnot, *Race Fatigue*   207

III. Exodus 213

Beverly Daniel Tatum, *Choosing to Be Black: The Ultimate White Privilege?* 215

Tim Wise, *White Like Me: Race and Identity Through Majority Eyes* 225

Colleen J. McElroy, *Traveling with White People* 241

Kiini Ibura Salaam, *Race: A Discussion in Ten Parts, Plus a Few Moments of Unsubstantiated Theory and One Inarguable Fact* 253

Touré, *A Funky Fresh Talented Tenth* 269

Lisa Dodson and Odessa Dorian Cole, *On* Acting *White: Mother-Daughter Talk* 273

Susan Straight, *Country Music* 283

Noel Ignatiev, *One Summer Evening* 291

Carlton Winfrey, *Spelling Lesson* 303

Bernestine Singley, *Jasper, Texas Elegy* 307

Michael Patrick MacDonald, *All Souls: Civil Rights From Southie to Soweto and Back* 317

Hanna Griffiths, *Pictures in Black and White* 323

Epilogue by Derrick Bell 327

ACKNOWLEDGMENTS

I AM ETERNALLY indebted to Gary Reaves, the extraordinary blessing who is my husband and without whom neither the luxury of my writing life nor my sanity would be likely; to Tina Wallace, my sister, for love, courage, and perseverance; to Derrick Bell for three decades of goading, challenge, and relentless affirmation;

. . . to Marilyn Milloy for turning me into a real writer; Barbara Neely and MK Blakely for things too numerous to name; Reiki masters Cynthia Johnson and Polly W. Russell for healing; Vanessa Jackson for coaching; Annette Lawrence for clarity; and the Negril Beach Posse for you know what;

. . . to the most generous, gifted, and daring group of writers ever listed in any table of contents and especially to Patricia J. Williams, Robert Coles and Derrick Bell for being my first lures;

. . . to Ann Collette for seamless support and enthusiasm; Yuval Taylor for valuing my vision, Jerome Pohlen for perfecting it on the page, and Jaime Guthals for spreading the word;

. . . to Ms. Barbara Ann Roberts, Ms. Ilda Sue Johnson (Greene), Ms. Lecora Lucas Mobley, and Ms. Margaret B. Booker, my teachers in the black segregated schools of Charlotte, North Carolina—you always knew; the West Charlotte Senior High School "Mighty Lions" Class of 1967, Dr. Spencer E. Durante, Joseph C. Champion, Jr., and especially my found brother and e-mail philosopher, Fredrick E. McGriff—we made it through.

. . . to Cameron Isaiah Wallace; Jaylon Muldrow; Cameron and Savannah Windham; Wesley, Rachael, Leah, and Ryan Holmes; Jay, Victoria, and Jacqueline Boatright; Kia Harper and Cherice Harper Jefferies; Tramassa Tellis, Daneen Berry, and Deshay Franklin; and Ashley and Keevonya Wilkerson. You are the future. Live free.

INTRODUCTION

FORTUNATELY, I DID not know when I started out how long or what it would take to complete this book. As David Bradley warns about studying American history, so it goes for race: you have to be crazy—or willing to go crazy—to seriously mess around with it. To mess around with a book on race—well, you have to be *real* crazy.

It also helps to have others who will join you in such a risky venture. Of course, if thirty of America's finest contemporary writers had not been willing to put their racial selves on the line, there would be no *When Race Becomes Real.*

Race. How did we arrive at the portal to the twenty-first century so entrenched in denial about what race means in America and who we are in reference to it? Is there really no cure for what Barbara Diggs-Brown and Leonard Steinhorn have diagnosed as "the integration illusion"— that affliction they describe in *By the Color of Our Skin* where our "public expressions masquerade as integrated when our lives clearly are not"?

And where the hell do we go from here?

When Race Becomes Real confronts these questions in a collective peeling-back that uncovers lessons of race, class, gender, and power. It is a re-membering of current events too often severed from our recent and distant past; it is observation from inside and out.

❧

I was determined to make this book different than all the other books about race. I wanted to gather a cross section of people, both black and white, and get them to do what most Americans refuse to do—honestly reveal their personal feelings and experiences around race. Baring your soul to public view or, more accurately, for public consumption, is not easy. We are, after all, a culture that leaps to destroy whatever displeases us. And race, no matter how you look at it, is rarely pleasing.

To handle this tough task, I devised a simple strategy: choose writers who had already demonstrated they would not tiptoe around the issue, but could stand up to the challenge to *stay focused on themselves, stay honest, and stay clear.*

I did not want white writers waxing nostalgic about their "best black friend," nor black writers preaching sermons to or being expert witnesses for white folks on racial issues. Instead of another collection of timeworn excerpts from the revered dead, I wanted original essays written specifically for this book, a book unconstrained by groupings of black-only, white-only, gender- or generation-specific writers.

To black writers, I said, "Drop the arm's length objectivity and write about race the way you talk about race when white folks aren't in the room." To white writers, I said, "Don't write about black people. Keep yourself at the center of the narrative and write about what it's like to be white at the end of the twentieth century."

Finally, I wanted *When Race Becomes Real* to appeal to the broadest possible audience. So, to create a book we could take to the streets, I gave writers one additional nudge: "This is a book intended for a general audience—not academics—though we expect it to be well received on college campuses. For that reason, we encourage clarity, humor, and emotional content of all kinds."

If that sounds easy, it has been anything but.

For the next two and a half years, I followed leads that came from everywhere. I pored over hundreds of books and articles in newspapers, magazines, and on the Internet; and scrolled through at least that many Web sites. Along the way, I chose the best authors. Among them are not only renowned academics and well-known professional writers, but also emerging voices telling truths we need to hear.

When I cast my net among well-known white writers, it came back empty. I was disappointed, though not surprised. Unfairly or not, I had assumed that writers who have built extraordinary careers writing about poor, brave, disenfranchised black people might not jump at the chance to turn that same spotlight on themselves. So I made my pitch more blunt and threw the net back out. "We believe that [your] presence would . . . embolden other white writer colleagues," I wrote to two writers of long-standing national acclaim for their race work and writing.

It worked. Pulitzer Prize winner and Harvard professor Robert Coles, M.D., stepped into the thicket of personal race revelations and, without further discussion, promptly became the first writer to submit a chapter for *When Race Becomes Real*. When his package arrived in the mail, I realized I could make this book happen.

I recruited one writer during a break at a writing workshop, tracked others down by word of mouth, and begged referrals from colleagues. I got a lead on one writer at a wedding, leapt on another at a book signing, snagged another with a follow-up question in a conversation. Whether by phone, fax, e-mail, or snail mail, I dealt with each writer one on one, inviting only those whose work I knew I wanted to publish.

Providence dropped some contributors right into the middle of my constantly evolving search. For instance, I thought it would be an interesting twist to have a parent and child writing from the same family. Then, nearly a year after Kalamu ya Salaam submitted his chapter, I "met" his daughter, Kiini Ibura Salaam, one night while reading her breathtaking reports from Fiji posted on his listserv. She accepted my invitation. The Salaams, writing independently of each other, storm the stage, proof that the sapling towers, brilliant and proud, right alongside the tree.

Much later, in an e-mail exchange with Lisa Dodson, she mentioned her teenage daughter's recent experience working in a job where she "felt really white."

"Does your daughter want to write a piece?" I asked. Lisa and her daughter, Odessa Dorian Cole, teamed up for their chapter, "On *Acting* White: Mother-Daughter Talk."

I am enormously pleased to have a range of other young voices offering a glimpse of what our racial future might hold: Michael Patrick MacDonald, Kimberly Springer, Shawn E. Rhea, Touré, Carlton Winfrey, Tim Wise, and Hanna Griffiths, the youngest writer at 12.

Three groups of writers deserve special mention.

"Race in America is perilous ground," Dodson cautions. "You walk into a minefield if you go there, and when you are white, you can choose not to." Yet Hanna Griffiths, Lucy Gibson, and Odessa Dorian Cole bravely chose to "go there" for their writing debuts. Theirs is an act worthy of imitation.

Three other writers earn special mention for daring to be funny about race. In stories covering a range of humorous encounters—from threats to a black girl for talking white; to the short-lived success of an interracial group of pint-sized thieves routinely raiding a church offering box; to the shocked reaction to three little black girls who adore country music—Kimberly Springer, Jim Schutze, and Susan Straight land their punches between the laughs.

Finally, there are the ones to whom I owe a special debt: those who started, but could not finish. One *New York Times* best-selling author eloquently summed up his struggle when, just days before the deadline, he sent his regrets:

> I gave it several shots and each time I found myself locked in writer's hell, each sentence its own Mt. Everest. I spent a total of 16 elliptical hours inside just two paragraphs!!! Every point I most wanted to make was ever elusive to put to paper—like trying to grab smoke. I worked right up until 4 A.M. Sunday night before throwing in the towel. I have been sunk in an irritating depression ever since. Perhaps it is that the subject is too nebulous for me—each thought actually a depth charge which explodes into a thousand other thoughts on contact. I'm sincerely sorry.

For those, like him, who found themselves stymied because the topic weighed too heavily upon them, here's a special message: finish what you started anyway. We need exactly what comes from that kind of conscientious struggle.

Veteran award-winning writers are here in abundance and spread across several generations: Natalie Angier, Derrick Bell, David Bradley, Robert Coles, Ira J. Hadnot, Robert Jensen, Julianne Malveaux, Colleen J. McElroy, Joycelyn K. Moody, Les Payne, Leonard Pitts, Jr., Kalamu ya Salaam, Jim Schutze, John Seigenthaler, Sr., Susan Straight, Beverly Daniel Tatum, Theresa M. Towner, and Patricia J. Williams. Prominent for their writings on race and a multitude of other subjects, they are the anchors for *When Race Becomes Real*.

No one here is hemmed in by an overarching agenda. There is no out-line to be fleshed out; the whole is not tidily packaged to go down smoothly. Yet certain threads connect one story to another.

The stories in "Genesis" speak to the origins of race consciousness: how we teach our children who is "up" and who is "down," whom to see and whom to render invisible, the language and the labyrinthine rules of engagement. Leonard Pitts admonishes, "Black people spend too much time talking about race and white people don't spend enough." These stories amply illustrate the reason why.

"Fear and Longing" takes us behind the curtain of race dialogue and interaction to reveal why we usually bite our tongue and what can happen if we don't. Chronicling what Kalamu ya Salaam calls "princi-pled engagements," these stories mark the shift that occurs when we decide to daily confront racism at home, at work, at play, or simply dur-ing an evening stroll.

Coming full circle, "Exodus" ends this anthology in the same place where it started: with parents, children, and race. Here we see cycles bravely broken and learn of lasting hierarchies yet to be toppled. When Noel Ignatiev calls for "race traitors" and turns the spotlight on the prison of whiteness, Beverly Daniel Tatum, Tim Wise, and Michael MacDonald call out in response, showing us more noble ways out.

There is a downside to this approach, this style of *res ipsa loquitur,* stories speaking for themselves. In an industry where audiences are cor-doned off in rigidly defined segments of race/class/gender/age and sales pitches are shaped accordingly, *When Race Becomes Real* is eclectic: a hodgepodge, all over the damn place. That is precisely what I hoped for.

If we have hit the mark, *When Race Becomes Real* will end up not just on college campuses, but also at bus stops, on subways, in beauty and barber shops, in middle and high schools, in churches, synagogues, mosques, and other spiritual and secular gatherings of all kinds.

❧

We are not now, nor have we ever been, a nation of just "blacks" and "whites." Yet black and white—what Joycelyn Moody calls "the false binary"—is what tortures us. The other ethnic divisions—between whites and Latinos, American Indians, and Asian Pacific Americans—all deserve to be addressed by those who claim these divisions as their demons. I urge them to jump in.

In the meantime, though, we offer *When Race Becomes Real* with this challenge: use these stories not to imagine some mythical color-blind future, but to stay in this moment of our often unyielding racial present and to confront all of what we are and might become, understanding what is required if we wish to live fully human.

༄

I am grateful and indebted to each of these writers. Whatever gems you find among the pages of *When Race Becomes Real*—and you'll find different ones each time you return—belong to them. I understand now that I was a vessel for their stories, a channel for the centuries of race wisdom and experience they represent. For me, that has been the most exquisite of race revelations.

I did not plan to end this project on a hopeful note. In fact, there is scant evidence in this nation's racial history to suggest that things will get any better than they are now. Still, I confess that these stories have changed me, proving that growth is possible even for a weary spirit. Surely, this counts for something.

If that sounds hopeful, so be it.

BERNESTINE SINGLEY

I. GENESIS

© Mariana C. Greene

Race Story

JIM SCHUTZE

IF THERE ISN'T a reason, there is at least a little story about why my brother and I, both white kids, attended an almost all-black school in Michigan when I was in the first grade and he in the sixth. My grand-father, a German immigrant who came to this country before the turn of the century, brought with him a bitter anticlerical bent. We were told that when the Lutheran minister came to his house in St. Louis to recruit my grandmother, my grandfather beat him up. Maybe it's an apocryphal family legend, but I do know from good sources that my grandfather was very seriously opposed to organized religion. Other than that, he was probably a typical, tough, self-made, first-generation, conservative businessman.

My father, I believe, was rebellious in his own way. When my mother and father were in their twenties, they were Depression-era Roosevelt liberals, living in public housing in downtown St. Louis and dabbling in good works. Somehow I know—they told me or I gleaned from the conversational crosscurrents of the house—that the public housing days were heady times for them: they drank cheap wine in the kitchen with people like William Inge, the playwright who went on to write *Come Back, Little Sheba* and *The Dark at the Top of the Stairs*. For most of my mother's life she continued to correspond with Martha Gellhorn, whom she met in St. Louis during those days and whom I guess history now remembers as one of Hemingway's wives.

In this milieu my father came under the sway of the social activist dean of the Episcopal cathedral and experienced a religious awakening. To the serious dismay of my grandfather, my father went off to the Virginia Seminary and became an Episcopal minister. It's clear to me in retrospect that my father's decision was driven by religious feeling and political idealism, and that he had little, if any, idea until later in life what role the Episcopal Church plays in the social and business hierarchy of the nation. If anything, my father always seemed a little clueless about the finer distinctions of the American caste system. Maybe it just takes more than two generations to figure some of that stuff out.

When I was very little we lived in a succession of hick towns in Maryland and Michigan. Back then, not many people had romantic notions about small town life. Sinclair Lewis had made living in a small town in the Middle West a kind of intellectual sin. I have to imagine their sojourn in boondocks Michigan was a tough price to pay for their religious convictions. I think it was an especially tough price for my mother to pay for my father's convictions.

His first big career move was to Ann Arbor, Michigan, a university town, where he became the associate rector of the big downtown Episcopal church, St. Andrews. Ann Arbor, which described itself immodestly in those days as "the Athens of the Middle West," was a northern town, of course, and a place of learning and enlightenment where people looked with dismay and disgust on the racial habits of the people of the former Confederacy. The Union had militarily vanquished the rebels only eighty-six years before my family moved to Ann Arbor, placing the War of Rebellion well within the living memory of the national culture at the time.

The Civil Rights Movement was still ahead. During the movement years, Ann Arbor would send both money and people to the South to fight the abomination of racial segregation. Tom Hayden, a founder of SDS, husband of Jane Fonda, and so on, preceded me on the staff of the University of Michigan student newspaper, the *Michigan Daily,* by only a few years. It was while he was writing for the *Daily* that he traveled south to witness and take part in the great struggle for universal voting rights, sending back missives that helped ignite the fires of white student activism.

I always loved Ann Arbor—its gentle hills, lush green canopy of trees, generous parks, ivied walls. I remember thinking even as a little boy that I lived in a beautiful place. But later, when I returned as a university student and found the place champing at the bit to reform the racist South, I was seized by memories of my own first grade year there. (Unlike the years on either side, I do remember that year fairly clearly.)

Just to heighten the irony, in the mid-1960s, at about the time I came back to Ann Arbor to go to college, someone was suing to force the closing of Jones School on grounds of de facto segregation. The town, especially the university community, was enraged. Almost everyone in Ann Arbor seemed to believe it was unthinkable, preposterous, wrong-headed, and absolutely upside down that anyone would even think of accusing the Athens of the Middle West of racism.

I kept quiet. I didn't know what to say. I was a kid, of course. But I did know for certain that in the early 1950s when we had moved to Ann Arbor there was a street down the middle of town called Division Street, and most of the people on one side were black, and absolutely everybody on the other was white. I continued to grow up in the North after we left Ann Arbor, so I was raised with the impression that the division of northern towns and cities into separate white and black enclaves was not segregation. Nobody ever said what it was. I try now to think my way back into a town with a real Division Street right down its middle like a big skunk stripe, and where the people were shocked and dismayed when someone dared suggest that this arrangement amounted to racial segregation.

But it's too far back. I can't do the math. It's just how it was. Racism and segregation were the debased practices of those bad people we had righteously smote in the Civil War, and the deal with Division Street was something nobody ever talked about. Lucky for us.

The rector of St. Andrews lived in a Victorian mansion out off Hill Street in the neighborhood where the senior university faculty lived.

As associate rector, my father was assigned a little stone Englishy-looking cottage across the parking lot from the church. The previous inhabitant had been the former sexton (Anglican janitor), now retired. The church was on Division Street. Jones School was one block away.

I don't know this as fact, or I don't remember it well enough to say I do, but judging by all that happened later it must have been assumed by the church and the community when we first showed up in Ann Arbor that my parents would find some way, some hook or crook, to get my brother and me across town to the white grade school. (And, of course, that school was never thought of at all as the white grade school, and no one would ever have called it that, even though I distinctly recall adults referring to Jones as the colored school. The liberal North was a complex place.)

I do know, and my brother confirms, that it was the conscious decision of my parents, with their Roosevelt-liberal St. Louis public housing social-organizing years still fresh in their hearts, that Bill and I would do good works by attending the neighborhood school.

I had never been close to black kids before, but, more important, the first graders at Jones must never have been up close and personal with very many white kids before that day, either. It wasn't like the segregated South, where white and black children often grew up playing with each other before institutional segregation intervened and walled them apart in the schools. In Ann Arbor, which was not segregated, white and black kids barely even caught glimpses of each other across Division Street until the first day of junior high school.

Clearly etched in my memory of that first day at Jones is the moment my one white face came into the midst of their many black faces. I found myself in the center of a mob of children on the front steps of the school, all of them very curious to know who I was but, more urgently, what in the hell I was. A child approached me and clamped fingers on my sun-whitened burr-cut head. A boy came up to me slowly and leaned forward to peer into my face. He took a step backward down the steps and then announced to the crowd in a tone of evenly mixed amusement and revulsion, "His eyes are blue!"

The next several weeks on the playground were sort of like medical experiments: if you hit one of these white things in the mouth, what might come out? I remember only fighting, fighting, and fighting. One afternoon when I came home bloodied and tearful, my mother took me to the living room and sat me down on the sofa. I remember this speech clearly, and I still think it was probably a good speech in the longest view of life.

She told me all about slavery and the evils that white people had visited on African American people. It was a terrible story, and for a while my tears shifted from self-pity to compassion. The moral of the story was that I needed to feel sorry for the little colored children at Jones and I needed to try to help them become better people, by which I assumed she meant they needed to be more like us.

I was a first grader, and I would guess now that the story probably worked well while we were on the couch. But the next morning when I was running down Division Street as fast as my feet could carry me with the Mike Burns gang inches from my back and snatching at my shirt, I assume my effort to feel sorry for Mike was a failure.

My mission as the Great White Liberal Hope of my first grade class suffered another challenge, because not too far along in the school year the psychological lines of color began to blur and fade. We were very little, after all, and we were not yet fully imbued with the importance of our differences.

I'm certainly not saying the lines ever disappeared entirely. I have a specific memory of the day the teacher—the only other white person in the room, as I remember it—called us to her knee to read us the story of *Little Black Sambo*. And who knows? Maybe in the relative context of the early 1950s, she saw *Little Black Sambo* as culturally relevant.

Depending on your age, you may or may not remember *Little Black Sambo* as the story in which an African boy climbs a tree and taunts the tiger to rush around and around at his feet until finally the tiger churns himself into butter. She introduced the story by saying something to the effect of, "Sambo, like many of you in this room, was a little colored child."

I remember distinctly that the eyes in the room drifted and turned, whirled and lifted until finally every eye was on me. Someone said, "Jimmy's the only one that's not," and there was laughter, for which I was grateful. But even when the laughter had subsided, I still felt eyes lingering on my uncolored skin. I was Little White Sambo, and I remember that I hated my difference.

At some point during the months between the first day of school and Christmas vacation, a miracle transpired. I was approached on the playground and offered a position in the gang, which I learned was not the Mike Burns gang at all but the Eugene (last name forgotten) gang.

Mike was just enormous. He must have been held back. But Eugene was the boss. He was cool and slick. I remember only one of the other kids—Johnny Johnson, a happy, funny guy who always had a big buck-toothed grin, even when he was caught red-handed. Especially when he was caught red-handed.

I don't know if I knew then why I was so honored. Of course I know now. The Eugene gang was in the after-school business of robbing coins from the religious pamphlet racks at St. Andrews Episcopal Church, the big white church across Division Street. Eugene had picked up on the fact that I was the preacher's kid. The Eugene gang had their act fairly well down. They knew where the good racks were that got filled up with money every Sunday. Mike was able to pry the coin boxes off the racks with his bare hands.

But they needed a white lookout. If they stood around the white church with their hands in their pockets trying to look innocent, the people over there called the cops. As I learned, the white people across Division Street would call the cops on them sometimes just for cross-ing Division Street, let alone entering a place of white worship.

Who could be a better good-eyes than the white preacher's kid? I was thrilled. Maybe I was thrilled because it meant that Mike now would be working for me. But I remember that I also was thrilled by the robberies themselves. It was dangerous work and very exciting. I stood in the half-dark echoing caverns of the church corridors and sang out my warning cues: "Oh, hello, Dr. Lewis! (The scratchy whisper of escaping feet around the corner.) It's nice to see you. (My eyes on Dr. Lewis's eyes to gauge whether he has heard.) I was just looking for my father. (He nods, maybe only now recognizing me, and turns his hear-ing aid toward me.) And now I have to go to the bathroom. (He turns curtly away.)"

We made great money. I had money for all kinds of candy. I don't know why my parents didn't notice. My father was busy with his career and, like most men of that era, had little to do with hands-on parent-ing beyond his role as Household Minister of Justice. My mother was eccentric and kind, preoccupied with her own challenges. But I don't think parents in general noticed very much about kids in the early 1950s, because they didn't have to. They put their children out on the stoop every morning like empty milk bottles, serenely confident that society would come along in a clean white truck and fill them up.

My mother probably gets the credit for my ultimate social success at Jones. For all of her preaching about the white liberal's burden, she was really sort of a child herself, and nothing made her happier than seeing children running wild and having fun together. She invited the entire first grade class to my birthday party—there may have been thirty or more children—and we had the very best time I think I have ever had in my life. I don't remember details, but I do have a general recollection of kids flowing in and out of the house and over the furniture and through the shrubbery in an endless wave, shrieking and chasing, gobbling down cake and ice cream, and I remember my mother clapping her hands and laughing out loud because she was having so much fun. She wasn't big on housekeeping.

As a father myself now, I know that's what really counts. It's not playing in the neighborhood or on the playground but being inside each other's houses, with your mamas looking on and laughing while you eat cake and ice cream. If you do that, you're true friends. After that party, I was welcome and had a name in everybody's house. The birthday party my mother gave me was the real reason for everything that ensued.

At some point during the party I remember looking up—I remember this keenly, like a blade cutting skin—to a spot just across the church parking lot. High on the towering stone wall at the back of the church was a wrought-iron balcony outside the room in the church attic where the choir practiced. Standing on the balcony looking down on the mayhem at our house was a squadron of white church ladies, their faces darkened by scowls. They didn't like my party. I realized years later they hadn't liked my mother.

Between January and the end of the year, pressure must have grown for my parents to get us out of Jones and across town to the white school, which had the felicitous name of Angell School. For years I blamed my removal from Jones to Angell on the church choir ladies who had looked down on my all-black birthday party from the choir-room balcony. My childish understanding of things helped darken my subsequent adult feelings about church ladies in some unfair and unfortunate ways that I am still working to overcome.

I doubt now that the church ladies were the whole cause of my banishment. For one thing, a lifetime as a reporter and many years on the police beat lead me to suspect that the church literature rack scam probably was less slick than we thought. I wouldn't be surprised to learn they had yanked me out of Jones and away from the gang in preparation for busting all of the black kids. I know they did get caught some time after I left Jones.

But another cause—what I now think was the most compelling one—came to me more or less out of the blue just a few years ago. Somehow the subject of speech therapy came up, and I found myself drifting out to the edges of the conversation, privately remembering that I had gone through some form of intensive speech therapy during my first months as a second grader at Angell School. I don't know how scientifically advanced the business of speech therapy was in the early 1950s. When it came back to me I mainly remembered a speech lady—whom I recalled as red-faced and pretty mad at me—leaning into my face and telling me in an emphatic voice, "Jimmy, you must stop talking like a little colored boy!"

When I remembered it, I laughed silently to myself. I thought, "There's your social emergency."

It would easily have slipped by my parents. My father was busy and my mother preoccupied. But it wouldn't have eluded anybody else at St. Andrews. I bet I set off eighty-seven different varieties of racial alarm, phobic response, and social panic when I showed up at Episcopal Sunday school talking like a black kid. Just as peasants from time immemorial have feared witches and gypsies, so Middle Westerners in the 1950s must have loathed the racial changeling.

In personal terms, speech therapy actually wasn't my big issue at Angell. The really big one was the fighting. I doubt that I wanted to fight. I was pretty puny. I'm sure the thing I had liked about being in the Eugene gang at Jones was that I didn't have to fight much any more. All I had to do was look for Eugene, who looked for Mike. I don't think I was ever good at fighting, anyway. But at Jones, at least you learned to throw a punch and block a punch, no matter who you were. (I haven't had an occasion to test those skills since my freshman year in college—an incident that involved drink—and I don't want one.)

I do remember a few instances on the playground at Angell when somebody made a move on me, and I remember thinking it was absurdly easy to hit them in the face, like shooting fish in a barrel. I absolutely do not believe that I was a bully or a fight-picker. Maybe we don't remember that sort of thing from our own early childhoods, but I really think I was too small and too retiring. I was able to use my hands if I had to, but I don't think I wanted to.

One day in the water fountain line in the corridor at Angell, a boy behind me in line slapped me on the back of the head so that my teeth cracked against the stainless steel tap of the fountain, sending a quick electric shock of pain up into my forehead.

When something like that happened at Jones, it meant you had to stand and deliver. You had to start punching and hope you could last until Mike got there. So I wheeled around without thinking and shot my fist into the kid's mouth.

I don't remember him. But I do remember how he stood. He lifted his hand slowly to his lip, then held it out where he could see the blood. He stared at the blood in silence. And then he began to emit a scream which I still remember as being like one of those European police sirens, up and down, up and down, on and on, never fading in volume, echoing through the tile and linoleum hallways like a banshee wail from one end of Angell School to the other.

The other children in line took it up like a Greek chorus: "He has blood! He has blood!"

The school took it very badly. It was as if, finally having been admitted to Heaven on a conditional visa, the first thing I did was walk over and coldcock an angel.

I hit him one time only. One shot. I remember that, because it came up in the inquisition. Two teachers, one on each armpit, hauled me down the long corridor and down the steps with my toes dragging behind me to Miss Buckley's office. I came to love Miss Buckley in the years ahead. She was very tough but very warm. I think she liked me, years later. That day, she made the teachers tell over and over again what had happened, and she asked me several times to explain. She called in other students. Finally she ruled that I had been technically within my rights to defend myself, and she said it was worth something that I had hit the kid only once and then stopped when there was no longer any threat.

She sent everyone else out of her office. When we were alone together, she touched my knee with her hand to make me feel better, and she told me in a gentle voice that the real problem was not that I had struck the boy. She said it was that "you fight like a little colored boy."

Maybe we were still working on my speech problem at that point. I don't remember. But I do remember the moment, sitting in her office, when she told me in a very somber voice that if I didn't stop behaving like a little colored boy she might have to send me back to the colored school. Maybe my response was ingratiating. I was a preacher's kid, after all. Maybe I said something—in second grade vernacular, of course—along the lines of, "Miss Buckley, I want you to know how valuable I feel my experience here at Angell has been and what a fine institution this is. . . ."

Maybe I just started grinning from ear to ear. I don't remember. But I do know how I felt. It was the impossible dream. I hated Angell. I hated being different from the rest of them. I could think of nothing more wonderful than going back to Jones, getting back with the Eugene gang, and knocking over a few racks at my father's church. One way or another, I conveyed to Miss Buckley that I was ready to return to Jones right then, at that very moment, and that I would be careful not to let the door hit me in the backside on my way out.

I never got over the wall.

It was after the water fountain incident that I began having to spend long hours in a little room off the nurse's office at Angell School, trying to put round pegs in round holes and square pegs in square holes for a lady who sat across the table from me and never spoke, examining me as if I were a partially dissected frog. She may even have been the same person who was trying to do speech therapy on me. Whatever she really looked like, by now she has melded permanently and inextricably in my mind with Nurse Ratched in Ken Kesey's *One Flew Over the Cuckoo's Nest*.

My parents and I were called in at some point for a family conference with her. In the car on the way home afterward my father was irritated and high-strung. He hit the dashboard with his fist, which frightened me. He told my mother he thought he probably had tons more training as a counselor than the peg lady and that he didn't think much of her techniques. I don't remember anything at all about why he was so hostile toward her. I suppose at some point in the conversation she must have asked him what he had been smoking when he sent his kid to the colored school.

And you know, what were my parents going to do about it, anyway? They were Roosevelt liberals. Instead of helping the colored children in his first grade class become more like white children, their son had turned into a colored child. In the contest of culture and personality between noble white saviors and the indomitable survivors of oppression, the survivors had taken the day hands down. What could my parents do but ride it out? Nobody ever said squat to me. I probably figured the peg thing was a Chinese water torture for making that kid bleed.

For the next few years we continued to live next to the church, and I commuted to Angell School on city buses. I played with my white friends on the playground at school and continued to hang out with my black friends at home. Then at some point the church bought us a large, beautiful house on Onondaga Street, across from a baronial fraternity house and well within the area served by Angell School. And my world became properly monochromatic.

I never saw my black friends again until the first day of seventh grade at Tappan Junior High School. That day, I was so excited about being at Tappan that I could barely keep my feet on the ground. Tappan was a huge, gleaming new school, thronging with well-dressed shiny-faced kids, a temple of postwar American prosperity. On that thrilling first day, those of us who had come from Angell searched anxiously for each other in the crowded hallways and embraced joyously when we met.

And then at a certain moment in the day, when I was walking down a broad corridor with a big gang of my Angell friends, we rounded a corner and there in the distance, huddled like birds on a far branch, were my Jones School friends.

I ran even harder, and I remember clearly that they were very happy to see me. They called me "Jimmy," which I hadn't been called at school since the first grade, and we hugged and embraced. My sense—who knows how much of this I impose in retrospect and how much was really there?—is that they were a hundred times more excited and nervous and apprehensive than even I on that day. This was not just the first day at Tappan for them: it was their first real day in the white world.

The next vision is so clear and animate, even after all these years, that I do not doubt it in any detail. I had my arm around Eugene's shoulders. I turned, expecting my Angell friends to be standing inches behind me, having followed me down the hall to meet these new kids.

They had not moved an inch from where I had left them at the far end of the hall. The expressions on their faces were of shock and horror.

I said good-bye to my black friends. I hurried back down the corridor to my white friends.

They were aghast. They wanted to know how and why and when I had come to know colored kids. They wanted to know why on earth I was behaving in a way that was buddy-buddy toward the colored kids. They wanted to know what in the world was wrong with me. It was as if I had revealed myself to them as some kind of frightening avatar, a being totally unlike what they had always believed me to be.

I do remember clearly trying later in the day to think it all through by myself and, in that process, marveling at how huge was the difference my white friends perceived between themselves and my black buddies. It took my breath away. The white kids talked as if the black kids were not fully or truly human.

I hungered to be accepted and approved by my white friends. I was even a politician, one of the first seventh graders ever, I was told at the time, to be elected to the student council. One of the ways I won my white friends over and helped ease any misgivings they may have had was by turning my back on my black Jones School friends, erasing them with my eyes, never speaking, never even acknowledging a glance or nod or hesitant lifting of the eyes. I made them more than dead. I made them into beings who had never existed.

I wasn't only turning my back on kids with whom I had committed crimes against pamphlet racks. There were black kids in the larger circle of my friends from Jones School who never did anything wrong, who came from the sternly determined families who went on to do things like integrate the postal service and send their kids to Harvard. I treated them, too, as unworthy of my gaze. Dirt on the floor.

When the big things happened—the pep rallies and the assemblies and the elections and even the fooling around in the cafeteria—the black kids were invisible to all of the white kids. They couldn't be pretty or handsome or cool or important: they couldn't even really be present, not truly present, because we made them not there with our eyes. It's not child's play, that trick of the eyes. It's the first step, the very beginning of the process that ends with the trains and the ovens.

Once in a while I slipped. The black kids got me. As I moved down the hall with my group and passed one of the marginal little corners or nooks where the black kids were allowed to gather, Eugene or Mike or one of the girls would look at me and catch my eye.

Their eyes always spoke plainly. Their eyes said to my eye, "Asshole."

I envied the white kids who had never known black kids, because it seemed to me that their cruelty toward them was guileless and unwitting. Unlike me, I thought, the other white kids had never known that the black kids were human, had never been fed milk and cookies by their mothers or felt the joy of having them flowing in and out of the house, smeared with cake. I was the only dirty one, the only one who knew better, the only one who committed social annihilation by choice and for the sake of getting elected to the student council.

In the end we didn't make it in Ann Arbor. When Dr. Lewis retired, my father did not succeed him as rector and was banished instead to the boondocks of Michigan. My father never said anything about why we didn't make it, because he never said anything about anything. Family legend years later is that the cause of our exile had been his crusading liberalism. Apparently he had led a charge for a local open housing ordinance. After he had campaigned for some months, Dr. Lewis informed him coolly, I am told, that three-fourths of the housing south of Division Street was owned by the senior warden of St. Andrews Church and that the senior warden was not at all interested in either urban renewal or the dispersal of his tenants into rental properties owned by persons other than the senior warden.

But at the time we left my beloved Ann Arbor, my understanding of the causes was childish and personal. I blamed our banishment on the church ladies. I knew from overheard whispers and looks I had spied on their faces that they thought my mother was embarrassing. Perhaps I recognized their feelings because, with great guilt, I shared them. In my exquisitely self-conscious pre-teenage years, my mother made me cringe as well. She had never even tried to become an Episcopal church lady. By then the church ladies all drove Country Squire station wagons and drank martinis in the late afternoon. It embarrassed me to the point of breathlessness to see my mother careening through the narrow streets of Ann Arbor on her balloon-tire bicycle with her artist and potter friends, especially because she was always so insanely surprised to see me and because she never once succeeded in using the brakes to bring her bicycle to a halt. After school I hung out inside Moe's Sport Shop because the big window in front was tinted and I could see her coming before she could see me.

Whether she was the real reason we had to leave, the fact remains that she was too much for Ann Arbor. It wasn't Athens. It was just the Middle West.

History played a nice little joke with my father's exile to the boonies. In the last small town where he lighted—a typical old farming and light manufacturing community in southern Michigan—he seemed to have sunk his claws into the soil and made it his business not to be pried loose. No more Roosevelt liberal hanky-panky with this parish, not this close to the end of the journey. But in the years after his arrival there, Detroit exploded, fifty miles away. Immediately after the '67 race riot, white people by the teeming zillions loaded up their Country Squire station wagons and headed for the hills, terrified of black people.

The hick town where my father had made his last stand became a magnet for busing flight, white flight, urban flight, all the kinds of flight and panic and racial retreat that inflamed white culture of the period. Huge shopping malls and vast new traditional neighborhoods flew up all around the town like a tent army that had arrived in the night. My father briefly joined a local militia that was going to defend the community when the black people in Detroit all loaded up on chartered buses and came out to kill them. He was in the catbird seat, smack dab in the middle of Episcopal Heaven. Madonna went to high school in that town.

As a young man I moved to the South, where I have now spent the lion's share of my adult life. Early on in my Dixie sojourn, I heard white southerners tell a particular kind of story about their own childhoods that I found personally fascinating. I listened with an urgent secret interest while they rambled on about how when they were little they had played with and had been dear friends with black children.

I still don't understand why southerners tell that story or what point they think they are making. But I know what I heard in it. Those stories, when I first heard them, thrilled me. I thought, "Well, you're all worthless bastards, too."

Like me. If they played, if they sang, if they slept, if they shared the crystalline loves and joys of childhood with black kids, and if they only reverted to racial caste when it was imposed on them by the public schools, then they knew exactly what they were doing. Their racism was not guileless or unwitting. It was learned, decisional, and willful. I thought, "Home at last."

In the last twenty years I have come to enjoy Southerners, black and white, because they have manners. I even have some now myself.

I'm not sure how much permanent impact my first grade year had on me. A few years ago I found myself listening while some erudite white people were discussing *Huckleberry Finn* and the cultural/historical value of the original text. One person at the table said he thought there was a laughable arrogance in the assertion that Twain's words should in any way be censored in order to meet standards of contemporary political correctness, and he suggested that black kids who don't like the name of Twain's black character, Jim, probably should just suck it up and learn to deal with the culture as it was during Twain's time.

At that time I was the new father of a baby boy. I drifted from the dinner table conversation to my memory of the day the teacher read *Little Black Sambo* to us. I remembered a roomful of eyes on my skin. While my dinner guests chatted and laughed at the table, I mused on the possibility that someone might one day make my child feel that way about what he was . . . at school, where I would have to send him, where I could not protect him. I found myself wondering if it would help the man at the table get any smarter if I went upstairs, got my copy of *Huckleberry Finn*, brought it back down, and whacked him upside the head with it a couple of times.

So I guess *Little White Sambo* is still in there somewhere.

Another possible small legacy—something I hadn't really noticed about myself until I began working on this essay—is that I seem to be a bit of a student of religious pamphlet racks, which, by the way, have evolved significantly since the early 1950s. In many churches you now see racks in which the coin box is actually inside the rack itself. The modern rack is a locked container, like the boxes from which newspapers are dispensed. In order to get to the money, then, you would have to break open the rack and then somehow pry loose and get into the coin box. The coin boxes look to me as if they are much more solidly built mechanisms than the little tin enclosures of my childhood. So I must not have been the Lone Ranger on that one.

In fact, now that I'm old, I don't really feel like the Lone Ranger on anything. Eventually I deprived myself of even my sense of moral particularity on the race question. I decided the rest of my fellow Yankees had also been deliberate and morally witting in their racism. I won't bore you with all the details of this evolution in my private thought, except to say that I came to it by working my way logically backward from the teachings of Dr. King.

Martin Luther King, Jr., and the leadership of the Civil Rights Movement reformed the moral consciousness of white Americans by appealing to their consciences. The reason Dr. King could succeed was because there was a white conscience to appeal to. We all knew better. We always had. We didn't come to our racial sins because some deterministic clockwork of historical causes had impelled us there against our will or without our knowledge. We did it because we wanted to. We were Strom Thurmond's willing helpers.

The most terrible thing I can make myself say about white people is also the most wonderful. Somewhere, however buried and refracted by guilt, the truth lives in our souls. We know what we're doing. It's why we are susceptible to improvement. It's why we have no excuses.

Jim Schutze *is an investigative reporter, newspaper columnist, and author whose career has spanned more than thirty years. A graduate of St. Paul's School and the University of Michigan, Schutze joined the* Detroit Free Press *as City Desk Reporter in 1971. In 1978, he moved to the* Dallas Times Herald *where he remained for nearly fifteen years. While there, Schutze headed the investigative news team, was the Metro columnist, and was a member of the editorial board. From 1995 to 1998, Schutze was*

Dallas Bureau Chief for the Houston Chronicle. *He is currently a columnist for the* Dallas Observer, *where he has worked since 1998.*

In 1986, Schutze published his first book, The Accommodation: The Politics of Race in an American City *(Citadel Press), chronicling Dallas's failure to push toward racial justice. He has published five other books, among them* Bully *(William Morrow, 1996);* By Two and Two *(William Morrow, 1995); and* Preacher's Girl *(William Morrow, 1993).*

Since 1991, Schutze's movie projects have included Black Widow Murders: The Blanche Taylor Moore Story *(NBC/Lorimar Productions), a television movie starring Elizabeth Montgomery and based on Shutze's book* Preacher's Girl. Bully, *a feature film based on Schutze's book of the same name, premiered at the 2001 Toronto International Film Festival and La Biennale di Venezia. Directed by Larry Clark with a screenplay by David McKenna (*Blow*),* Bully *was produced by Don Murphy (*Natural Born Killers*) and distributed by Lions Gate Entertainment.*

For the third consecutive year, in 2001, Schutze won the national Unity Award for reporting on race.

© Leonard Pitts, Jr.

Crazy Sometimes

LEONARD PITTS, JR.

IT HAS BEEN suggested—and fairly so, I think—that black people spend entirely too much time talking about race. That we interject it into situations where it has no business, use it to explain slights that could just as easily be explained in other ways.

I can tell you why we do: It's because this thing makes us crazy sometimes. Race, I mean.

A story.

A few years ago, Ted Koppel was conducting a group interview on the subject of race. His subjects: a group of white Philadelphians who had bullied a black newcomer into moving out of their neighborhood. These people, blue collar, young, old, and middle-aged, had all kinds of excuses for what they had done. They were worried about crime, they said. About the woman's effect on property values. About what sort of neighbor she might have been.

21

Not one of them stood up and said, "By God, I didn't want that woman here because I'm a racist." Had they done that, I think I'd have had more respect for them.

Instead, the group was impatient with the idea that because of white animosity, black Americans have it harder than others or deserve recompense for their sufferings. Blacks, went the general consensus, have it as good or better than anyone.

Then Koppel asked a telling question. How much money would they each require, he wanted to know, before they'd be willing to give up their white skins forever and become black?

Surprisingly, a man in the audience was willing to answer. Fifty million dollars, he said. That was the going rate for white skin. That's what he'd require to be black. If he had fifty million, he told Koppel, "I could live anywhere I want. I wouldn't have to deal with any . . ."

And here there came a pause, a half-beat of stammering, at a word he didn't quite know how to confess. That instant of hesitation told you everything you needed to know about why black people get crazy sometimes. Because he finished his sentence with the word you knew was there, the one that was hiding all along behind the rationalizations, that gave the lie to him, his neighbors, and all their protestations and excuses.

". . . racism," he said.

I was watching this and didn't know whether to laugh or cry: laugh, because the idea that money buys an escape from bigotry is so ludicrous; or cry, because I knew the dissonance between what he said before and the word he just forced himself to stammer was probably lost on him, lost on them, lost on many of those watching. I wanted to holler at the TV, I wanted to grab this guy by the lapels.

In the end, I didn't holler, laughing and crying canceled one another, and his lapels were beyond my reach, so I just shook my head and wondered the same thing I've wondered so many days and nights after listening to people like this say things like that: can they hear themselves? It is the question that rises inevitably from the places black folks gather. It is asked in amazement, often. Asked with laughter, occasionally. Asked with glittering eyes, once in a while.

The thing makes us crazy sometimes.

Because if, by almost every available measure, it was more difficult to be black in America thirty or forty years ago, there is one area in which it is indisputably harder now: the area of knowing who and where your enemy is. In the days when segregation was a widely accepted political philosophy, those who bore black people ill will had no reason to deny it. Indeed, such people spoke openly and with no evident fear of contradiction—much less stigmatization—about the athletic and intellectual inferiority of blacks and their general unfitness to participate in the social and political life of the nation.

The Civil Rights Movement made those views unfashionable, drove them underground. Which is, of course, not quite the same thing as making them go away.

The result is that to be black in modern America is to feel the touch of hidden hands pressing down upon you. You know they're there. Their effect is clear in government and university statistics documenting that, in terms of education, employment, housing, justice, health, and other quality-of-life indicators, people like you lag behind the nation as a whole.

You know the hands are there, but when you turn around to catch them in the act of pushing you down, you encounter only white people with "Who, me?" expressions on their faces. Expressions perfected to such a degree that a group of white Philadelphians who bullied and browbeat a black woman until she fled their midst could then face the nation and, with straight faces, declare their moral innocence.

It's enough to make you miss Bull Connor and all the other unrepentant racists with whom Martin Luther King, Jr., and his generation clashed in the South. You wonder why these new people won't stand up and say who they are and how they feel about you.

If they did, you'd never have to guess. That job you didn't get, that grade you didn't deserve, that cold look you received . . . was the other person just having a bad day, or did he or she have something against a person like you?

And it occurs to you that if folks who hate you would stand up and declare it, you wouldn't have to go through your day on guard against the world, wondering.

But they don't, so you do. You flinch from the hits that come, and from those you only expect to come.

Crazy sometimes. Crazy enough to give up.

Like the time a fourteen-year-old friend of my oldest son said, "I can't get anywhere, because the white man is keeping me down." Fourteen years old and already convinced of his own defeat.

Crazy sometimes. Crazy enough to holler first and ask questions later.

Like the time folks in Washington went to war over a white bureaucrat who used the word "niggardly"—never mind that it meant stingy, cheap, tight, and had nothing to do with that word it sounds like.

Crazy sometimes. Crazy enough to feel that blow even when it's not even there.

Like the time a black woman I didn't know sent an e-mail alerting me to a "racist" message she claimed was hidden in a popular word-processing program. She gave me instructions on how to find this message: I was to type a certain chilling sentence—"I'd like all Negroes to die."—then highlight it and go to the thesaurus. I did what she said and the computer came back with, "I'll drink to that."

I started fooling with the sentence, changing words around. I replaced "Negroes" with "white people" and "die" with "live." I wrote a whole series of sentences beginning with "I'd like." "I'd like to play basketball like Jordan." "I'd like to win the lottery." "I'd like to teach the world to sing in perfect harmony."

Each time, the computer came back with the same response: "I'll drink to that."

So I wrote the woman and told her there wasn't some hateful hidden message. It was just a software glitch.

I figured that was the end of it. But she wrote back to say that what I'd told her meant nothing. Somehow, she was still convinced a software maker had it in for black folks, but I was too naïve to understand the machinations of the white man's conspiracy.

Crazy sometimes.

The people who feel we stand in the promised land, having already overcome, enjoy hearing these stories. The tales validate their notion that black folks operate on a hair trigger, with rage reserved like a Molotov cocktail carried in the briefcase, needing only a spark to become a bomb. More to the point, stories like these support the argument that we talk too much about race, that we're too ready to see its hand in innocent places, that we need to get a grip.

You cannot gainsay their arguments. Indeed, they eloquently speak of the need for African Americans to refocus their struggle for the new millennium and to spend their moral capital more wisely than they have recently. To be a little less crazy sometimes.

And yet . . . being crazy doesn't make you stupid, does it?

You feel the press of hidden hands and you're not fooled by "Who, me?" looks.

Another story.

A white kid once swerved a car toward one of my sons. The kid turned away at the last instant as someone inside the vehicle yelled racial slurs.

My wife, Marilyn, went to the house where these young people had gathered to talk with the adults. This is what we believe in doing when one of our children has a serious problem with another child in the neighborhood. Go to the parents. Talk it out. Get it straight.

But when Marilyn got there, about ten or fifteen white kids were jeering at her from the porch. And the mother of one of the children who had been in the car stepped down and challenged my wife to a fight. "I am so sick of you people," she said.

I learned all of this by phone from 3,000 miles away, and a coldness spread through me. It was a hit about which there could be no mistake. My thoughts were a pounding drum that said, "Here we go again again again again again."

I had been to this crossroad so many times before. You move beyond it, you think you've traveled to a far and better place, and then you look up and you're right there at that same ugly intersection of bigotry and fear. It wears on you. It tears you down.

And yet, in hindsight, the most troubling thing about that episode wasn't the fatigue it left me with, nor even the fact that it validated my flinching. Rather it was knowing that, if you asked her, the woman who pronounced herself "sick of you people" would tell you, like those people in Philadelphia, that she had reasons for the way she felt. And that racism was not one of them.

Racism, for people like this, does not exist. Or, if they concede it does exist, it can be explained away as rationality and common sense, not the atavistic stupidity it is. Not racism, but fear of crime. Not racism, but concern for property values. Not racism, but . . . fill in the excuse.

So yeah, you get crazy sometimes. Not just because of those times when you don't know, and can't be sure, but also because of those times when you do know, irrefutably and unmistakably, yet some white person will look at you, with a straight face, and insist you must be mistaken.

You get called crazy, even when you're not.

So here we stand, a generation after civil rights; more doors open, more opportunities available, and yet we have not overcome. We have only learned to flinch on the one side and deny on the other.

Meanwhile, the nation frays along seams of culture, race, and class. Black men still earn fractions on the dollar to what white men make for the same position. Black and Native American men have the lowest life expectancies in the nation. Black male unemployment runs at approximately three times that of white males twenty and older.

According to *The Real War on Crime: The Report of the National Criminal Justice Commission*, black people account for 13 percent of regular drug users, but 35 percent of drug possession arrests, 55 percent of drug possession convictions, and 74 percent of all drug possession prison sentences.

The Justice Department reports that, on any given day, one in three black men ages twenty to twenty-nine is under the control of the justice system, either incarcerated, on probation, or on parole. After reviewing statistics from the U.S. Department of Justice, Jerome Miller, founder of the National Center on Institutions and Alternatives in Alexandria, Virginia, has concluded that by the year 2010, the majority of black men ages eighteen to thirty-nine will be in jail.

And yet black unemployment is down. Black earnings are up. Black test scores are rising. College attendance among black women is skyrocketing. Black teen pregnancy is falling. And an unprecedented number of black women and men stand acclaimed by the white mainstream as role models.

Which picture tells the truth? Blacks and whites would tend to point in opposite directions. The fact is, both pictures are correct.

Together, they point to the unfinished business that remains between those who flinch and those who deny.

Because the truth is this: Black people spend way too much time talking about race.

And white people don't spend nearly enough.

Leonard Pitts, Jr., *a Pulitzer Prize finalist and a syndicated columnist for the* Miami Herald, *writes about pop culture, family, and social issues. His column appears in more than 150 papers nationwide. In addition to writing for* Spin, Parenting, TV Guide, Reader's Digest, *and* Billboard, *he also writes and produces radio documentaries on such widely diverse subjects as Madonna and Dr. Martin Luther King, Jr.*

In the summer of 1999, Pitts published Becoming Dad: Black Men and the Journey to Fatherhood *(Longstreet Press), part case study and part memoir of how fatherless sons make fathers of themselves. The winner of many awards during his career, Pitts has thrice received National Headliner Awards.*

© Robert Coles

Experiences and Memories

ROBERT COLES

I HAVE NO childhood memories of racial awareness. I was born in a suburban town outside of Boston where only white people lived. My dad was born in Yorkshire, England, and moved to America in order to study science and engineering. My mother was born in Sioux City, Iowa, and moved to New England for a college education. They were both devoted to Victorian novelists, and read to each other from books by George Eliot, Dickens, and Hardy. My mother loved Tolstoy's writing—his moral essays as well as his fiction; my dad immersed himself in Orwell's documentary works, and occasionally tried to follow his literary hero's lead by exploring certain neighborhoods, trying to figure out who lived in them and why—though he didn't venture much into Boston. When he and my mom traveled, they both shunned tourist guides, and tried to pursue their own bouts of curiosity and observation.

Sometimes when our parents would drive us into Boston's downtown to go to the movies, hear a concert, or visit a museum, they would point out street scenes, particular stores, or individuals. In that regard,

my first memory of race as a subject of parental mention, and consequently, as an aspect of my awareness, goes back to 1936, I know, when
I was around six. My dad was driving my brother Bill and me, with our
mother at his side, and a red light had us stopped. A hurricane was
threatening Boston, and our parents were anxious to get home after
some hours of shopping in the city, with every anticipation of a storm's
damage—fallen trees and wires would make automobile travel hard. I
clearly remember, even now, sixty years afterward, my dad's hurry, but
also his spoken anxiety and fear as that light held us up longer than
usual. The light wouldn't turn green, and the two cars ahead of us
weren't budging. All of a sudden, dad beeped our car's horn—to no
effect. Our usually quiet, calm, controlled dad turned outspoken, angry,
muttering something about the cars ahead and the street where we were.
He abruptly pulled into the lane where the oncoming traffic might have
confronted him, but fortunately didn't; so, in no time, he drove ahead
of the other two cars, ignored the light, and proceeded toward our
home.

I can still see dad looking at the drivers of those two cars; I can still
hear him telling our mother that those two drivers obviously lived in the
neighborhood where our car had been kept waiting a minute ago—and
thereupon some further comments from him that addressed the world
of streets and people he had done his very best, foot heavy on the gas
pedal, to leave behind. By then we were well on our way, and I can still
remember the relief my father's face showed, and the consequent pleasure my brother and I felt—even as one word crossed our dad's mouth:
"safe." Immediately he turned on the radio, and right away we were
attending a radio program, an announcer's remarks about the weather,
and classical music (to which our parents were forever listening, whether
in the house or in their car).

When we got home, we asked our mother why dad had been so
upset—and her quick and brief remark stands in my mind as my first
occasion of racial awareness. I can even see her, today, making supper
in the kitchen as she spoke: "That was scary because there is crime
there—your dad wanted us out of there." But we wanted to know
more—those endless questions of the young. What kind of crime? Is it
different there than anywhere else in the city? Our mother kept quiet
as we posed our inquiries, and held us off by reminding us of the obvi-

ous—that she had to prepare food, and had no time, then, for the kind of talk we seemed to want. She settled the matter by suggesting that we go see our dad, who was upstairs in his study. We were all set to comply with her recommendation—but suddenly, she had some second thoughts. She stopped cutting vegetables for the soup she was making, and suggested we all sit at the kitchen table—a move that added suspense and drama to the proceedings, I would later realize. Then, her announcement—the words an important part of my later social awareness, I came to understand gradually: "That was a neighborhood where poor people live"—a brief pause, and then the qualification "poor colored people." She must have seen the quizzical looks on our faces, because she immediately went into an explanation that I also remember clearly, and that stopped us all short: "Some people call them colored, some people call them Negro."

My brother and I looked at one another; meanwhile, she was looking at us. Herself a former teacher, she now spoke like one of our elementary school teachers—told us about the Civil War, the history of slavery in the American South, the migration of Negroes north to escape their grim social, economic, and legal fate. I am now turning that discourse of hers into a formal narrative account of a segment of American history—whereas back then, a mother was trying her best to explain a family incident, supply it with some social and historical context, though she evidently had been made nervous by what had happened, by our interest in knowing about our dad's words, and by his short spell of irritation, frustration, anger. Finally, this remark—a valiant effort on her part to be psychological and morally evenhanded which I'd appreciate much later (years later, actually): "White people are often afraid of Negro people, the colored—it goes both ways."

She had to return to her cooking, she wanted us to know, and she indicated this loudly and clearly through her own frustration (not irritation)—an echo, at home, of what we'd experienced on a distant downtown street. Now it was for Bill and me to figure out what had happened—the why of our mother's remarks, blunt in one aspect, but also enigmatic. Together, we wondered who "Negro people, the colored" were, and how our parents knew who they were—because we had never seen such people in our neighborhood, our town, nor had we seen any such people on that Boston street, as our dad had tried to speed us away. Our mother and father had been referring to individuals whom we had no way of knowing, even (at that moment in our young lives) recognizing—hence the perplexity, the confusion of it all.

Soon our dad appeared, and we told him what we had heard from mom. "Yes," he remarked and then he bore down on race in an all too concise and unqualified manner: "White people have skin like we have, and Negroes have brown skin, so they're different from us." To this day I recall what my brother said after a few seconds of puzzled silence on our part: "But we get tans in the summer, and then our skin is brown." At that dad nodded, and laughed. Another of his explanations followed: "A tan goes away, but if you're a Negro your skin is always tan—that is why they are called 'colored.'"

We could tell that there was more on his mind, that he felt there was more to say, but we could also tell that he didn't want to pursue this subject any further. We mentioned what mom had told us about (I'd now paraphrase it as the reciprocal distaste of whites and African Americans toward each other) and he assented, told us mom had put it just right. But he went further, and those words I still can recall, as well as his head's movement, then that of his right hand. He shook his head and, pointing to the Boston newspaper in his hand, offered this: "The papers tell of crimes in Negro districts [of Boston]—that's why I wanted us out of there fast. You shouldn't say all Negroes are guilty of crimes, but you have to look at the news, the statistics." Thereupon a long explanation from him of violence among the poor (and, as he kept pointing out), of *noticeable* violence among the poor. By no means do I remember every word, but I do certainly recall his line of articulated thinking, and I especially well remember his emphasis on the word *noticeable*—the beginning, I'd now say, of an extended riff, were he by some miracle here on earth, and I, a grown-up, listening to him speak. He wanted us to realize that people often pay attention to some people, some events, and ignore what others do or say. He was giving us a memorable lecture on perception, its causes or reasons. Indeed, he went further, turned a bit biographical, if not confessional—insisted that he might "hold against" (his phrase, used often) Negroes what they might otherwise ignore, even forgive, or find ways of understanding, then condoning, in others.

I am, of course, speaking for my dad, imposing on a past event my contemporary way of seeing and talking about things—but I can see my father's face, hear the themes of his intended communication. Most of all, I can hear him lowering his voice, yet inclining his body toward us—as he let us know that if we'd been driving through other sections of Boston where the crime rate was also well known to be high, he'd have been far less worried. Then, his way of summarizing so very much—and here I certainly do recall his observations (or self-observation) faithfully, if not word for word: "If I actually knew any Negro people, I think I'd have been less scared. I was scared—I said that street was scary, but I was scared." We weren't accustomed to that line of introspection and self-arraignment from our scientific father, so often a forthright and formidably knowledgeable person. Yet there he was, determined to tell us what had crossed his mind, what he felt, as he pushed more and more gas into his car's engine. Abruptly, he ended our conversation; his favorite news commentator on the radio, Elmer Davis, was about to begin announcing what was happening across America, over the world's continents—so the end of an experience, soon to become a life-long memory that has prompted me to realize at least some little bit of what racial fear (if not outright racism) is all about. In a reasonably comfortable home, maybe even, relatively speaking, a privileged one, two parents had acted and spoken in such a way that they had to explain themselves to their children, giving us both pause and thought—making us wonder what had gotten so much going, all because a red light wasn't operating with normal dispatch.

A few years later, when I was in the sixth grade, a wonderful teacher, Miss Avery, dared pour out her heart and soul as she taught us American history, and particularly (at great length and in mighty detail) the stories of the Civil War, of slavery, of "Negroes as victims of bondage, exploitation, and persecution"—those words mine, copied from what Miss Avery wrote on the blackboard, and saved by my mother and dad, among other of my school notes and compositions. To this day (another experience become, at times, vivid memory), I can hear our Vermont-born and -reared teacher (so she told us many times) speaking of her favorite American president, Abraham Lincoln—speaking, too, of why: what he did on behalf of whom, for which reasons. Once, in the midst of such a lesson (about slavery), Miss Avery asked us please to "look around." What in the world did she mean for us to do? We sat silently, awaiting elaboration, a clue or two. But she kept staring back at us, and so we began, at last, to "look around" at one another, not sure what to notice or attend to, but as loyal members of a reasonably well schooled, obliging class. Suddenly, words came at us—and they are still loud and clear in my auditory memory: "Well, what have you seen?" We knew not her intended line of inquiry. She knew we sat there uncomprehending. She answered for us, and also told us what she wanted to get across: "You see one another, but there is no Negro for you to see in this class, or in this school."

Surprised, stunned even, we became fidgety. Now our eyes were lowered—no longer directed either at her or one another. She then turned us around, asked us why she had just put us all through that "exercise," she called it. We were silent—until she wanted us to explain out loud *why* there weren't any Negroes at school with us; and I can remember my spoken answer when she recognized my raised hand: "The Negroes don't live here. So they don't go to school with us." No brilliant discovery or formulation, that, but our teacher was never one to let things go, let our earnest or well-intentioned efforts pass her uncritical muster. "But *why?*"—she wanted to know; and then a long rendering of her question: "Why are there no Negroes living in this school district?"

None of us knew how to reply, for a time long enough to make us all restless and anxious—I recall moving my feet on the floor, staring at my seated classmates, and remembering what I'd recently heard my parents say. Nervous about the silence in the room, and nervous about quoting my parents, I blurted out: "The whites are scared of the Negroes, and the Negroes are scared of the whites"—my version of what I'd heard, learned at home.

"Yes," our teacher bellowed—and then another of her *whys*! We were certainly dumbfounded—me, the answerer, included. In moments we were told about the way people treat others badly, then earn their resentment. We were told about the way people feel when they sense they have done wrong—they try to blame others for what they themselves have done to those others. I don't, of course, have every word of Miss Avery's down, or tape-recorded, but I can sure hear her, even now, trying to get us to understand the elements of crowd psychology she was hoping to convey to us in that elementary classroom—and here I am, decades later, harkening back to what happened there, as well as on that aforementioned Boston street: two experiences that became part of a memory, part of a child's racial awareness—that got furthered amid a long stretch of ignorance and indifference with respect to racial matters.

No wonder, decades later, when I went South to serve my two years owed the military (under the old Doctors' Draft) and lived, consequently, in Mississippi and in Louisiana, I kept going back to those childhood moments, kept hearing my parents and a much-favored teacher, kept trying to find my own responses to the statements and questions I'd long ago heard, to the attitudes and customs up North I'd taken for granted. For I was, in the 1960s, living in a South challenged decisively about its prevailing attitudes and customs—life's social and racial confusions were ever ready to assert themselves, impress themselves on me, just as they have, historically, on others up America's North, or down our South.

Robert Coles, M.D., was an Air Force physician stationed in Biloxi, Mississippi, in 1958 when he first saw extremely friendly southerners who were also comfortable with violently enforcing the racial divide. Later, as a child psychiatrist studying the process of school desegregation in New Orleans, he met Ruby Bridges, a six-year-old girl who faced down racist mobs to become the first black child in the city's public schools. Inspired by Ruby's courage, Coles devoted himself to anti-poverty and desegregation programs that eventually led to his work with Martin Luther King, Jr., and Robert Kennedy.

The author of more than sixty books, among them the Pulitzer Prize–winning "Children of Crisis" series, Dr. Coles is widely revered as an author, a doctor, a professor, and a civil rights activist. In 1999, President Bill Clinton awarded him the United States' highest civilian honor, the Medal of Freedom.

© Les Payne

The Night I Stopped Being a Negro

LES PAYNE

A WHITE LAD once delivered a telegram to our Tuscaloosa home and my grandmother, as was the peculiar Alabama custom, addressed him as "sir." Her deference to a teenager broke my six-year-old heart. Some will argue, and psychologists among them, that a child of such a tender age could not have been so repulsed by a community custom that his parents steadfastly embraced. But I suffered the incident in silence, and I was indeed only six years old.

Other such contradictions riled me periodically. I once refused to answer "Yes, sir" to a white shoe salesman and my mother slapped my face crisply, and hard. Despite her maternal entreaties, and another cuffing right there in the store, I refused to utter the requisite "sir." This unreadiness seized me involuntarily, like the hiccups, quite without warning. I had no reasons, only questions I dared not ask. Children in black, working-class families, even loving, fundamentalist Baptist ones like mine, simply did not talk back to their parents. We were to be seen and to obey in silence.

Honorifics were prized among us and had specific application. "Sir" and "ma'am" were reserved for parents, elders, and adult strangers. Youngsters shy of their majority were spared. There were certain exceptions among family. My brothers and I did not, for example, answer "ma'am" to our Aunt Lizzie, or "sir" to my Uncle Edward, whose nickname was "Deadwood Dick." Both of these family elders had strayed from the teachings of Christ Jesus and, we learned later, drank whiskey.

Strangely, my brothers and I were not required to answer "ma'am" to our mother—with her tacit approval. She was not a backslider and didn't drink whiskey, so this was puzzling to me, the youngest following the lead, but again, I didn't ask questions. Later I surmised that it was because mother was a very young woman, looked even younger, and was separated from our father.

This matrix of Southern behavior was straightforward enough, until whites entered our small, homogeneous universe. Race etiquette of the day had white strangers addressing my grandmother as "girl," or "Annie." My sixty-eight-year-old granddaddy they called "boy." Negroes, on the other hand, were required under penalty of law, vigilante violence, and hellfire to address all whites, of whatever age or station, with "sir" or "ma'am" and "Mr." this and "Mrs." that.

The telegram boy was the first white person I'd encountered up close. He was not, however, the first teenager I'd met. Teenagers, in my six-year-old mind, were never answered "sir." Yet here was my grandmother, the person I respected most in all the world, humbling herself before a teenager. It sent my whole world crashing. As for the incident with the shoe salesman, I just couldn't bring myself to utter the respectful "sir" to a stranger in the presence of my mother.

It would be a stretch to conclude that my childhood refusal to address white strangers by polite titles of respect was some existential reach for justice. Albert Camus majestically argues such a point in his philosophical treatise, *The Rebel*, where the first insurrectionary word out of the mouth of the hero is "No." Unlike the Rebel, I was quite diffident as a child, though a bit stubborn. I suspect that my unreadiness, initially at least, stemmed from the fact that, like all children, I was born free of racial bias. In my innocence, I also held the naïve notion that words meant something specific and that their application was immutable. This concreteness emboldens some primary students hard off their first grammar lesson to correct their parents' syntax. I dared not correct my elders, though my knees buckled at certain constructions, to say nothing of the contradictions. We didn't answer "sir" to teenagers, so why did grandma answer "sir" to a white teenager?

My push for justness in conversation earned me a few beatings and some alienation, and cost me a new pair of shoes. Still, my abstinence persisted, not so much as an act of rebellion, but as an outcry for clarity in a confused young life knocked topsy-turvy by race. More specifically, I balked unknowingly at this early parental pressure to get me converted, born again, and socialized into a state of inferiority—to be made a Negro.

I faced my first race-based conundrum.

The Eden into which I was born was the Tuscaloosa of the 1940s, a taut mill town on the disturbed banks of the Black Warrior River. Like most of the state, the city was garnished with the plundered culture and pilfered nomenclature of the vanquished Native Americans, mainly the Choctaw, who once roamed the Alabama woodlands. Tuscaloosa got its name from the chief who was defeated in 1540 by Hernando de Soto. Negroes of my day stood instinctively against the descendants of de Soto, instead identifying—many even claiming bloodlines—with Chief Tuska (warrior) Lusa (black), the Black Warrior.

Like a dagger of the Devil, the railroad tracks split Tuscaloosa between working class Negroes and the whites who ruled everything. On our side were wood-frame shotgun houses, segregated schools, Bar-B-Q juke joints, choke-dusty roads, bootleggers, and, proliferating everywhere, holy roller churches of the Lord. Snaking through the neighborhood, the blue and orange city buses would deliver our parents across town to menial jobs at the Gulf States Paper Mill, Holt's iron foundry, downtown stores, and the white folks' yards and kitchens.

Their side of town featured the lily-white University of Alabama, home of the nationally ranked Crimson Tide football team coached by the legendary Bear Bryant. Though barred from Alabama games, Negroes were recruited at five cents an hour to clean up Denny Stadium and mop the campus dormitory floors. As for Negro higher education, there was Stillman College. Founded in 1876 by missionaries, Stillman was operated by white Presbyterians who graduated black homemakers, ministers, musicians, teachers, frustrated handymen, and more missionaries.

Other than Bear Bryant, the closest thing Tuscaloosa had to a reigning hometown hero was Robert Shelton, the Imperial Wizard of the Ku Klux Klan. Whites preached that God Himself had anointed them to rule from their separate Eden. This grand design had Gov. James E. (Big Jim) Folsom as the equal of Charlemagne, Bear Bryant as a plaid-hatted Apollo, and Wizard Shelton as a housebroken Attila the Hun. So beloved was this White Knight in bed tick that an official sign at the city limits announced that Tuscaloosa was "The Home of Robert Shelton, Imperial Wizard of the KKK." Everything in those days was segregated: churches, water fountains, bus and train stations, rail coaches, schools, the hospital, drugstores, toilets, graveyards, the five-and-dime, even the sidewalks. Sheriffs enforced this apartheid by day; Robert Shelton and his hooded terrorists enforced it by night. A caravan of his Klan nightriders once rode through our community and kindled in my young soul more curiosity than fear. Every God-fearing Negro, save my uncle Deadwood Dick, quaked in their brogans for weeks. I got the message.

Despite the breast beating about supremacy, it took those redneck pets of God the dint of church, law, and many weapons to suppress Negro competition that might otherwise challenge this white preeminence. Competition, especially in the job market, was the great fear of these superior beings of Tuscaloosa. Their clown show as the Chosen Ones was orchestrated by a small, seldom-seen elite who had grown wealthy from recent wartime light industry, cotton plantation profits sweated from Old South slaves, and cheap labor of post-Reconstruction sharecroppers. This oligarchy manipulated the more visible mass of bamboozled white proletarians who ran the apartheid goat that chewed up the lives and resources of Negro families. Key to this terror regime was the Alabama judicial system that secretly supported armed bands of murderous, liquored-up, white degenerates like Robert Shelton, and loosed them upon agrarian blacks a generation out of slavery striving to improve their stake in America.

Our parents conspired with this Southern reality. They curbed all signs of rebellion in their offspring, especially in their boys, fearing that it would land them in harm's way. Getting arrested, they taught, was unchristian, yet the white sheriffs made it all but unavoidable. This brutal irony drove some parents preemptively to call the police to haul their rebellious children off to the penitentiary. Example made, those who stayed home dared not aspire to equal the measure of whites. Adolescence was a twilight zone. Manhood was unfathomable.

This inferiority, inspired in us at the hearth, was reinforced by every shred of evidence on public display: the Little Black Sambo schoolbooks, the billboards, the *Amos 'n' Andy Radio Show*, the drinking fountains, the sales clerks, the hillbilly governor's mansion, and the Jim Crow laws at every turn.

Occasionally, enlightened teachers would confuse us. They proffered the notion that we were just as good and as smart as anyone else— even the white students across the tracks whom we never saw, but whose tattered, second-hand books we were fortunate enough to inherit. What little we learned of those little darlings, whose parents ran our world, was picked up in snatches of conversations from our womenfolk who daily cooked their meals, cleaned their bedrooms, washed their clothes, and sometimes nursed their siblings.

We were bent like saplings to the circumstance of a permanent underclass. The process was at least as old as the Spartans' art of dominating the Helots by weeding out each generation's allotment of brave warriors who would otherwise break the cycle of fear, passivity, ignorance, and dependency. Without the courageous ones—so brutally ripped away—the others, no matter how deep their intelligence, could not mount and sustain an insurgency against Jim Crow. Police brutality, with its round-up tactic of racial profiling, served the state's purpose of maintaining white supremacy and had the tacit approval of the white majority.

The quiet kitten of self-loathing came subtly upon me as a child. My resignation to this inferior status in America was occurring in sinister, well-calibrated, almost scientific stages. Born free, I was, within the borders of my circumstance, becoming colonized. There were no pitched battles, no changing of the flag, no fanfare of surrender. Indeed, no internal war of the psyche was ever declared. All I know is that by age twelve—the year I found the Lord and was baptized—I was no longer digging in my heels against racial slights, indignities, and humiliations. When my eyes were not fastened on the hereafter, I noticed how few earthly rewards Negroes got for their efforts. In time, I began thinking maybe we Negroes just didn't deserve any better.

Caught up in this zephyr, I began trimming the sails of my dreams and expectations. I scrapped the idea of becoming a train engineer, an artist, a scientist, and even a fireman.

There were no black models to fix on, no tracks on the choke-dusty road. Tuscaloosa had seen to that. The strong men, so indomitable in our world, shrunk to insignificance in the presence of white folks. Proud, boastful lions at home, they were lambs on their jobs across town. Mr. Hughes, my junior high school principal, was so intimidating that when juvenile toughs heard his voice roaring near the boys' bathroom they would swallow their cigarettes, sometimes ashes and all. On those rare visits from white officials, however, the man we called the "Bear" put on his dance of the kowtow. His *basso profundo* would lose its deep timbre and regain it only when the white functionaries cleared the railroad tracks.

At age six, such obsequious behavior might have hit me like fresh manure in a closed stall. Approaching puberty, however, with the stench of segregation still wafting in the air, something within me had changed. I had started out with zero tolerance for the etiquette of Negro behavior. Once it had contorted me like a seizure of the hiccups. Now, at the age of twelve, thanks to socialization within family and community, such petit apartheid drew barely a yawn. My emerging generation was newly primed for our post-slavery role as hewers of wood in a rich, industrialized America.

I had become a rail-thin, down-home, born-again, Tuscaloosa Negro boy.

&

My family migrated north to Hartford, Connecticut, when I was twelve and going into the ninth grade. Just as the immigrants pouring in from Hungary, Italy, and the rest of postwar Europe, we too were seeking better economic conditions, and escaping political oppression and state terror. Unlike the Russians, the Poles, and the Hungarians, my family had endured eight generations of slavery, oppression, and misery, not in some foreign police state, but down on the Alabama steppes of America.

"I knew I didn't have the kind of boys that could make it down there," mother said of my two brothers and me. Despite careful grooming at home, school, and church, my parents judged us poor candidates for the kowtow. My increasing lapses in racial deference, my grand-mother feared, would surely attract the sheriff's attention, if not Robert Shelton's. The penitentiary beckoned, she warned, and behind it—an early grave.

The Tuscaloosa educational system had not prepared me for the shock of Hartford Public High School. All the teachers and 95 percent of the students were white. Plucked from an *Amos 'n' Andy* world, I had been put down in the classroom of *Our Miss Brooks*. For weeks I could barely speak around classmates I took to be one part Aristotle to two parts Captain Marvel. Though an honors student in Tuscaloosa, I felt totally compromised academically, forsaken, alone, alienated, afraid, country-dumb, and inferior all the way down my genomic chain. I felt even my God had failed me.

The tissue of the indomitable white student, in time, began to peel away from my classmates like a suntan. They spoke proper English, but their answers in class were no better than the ones I was too frightened to utter. Hiding in the second row of Mr. Nathalie's geometry class proved difficult. I was swept up into participation. My first test paper came back marked "92." The white kid a desk over got a 78. How, by the name of Tuscaloosa, could this be possible? Perhaps our test papers had somehow been switched. The scenario was repeated in English, earth science, and civics.

My guidance counselor, Carl Olsen, seemed impressed with my sophomore honor-roll grades, but the tall, bushy-haired teacher grew wary when I told him I'd like to become an electrical engineer. The Soviets had launched Sputnik, and the space race with the United States was on. Engineering was a hot field in Connecticut with key aeronautical firms such as Pratt & Whitney, Sikorsky Helicopters, and Hamilton Standards. Despite my grades, Mr. Olsen recoiled at my ambitions as if I had offended him personally.

"I don't think you should plan on going into engineering," he said. "It's just not realistic. I think you should (take courses that will) prepare (you) for a career where Negroes can get jobs." (When I read later that a Michigan teacher in the 1930s had similarly dismissed Malcolm X's plans to become a lawyer, I thought perhaps there was a national script that these white gatekeepers read from.) Mr. Olsen flatly refused to register me in requisite algebra and advanced physics courses. I don't know how many other black student wings he had clipped. Grades weren't discussed in my circle of street buddies. We talked girls, baseball, girls, cars, girls, gang colors, girls, pinball machines. Good grades were frowned upon. Some had the growing suspicion that, despite holding up my end in gang fights, I was something of a closet bookworm.

Mr. Olsen was the first in a long line of white gatekeepers to underestimate me.

I encountered Max Putzel as a sophomore engineering student at the University of Connecticut. The first literary essay I wrote for this English professor came back marked "BS." After class, I waited for the white students to clear the area around his desk before politely requesting an explanation of his rather strange grade.

"You know what it means," Putzel said gruffly. "It means bullshit. You know you didn't write that paper."

Speechless, I stood before the honored professor, perhaps, like Melville's Billy Budd, stuttering before Claggert. Unlike Budd, who struck a telling blow, I withered under the hot lights of Professor Putzel's false accusation and turned meekly for the door, tears welling from some place deep down in Tuscaloosa. I couldn't bring myself to plead my case or even to face my accuser.

At semester's end, Professor Putzel's postcard arrived at home bearing my final grade, a prominent B, this time without the S. A handwritten apology explained that he had been "hasty" in prejudging me incapable of writing a competent English essay. My performance convinced him finally, he wrote, that my initial essay had been my "own work."

Authority figures such as Putzel, Carl Olsen, and dozens of others were devastating setbacks. After departing Tuscaloosa, I had worked to overcome my crippling sense of racial inferiority. With no human reinforcement, it was through extracurricular reading that I came to grips with one aspect of my condition. This self-medicated therapy came through reading the works of psychiatrists Frantz Fanon, William H. Grier, and Price Cobbs and writers such as Gunnar Myrdal, Herbert Aptheker, I. F. Stone, Jean-Paul Sartre, Richard Wright, and James Baldwin. These prescriptions set me on the road to a cure. The most meaningful counterattack upon racism in America was Baldwin's magazine article on the Black Muslims. This was my first glimmer of the possibility of achieving peace, if not parity, on the race question.

My racial transformation, which started in Mr. Nathalie's geometry class, had been only a fleeting, easily reversible sense of academic parity. White students enjoyed no greater insight into Chaucer, Camus, or Dostoyevsky than I, yet they flew in an orbit far beyond my reach. I'd never met a white person, South or North, who did not feel comfortably superior to every Negro, no matter the rank or station. Conversely, no Negro I'd met or heard of had ever felt truly equal to whites. For all their polemical posturing, not even Baldwin, Martin Luther King, Jr., or the great Richard Wright, with all his crossed-up feelings, had liberated themselves from the poisoned weed of black self-loathing with its deeply entangled roots in the psyche.

One night during my college days, I came face-to-face with my own psyche of self-loathing.

It was June 6, 1963.

~&

Entering from stage left, the speaker of the evening loped into such a hush up front that his shiny Stacey Adams could be heard clacking on the oak floor. Settling quickly at the lectern, Malcolm X clenched his teeth against a fresh challenge from the local newspaper to his status as a national black leader.

His subject, that Wednesday night in Hartford, was "God's Judgment of America and the Only Solution to the Race Problem." He had been refining the speech since his "homecoming" appearance at Michigan State University four months earlier. Several of his white childhood classmates had attended that address on January 23. Proud, curious, and disbelieving of the fearsome aspects of his national image, they had not seen Malcolm in the flesh since he left East Lansing for Boston as a gangling teenager, with a twinkle and a yen for the fast life.

One white classmate from nearby Mason left the hall, bewildered that this fierce, podium Malcolm had shown no trace of "Harpy," her gentle friend and class president of her eighth grade. That was his last year of formal education, an ordeal his English teacher shut down by berating him for aspiring to become a lawyer. The white teacher proposed instead that young Malcolm Little make peace with his birthright as a Negro and aim at becoming a carpenter.

On the night of Malcolm X's speech, I was among the audience in the half-filled auditorium at Bushnell Memorial Hall. Connecticut was Martin Luther King, Jr.'s, country. His nonviolent Civil Rights Movement was Southern based and he came to New England not to scorn but to raise funds. King acknowledged that Southern history and tradition—codified in Jim Crow laws—had imbued "blacks with a false sense of inferiority and whites with a false sense of superiority." While King sought to change the behavior of the dominant society, Malcolm X hammered away at blacks' "false sense of inferiority." He conducted his scorched-earth polemics all over New England and elsewhere in the North, hell-bent on exposing whites as "blue-eyed devils" and changing the mind of the Negro.

Recommending black self-help, Malcolm X exposed the white hypocrisy of de facto segregation in such areas as Connecticut housing and education aimed at its 125,000 resident Negroes and Puerto Ricans. Segregation was not a Southern phenomenon, he argued, but an American one that also infected New England institutions of higher education. Among the 1,700 University of Connecticut graduates in 1960, for example, there were but two Negroes. At the time, I was one of less than sixty blacks in UConn's student population of some ten thousand.

I had first heard of Malcolm X and the Black Muslims in 1959 when CBS televised "The Hate That Hate Produced." Occasionally I would encounter Muslims "fishing" after North End church services or hawking *Muhammad Speaks* downtown. I had even come face to face with Malcolm X near the group's small, makeshift temple on Albany Avenue, but was too astonished to utter a word. Impressed with Malcolm X, but wary of his leader Elijah Muhammad and his cult, I had followed such news of the Muslims as reached my quasi-cloistered campus life. The image I had of the Muslims was of stereotypical ex-cons in bow ties shoving *Muhammad Speaks* into the faces of frightened white shoppers. Among others, Woody Allen popularized this image in his spoof of a dubbed Japanese movie, *What's Up, Tiger Lily?*

I altered my opinion of the Muslims in 1962 when I read, in *The New Yorker*, James Baldwin's "Notes from a Region in My Mind," a prophetic rendering of the writer's encounter with Malcolm X and Elijah Muhammad. (It was later printed as the best-selling *The Fire Next Time*.) Adding his oil to Elijah Muhammad's fires, Baldwin warmed me to the notion that whites were not fit models for how to live one's life. Negro students across the nation read Baldwin and took in his lectures, but wouldn't dare visit the forbidding Muslem mosques, with their body-and-handbag searches, hard security in the pews, and strict segregation of men from women. For his analysis of the Muslims, Baldwin, who had debated Malcolm X on several panels, went directly to the source, Elijah Muhammad.

At the Muslim headquarters in Chicago, Baldwin stood his ground as a writer when Elijah Muhammad, at his dinner table, asked him, "What are you now?" Refusing to be stampeded into saying "Christian," Baldwin said, "I don't, anyway, think about it a great deal." Elijah replied that, "[Baldwin] ought to think about it *all* the deal."

Despite the word from the top man, it would be Malcolm X, not Elijah, even under Baldwin's hand, who moved me to thinking more than *I* otherwise would have about my circumstance as a young Negro in America.

On the night of the lecture, I noticed that Malcolm X alternated his flat reference to "blacks" with a qualified "so-called Negroes." The former loosed a rustle of unreadiness among the brethren in the mixed audience. We were "Negroes," thank you, and proud of it. Malcolm's revisionism was rejected as name calling, bordering on the dozens. For generations, running back to slavery, black was pejorative—period. It conjured up evil, dirty, lowlife, unwashed, tarnished, polluted, squalid, inferior, and all the other negative connotations so well documented in the dictionaries of the early 1960s—and the one Malcolm X himself had pored over during stints in those Massachusetts prisons. Back home in Tuscaloosa, for example, whenever I would call my oldest brother "black" (though both of us were as dark as a pocket), I'd have to run for my life. If I had thought of calling him "African," God forbid, he would have chased me mercilessly to the ends of the earth.

The Negroes in the Hartford audience, as elsewhere, brought acquiescence, if not pride, to our contemporary racial group designation. This same year, 1963, a group of Negro students at a Toledo, Ohio, high school organized an angry demonstration after an assistant principal referred to them over the intercom as "black students." Like the other Negro Baptists in the hall, I had, with the faith of little children, believed in every Christian tenet and American orthodoxy including— down deep—our own racial inferiority.

Every jot and tittle of this Judeo-Christian-American credo Malcolm X shredded this night with his terrible, swift sword.

Sensing the misplaced racial pride as strong in Hartford as anywhere he had visited, Malcolm X took pains to address the issue head on. "Now I know you don't want to be called 'black,'" he said, isolating his targets scattered throughout the mixed audience. I got the feeling he was speaking directly to me. "You want to be called 'Negro.' But what does 'Negro' mean except 'black' in Spanish? So what you are saying is: 'It's OK to call me 'black' in Spanish, but don't call me black in English."

This simple analysis struck me dumb! Sitting in my cushioned seat, a shiver of enlightenment swept over me. It was as profound as a haiku moving a Buddhist novice to achieve "satori" under the prompting of a Zen master. After shovels of Muslim theology, horse-doctor doses of racial counterrejection, and trash talking about the "blue-eyed devils," Malcolm had finally done the job with an eyedropper.

My mind raced back to Tuscaloosa and every parent and teacher urging that I was "just as good as white kids," only to get contradicted by the Alabama reality of the 1950s. The "whites only" signs rolled by, as did the juke joints, the Klan, the railroad tracks, the Jim Crow bus station, the redneck sheriffs, and Mr. Olsen. All of it patched into a crazy quilt of white superiority with the obverse side black inferiority.

If Negroes were "just as good," then why were we janitors but not landlords, cooks but not city councilmen, pickers but not farmers of cotton, hewers but not owners of the timberlands and lumber yards? Where, I had also wondered, were the Negro professionals: the doctors, architects, lawyers, judges, mayors, governors, and engineers? Where were, as Marcus Garvey had asked in 1916, the black men of big ideas? Why indeed did we so totally reject Garvey's notion of the African man?

The lightning Malcolm X loosed that night scored a direct hit on the tin shack of my own psyche. That conditioned sense of Negro inferiority, hothoused during my Alabama childhood, dissipated like ground fog under the bright sun. Perhaps because he had personally undergone

a Damascus Road conversion, Malcolm X was able to communicate—
and demonstrate with his life—how Negroes like myself could throw
off the damnable curse that blocks our potential and keeps us from taking our place among men.

By the end of the lecture, I felt—and knew—that something
within me had changed again, this time irreversibly. Whites were no
longer superior. Blacks—most important, I, myself—were no longer
inferior. This cardinal message would make Malcolm X a treasure for
black liberation and a serious threat to white America.

By stripping "black" of its magic powers to dehumanize, Malcolm
X single-handedly reoriented the "Afro-American" masses toward a
healthier sense of our color and an appreciation of our African roots.
He was the leader most responsible for condemning the term "Negro"
to the scrap heap. He also purged and popularized "black" and paved
the way for "African Americans" as accepted usage, driving both into
the *Webster's Collegiate Dictionary.*

My own group birthright, so indelibly stamped upon the souls of
black folks in America, was as difficult to remove as a tattoo. It was
finally stripped away by Malcolm's acid bath of racial counter-rejection,
tough-love logic, and bottom-up primer on American history. Since
Tuscaloosa, I had carried deep within me the mark of the conditioned
Negro, the most despised—and self-despising—creature in America.
Up until this June night I had been lost, but all praises be to Malcolm
X, my dungeon shook, and, as the poet said, my chains fell off.

I entered Bushnell Hall as a Negro with a capitol "N" and wandered
out into the parking lot—as a black man.

*Les Payne, a Pulitzer Prize–winning reporter, is deputy managing editor
at* Newsday *and a columnist for the* Los Angeles Times *syndicate. The
recipient of dozens of national and international journalism awards, Payne
was a permanent TV panelist on WCBS's* Sunday Edition, *and is the inaugural professor of the Laventhol Chair at Columbia's Graduate School of
Journalism. He has appeared on numerous radio and television shows including* Nightline, Good Morning America, The MacNeil/Lehrer News
Hour, Meet the Press, Washington Week in Review, The Phil Donahue
Show, *and CNN's* Year in Review.

Son of the South

John Seigenthaler, Sr.

I am a son of the segregated, racist South.

I declare it neither as a self-condemnation nor as a confession, but simply to acknowledge a grotesque fact of life in a conflicted and cursed time and place.

Those who look at the region as it is today are entitled to wonder why we who were acculturated to the ways of an earlier time could not (or would not) recognize either the conflict or the curse. Here, I wonder myself.

From birth through childhood and well into adulthood, my hometown, Nashville, Tennessee, was as racially partitioned by law, custom, and white preference as any city in South Africa at the peak of apartheid. White Nashvillians of my generation are quick to explain that our town was not as racist as Selma or Montgomery in Alabama, or Stone Mountain in

Georgia, or Oxford or Philadelphia in Mississippi. Black Nashvillians will tell you it was a difference without distinction.

Think of any public place where a resident of my city might need or wish to go—a hospital, restaurant, restroom, hotel, school, park, church, theater, trolley, or bus—and that place was ruled by Jim Crow laws and the Confederate tradition of enforced racial separation. Every government-owned building where citizens were required to do business—the courthouse, city hall, state capital, or health department—was required to have separate "white" and "colored" restrooms and drinking fountains to protect "the health of the community."

In courtrooms, there were only white judges and white jurors to decide disputes over property, liberty, and sometimes life. People of color who could afford it often hired white lawyers to represent them and spoke and thought of the word "justice" in quotation marks.

Department stores and government office buildings opened their doors to all citizens, but once inside, white customers and taxpayers routinely received preferential treatment by white sales people and white bureaucrats—and there were only white sales people and bureaucrats. "First come, first served" could mean that the second or third or fourth person to come, if that person was white, was served first. Everywhere posted signs mandated the Jim Crow law:

> *Colored to the Back*
> *Negroes Sit in Rear*
> *White Drinking Fountain*
> *Colored Drinking Fountain*
> *Negro Balcony Upstairs*
> *White Men Only*
> *Black Men Only*
> *White Ladies Only*

Even those who could not read had no trouble understanding. The signs silently declared what white southerners demanded, what state law and local ordinance required, and what the United States Supreme Court said was constitutional. African Americans had no option but to accept the obnoxious directives or face public insults, verbal or literal slaps in the face, and possible arrest.

Behind the meaning of those signs was the ingrained Southern certainty that people of color were less intelligent, less capable, less moral, less clean, and less deserving. There was an innate Southern sense that "they" were inferior.

~&

It was as if white people had embraced the blind ignorance of H. L. Mencken, the columnist and cynic (who was neither blind nor ignorant on other issues) when he wrote on "the failure of the educated Negro." "His brain is not fitted for the higher forms of mental effort. His ideals . . . are those of a clown. He will remain inert and inefficient until fifty generations of him have lived in civilization. And even then the white race will be fifty generations ahead of him."

To grow up white in the South at that time was to see black people in streets every day and yet (as Ralph Ellison's *Invisible Man* explained) never to see them; it was to ignore the gross unfairness that was so starkly visible; it was to believe the lie of "separate but equal"; it was to deny the emotional pain suffered by blacks; it was to adopt the myth that racial segregation was permanent, proper, ordained by God, and endorsed by government; it was to laugh hilariously at Stepin Fetchit, Hattie McDaniel, and Amos 'n' Andy, as if they were prototypical.

It also was to hear every day the word "nigger" from the lips of somebody—and most days from several somebodies—in the workplace and in most homes. That word was part of daily childhood discourse in grade school with classmates and, at times, from teachers. "This nigger who works for my daddy . . ." "That nigger janitor . . ." "Eenie, Meanie, Miny, Moe . . ." "There was this nigger Rastus . . ."

The one place I never heard that word was at home. My mother told my siblings and me that it was "common" and "vulgar" and "trashy" to utter that word. And if our wish not to be common or vulgar or trashy was an inadequate muzzle, my father believed that to spare the Biblical rod was to spoil the child.

My Aunt Delia, a Dominican nun and a kindergarten teacher, loved me and was a special person in our family. Still, the forbidden word crept innocently into her conversation, usually as part of some anecdote reflecting her benign and benighted view of black people. Once I asked my mother why she had not admonished her sister, the nun, about being common, vulgar, and trashy.

"Delia is just Delia," she said. Perhaps my mother meant that the South was just the South, Nashville was just Nashville, and she could not influence anybody outside her household.

The realization that it was all right for my classmates, teachers, and aunt to speak a word, but wrong for me to do so, should have sharpened my psychic sensors to the moral contradictions at the core of Southern culture. It didn't, at least not for a long time.

❧

Most of my prepubescent memories are vague and vagrant six decades later, but several poignant race-related anecdotes survive.

I must have been in early elementary school when I discovered that the Paramount Theater had one more balcony than I had realized on previous visits. My mother and grandmother had taken me to see a Shirley Temple film, probably *The Little Colonel.* As the movie ended, the house lights came up and I glanced toward the huge chandeliered ceiling. There, high up near the roof, I saw a line of black faces peering down at me. I had known there was a first balcony. It was my favorite place to sit during the Saturday morning *Popeye Club* flicks. But this second balcony was a revelation. How, I asked, did those people get up there?

"They have their own private entrance," my mother said, as if "they" were privileged.

My grandmother, noting their large number, said, "They all came to see Bill." I was sure they had. Bill was Bill Robinson, the famous black entertainer who had tap danced in the movie with little Shirley Temple. Within a couple of weeks, attending the *Popeye Club* alone, I discovered "their own private entrance." It was down an alley off Church Street and led to three steep flights of narrow stairs.

A far more disturbing memory emerged from a story my grandfather told me at about the same time. He had taken me one Sunday afternoon during a rainy season to the lower Broad Street riverfront to view the waters of the Cumberland swirl above flood stage and spill across cobbled First Avenue. Suddenly he pointed to the towering Woodland Street bridge some 300 yards away.

"I was just about your age," he mused, "and I was standing just about here on the sidewalk where we are now."

His mother had sent him on an errand that afternoon but had instructed him not to go near Public Square. She had heard that there might be "trouble." He had obeyed, but here he was, a mere three blocks down the hill from the very trouble about which his mother had spoken.

"I heard the hollering and shouting and looked right up there to the middle of the bridge," he told me. "It was a big crowd. And they had this colored fellow with a rope around his neck. When they flung him over the rail I could hear his neck snap all the way down here. It was the only time I ever saw a lynching."

"They killed him?" I hoped I had misunderstood. He nodded.

"Just to be sure he was dead they shot him maybe eight or ten times. I could hear the shots and I saw his body jerk when the bullets hit him." It was a stunning story that hurt to hear.

"Where were the police?"

"Some of the police shot him."

On the day before, he said, the black man had been arrested and charged with killing a white man. He was jailed without bond but the mob, obviously in collusion with policemen, had kidnapped him from the jail on Public Square.

My grandfather was a genial, jovial man who doted on me, his first grandchild. That moment was the first time I remember him somber and brooding. I am not certain that every detail of the story was accurate. I doubt from that distance he could have heard the cervical cord crack as the rope wrenched taut. I suspect he later dreamed that and imagined he had heard the victim's neck break. As I stood there with him I thought I heard it, too.

I have no idea why he shared that horror story. The memory had lived long with him—as it has with me. Later, at home, I asked him to relate the story to my younger sisters and brothers. No, he said, they were too young. So was I too young, my grandmother said sharply, scolding him.

Perhaps she was right. Today, more than sixty years later, whenever I drive up First Avenue from what now is Riverfront Park, I find it impossible not to glance up at the more modern Memorial Bridge and revisit in my mind's eye that ghastly scene he described.

I was probably a bit older when I received my first lesson on slavery. It came at Cathedral parochial school from my fifth grade teacher, Sister Mary Florence. She must have taught me many things I cannot now recall, but this lesson I remember with clarity.

"The War Between the States," she told our class (it was never "the Civil War" with Sister Florence, but sometimes was "the War of Northern Aggression"), "had nothing to do with freeing the slaves. The real cause was simple economics—the plantations of the South against the industries of the North.

"The nigger slaves," she explained, "were far better off on plantations in the South than white workers were in Northern factory jobs."

At age eleven I guess that made sense to me. By my teens I had read enough to know that her lesson on this subject deserved rethinking.

Then there was my first Klan sighting. On a Sunday morning my parents and I walked out of ten o'clock mass at the Cathedral and there, standing in two ranks across the street, were some two dozen hooded, robed, masked Klansmen. They were silent, but I felt their glaring eyes on me.

"Who are they?" I asked my parents.

"Damn fool Ku Kluxers," growled my father. In the car on the way home he told my mother he thought he recognized a couple of the men despite their disguises. "They should know better," he said.

My mother had her own term for them: "Yaps!" It was her synonym for "trash." "The Ku Klux Klan," she explained, "is against colored people and Jews, but against Catholics, too."

Why, I wanted to know, were these people I never had laid eyes on against us Catholics?

"They don't like the Pope," she said. She had equally facile explanations for the Klan's anti-Semitism and racism. "They think the Jews killed Jesus and they hate the colored people, well, because they are colored."

I must have pondered then and later over the invisible link that joined me with Jews and African Americans. At least I grasped that the Klan was the common enemy of the Pope and me—and others I had never considered allies.

❧

One afternoon I finally got up the nerve to correct Aunt Delia. It was my birthday and she was home for vacation from teaching kindergarten in Memphis. As a present she gave me a small copy of Francis Thompson's *The Hound of Heaven*. Then she related the story of a school year experience she thought entertaining.

"There was this nigger man," she said, "a Yankee who had just moved to Memphis from somewhere in the North." He had brought his little girl to enroll her in Holy Child kindergarten.

"The child was just a darling little pickininny," she told us, not thinking, of course, of the skin coloring of the holy child for whom the kindergarten was named.

"But it was so funny that he thought we might admit her . . ."

"Mother says it's vulgar to say nigger," I blurted. The beatific smile that usually wreathed her face beneath the veil vanished for a few seconds, reflecting her hurt.

My mother looked crossly at me. Then Aunt Delia said, "Your mother is right. It is vulgar." And she hugged me. If she ever was vulgar again I never knew it.

Finally, there is a perception of the hundreds of times I sat as a young boy, unmoved and unmoving, and watched black women—Nashville's counterparts of Rosa Parks—struggle, laden with shopping or laundry bundles, aboard city buses. I saw them but, as Ralph Ellison said, I never saw them as they stumbled toward "their" area in the rear, passing vacant seats reserved for whites. They had paid the identical passenger fare as white riders, but if they collapsed from exhaustion in a forward seat, blind whites suddenly had the gift of 20/20 sight. There were hostile, disbelieving glares.

Then the motorman would sternly state, "All right back there. You know what the law is. We are not going anywhere until you either get on back to the back or get on off this bus."

Never once did I move to assist them. Never did I leave my seat to move forward and ease their journey to the rear of the bus. I was a polite youngster who had been taught to rise and offer my seat to any woman who was standing. But never was that a black woman. And for too long it did not occur to me to be shamed by it.

In retrospect, I can only wonder: Where was my head? Where was my heart? And where were the heads and hearts of my parents? And my teachers? How could they not have taught me what they certainly knew? Yes, it was the law, but it was wrong. Segregation offended the most basic Christian teaching. It made a charade of any pretense at common decency. How could we have accepted, without comment or concern, a way of life that was so unjust, so corrupt, and so cruel? And where was the press that never bothered to expose these wrongs in society? Reporters, of course, were all white. They, like the rest of us, saw but did not see.

Never did I try to imagine what life was like across the line of segregation. I should not have had to read Ellison's *Invisible Man* years later to comprehend the frustration that was part of enforced anonymity. "I am invisible, understand, simply because people refuse to see me . . ." says Ellison's protagonist. "You often doubt if you really exist. You wonder if you aren't simply a phantom . . ."

I should not have had to read Richard Wright's *Eight Men* to appreciate the anxiety that was part of the stunted ambition of an entire race. "Like any other American," he wrote, "I dreamed of going into business and making money; I dreamed of working for a firm that would allow me to advance until I had reached an important position. Yet I knew with that part of my mind whites had given me that none of my dreams were possible. Then I would hate myself . . ."

I should not have had to read James Baldwin to understand the anger provoked by the ethos. "To be a Negro in this country," he wrote, "and to be relatively conscious is to be in a rage almost all the time."

I wish, looking back, I could claim some road to Damascus conversion that lifted scales from my eyes, or that there had been some startling lesson that cattle-prodded my lethargic young mind, or some thunderbolt sermon from the pulpit that jolted my conscience.

❧

There was one memorable, animating experience from my high school junior year that made a difference. I was approached outside class one day by Theophane Goett, a Franciscan priest who taught math. He presented me a book he thought I might like. It was *The Mind of the South* by W. J. Cash, published a couple of years earlier. It was an unexpected gift, more than a little puzzling since Father Theophane had spoken to me previously only inside the classroom, and then only about algebra, a subject I pursued like a flu germ. He was a stern and strange man, this priest, born, raised, and educated in the East. He spoke with a clipped Yankee accent, wore sandals in winter and, in addition to teaching duties, served the all-black congregation of St. Vincent de Paul's parish.

I had not heard of Cash's book and asked him what it was about.

"Read it and see," he said.

I found it fascinating. Probably because I wanted to impress him, I waded into the book at once, hoping that my enthusiasm for Cash might improve my algebra grade. Within a few days I felt for the first time that I better understood my hometown, my region, southern-born people generally—and even myself.

It was a book with shelf life. Later as a Nieman Fellow at Harvard, Tom Pettigrew, a social scientist with Virginia roots, exposed students to Cash's thesis: that there were many Souths, but also one South—a region dominated by distinctly separate white classes with a shared polity that blended romanticism, religious fundamentalism, hedonism, heroism, and violence. The threads ran together to form the rope by which a common brotherhood of white men controlled the black race.

My reading of Cash did nothing to raise my algebra grade from C, but it otherwise did a great deal for me. For one thing, it gave me a logical rationale as to what made southerners the way we were. It also gave me a deeper self-understanding of the sad and fuzzy, black and white, love-hate ambiguities that were so much a part of our nature. More than anything else, it stimulated my interest in reading more broadly and questioning more deeply.

By the time I enlisted in the Air Corps, where I was trained as a control tower operator, I had come to grips with an inescapable truth: the city and South I loved were flawed and scarred by racist legacy. Any thinking person in the military service had to recognize it.

I was assigned to MacDill Field at Tampa, Florida. From my glass-walled perch atop that Air Force base I had a picture-perfect bird's-eye view every morning of the senseless hypocrisy of segregation. This, of course, was before President Truman ordered desegregation of the armed forces.

As reveille sounded over loudspeakers, I gazed down to my right and watched black airmen file out of "their" barracks, answer roll call, and march off to "their" mess hall. Simultaneously, from barracks on my left, white airmen filed out, answered roll call, and marched off to "our" mess hall. We all were in the same Air Force, defending the same freedoms for the same country, but divided by skin color. If I could see the profound stupidity of the policy, why could not the federal government?

I have no doubt that the random incidents above gradually enlivened my interest in at least intellectually challenging the base inconsistencies around me. By the time I joined the reportorial staff of *The Tennessean*, Nashville's morning newspaper, I had some sense of the systemic injustice that had been a way of life for too long. It was 1949 and I was aware that the news and editorial policy of this newspaper was on the cutting edge of progressive change. Its priorities would include positive positions on the issue of race.

The 1950s were exciting years to be a journalist with that newspaper. Communities and the country were struggling to come to grips with shifting values. Soon after I signed on as a reporter, the newspaper attracted some bright, able, aggressive, young staff members who later would have a national impact on the news media. *The Tennessean's* reputation for aggressive news coverage served as a magnet for them. David Halberstam, Tom Wicker, Wallace Westfeldt, Creed Black, Richard Harwood, and Fred Graham were among those recruited by editor Coleman Harwell. Harwell was a tough news executive who kept our substantial egos in line with blistering daily memos that critiqued our work and demanded perfection. And he motivated us by respecting journalistic initiative, always encouraging fair and accurate reporting and clear, cogent writing.

When race was an issue—and with the furor surrounding the U.S. Supreme Court's 1954 decision in *Brown v. Board of Education* it increasingly was—*The Tennessean* reported on it and on the inflammatory political rhetoric it stimulated. Our paper's editorials urged respect for the Court and adherence to its desegregation mandate "with all deliberate speed."

Years later, Hodding Carter, Jr., and I sat together during a program at the University of Mississippi and acknowledged, in reminis-
cence, that those editorials from "liberal" Southern papers were hardly
models of journalistic courage. They were, rather, modest, moderate
appeals to reason. Still, they attracted angry, threatening, verbal attacks
from that mass of readers wedded to the past and loyal to that racist
present. *The Tennessean* was attacked as a "nigger-loving rag" and "Com-
munist propaganda." Those of us who worked there considered the
insults a badge of honor.

In the view of Silliman Evans, *The Tennessean* owner, and Harwell,
his editor, the South was a mosaic—pieces of a part. Violence in Little
Rock or Montgomery or Oxford or Birmingham was of compelling
interest to those who read our paper in Nashville. Members of our staff
were sent across the region. And when racial conflict visited Nashville,
reportage was intense.

My first important articles on racial violence came as a young investigative reporter. They concerned the slaying of an African American
sawmill hand by a white cab driver in a rural West Tennessee town.

The news tip came from a black Nashville lawyer, Avon Williams,
who later would become a giant among the South's civil rights litigators.
It was in December 1954, a few months after the Supreme Court had
shocked the South with the *Brown* decision. Williams telephoned the
paper and asked for me by name.

"I want to tell you about a murder of a Negro by a white man down
in Camden, Tennessee, a month ago," he said. "No other reporter
knows about it." I understood. He was giving me an exclusive. He
sketched out the details I would have to verify.

Owen Travis had been slain by Ernest Cole over an eight-dollar cab
bill. Within thirty-six hours the Benton County grand jury returned a
"no true" bill clearing the cab driver. Cole's father-in-law was on that
grand jury. It smacked of a racial killing with lynch-law justice.

Why, I asked the lawyer, had he chosen me for this exclusive tip?

My name had been recommended to him by a Catholic priest he
knew, Father Theophane. "He vouched for you," Williams said. I had
not heard from the Franciscan since algebra class. The tip turned out
to be more valuable to me than an A in algebra.

I shared the information with my editor and shortly after the New Year I was in Camden, digging up hard facts. The lawyer's sketchy tip turned out to be true: Owen Travis worked at Dobson's saw mill in Camden. Ty Dobson, his white employer, considered Travis his most reliable worker.

My first encounter with Dobson was perhaps the most powerful interview I ever conducted as a reporter. His rage spilled out as he recounted the slaying that had occurred at midnight in his front yard. His memory was sharp, his description of Cole acerbic, his affection for the slain man real.

Late that November night Travis had come knocking at his door, asking for an eight-dollar advance on his wages. Cole, the taxi driver, was with him, demanding the money.

Dobson, already retired for the night, did not open the front door but called out to Travis that he would give him the money first thing Monday at work. Dobson heard a skirmish, but by the time he got to his front porch, Travis's body was sprawled on the front lawn, stabbed through the heart, his neck broken by the wheels of the cab.

On the following Monday morning, the County Sheriff reported to the grand jury that he had investigated Travis's death after Dobson reported it. The Sheriff had questioned Cole, who claimed he stabbed Travis in self defense. He had thrown the knife into the Tennessee River. Cole's father-in-law, Allen Elmore, an influential farmer in the county, was a grand jury member. The jurors, with Elmore abstaining, voted a "no true" bill absolving Cole of the crime.

My articles about the case had a double impact. A new grand jury was empanelled. I was among the witnesses subpoenaed to testify. This time Cole was charged with first-degree murder. But the stories I wrote infuriated many whites. There was a storm of protest and a campaign was launched in West Tennessee to boycott *The Tennessean*.

As the trial date neared, tension over the case grew. Law enforcement authorities asked my editor to keep me away from the trial, fearing that friends of Cole would try to harm me. The District Attorney told my editor that my presence in the courtroom would encourage defense lawyers to "try Seigenthaler and divert guilt away from the killer." My colleague, Gene Graham, was sent in my stead to cover the trial.

I felt cheated. Graham, later a Pulitzer Prize–winning reporter, understood that this was my story and thoughtfully phoned from Camden each afternoon to keep me abreast of trial developments.

The all-white jury convicted Cole of manslaughter and a white judge sentenced him to ten years in prison. It was, I thought, hardly an adequate sentence for such a brutal crime—but it marked the first time since Tennessee's Reconstruction that a white man had been found guilty and imprisoned for slaying an African American.

Already reaction to the *Brown v. Board of Education* decision was creating emotional quakes among Southern politicians. School boards were struggling with decisions about how to desegregate "with all deliberate speed." Nashville dallied with its decision until the fall of 1957 when it adopted what was called "a stair-step integration" plan; that year, it would integrate the first grade and each year thereafter a subsequent grade. The result: a twelve-year desegregation process. "With all deliberate speed," indeed!

On September 9, 1957, the first step in the first grade was taken. There were street protests, threats, and vicious crowds of angry white people outside the schools targeted for integration. That first night, Hattie Cotton School, where a lone six-year-old black girl had enrolled, was dynamited and blown off its foundation. The criminal who set off the blast was never charged.

I remember our reporters and photographers arriving at the bombsite before sunup. Already a crowd had gathered, including students and their parents. Many were in tears. The black child and her parents, now under police guard, stayed away.

The next morning's news story reported the tears and cries of anguish from students and their parents who came to view the wreckage of their school. Among most white citizens, there was an outpouring of sympathy both for the six-year-old black girl who wanted to attend Hattie Cotton and for the white children who loved their school. The town's leadership denounced the bombing. Voices of reason subdued voices of hate.

In record time, the school board restored the bombed building and reopened its doors before the close of the virgin integrated academic year. It was inevitable that the board would decide to abandon its stair-step desegregation plan in favor of immediately admitting blacks to all grades.

As I think back, I am amazed at how often—in Nashville and else-where in the South—an act of violence designed to destroy the Civil Rights Movement transformed the minds of people who had previously favored Jim Crow laws. Racial hostility did not evaporate, but violence often begot intolerance for more violence—and tolerance for racial progress.

Then came the Nashville sit-ins. David Halberstam's 1998 book, *The Children*, recounts the graphic story of Nashville in the late 1950s. His narrative is enriched by his personal recollections as the lead reporter who covered the story. A group of African American students from Fisk and Tennessee State Universities, American Baptist Seminary, and Meharry Medical College found themselves unable to live with the contradictions between the revolutionary rhetoric they read in their history texts and the racist rhetoric that ruled the segregated commu-nity. Under the guidance of James Lawson, a young African American ministerial student at Vanderbilt Divinity School, the students launched the sit-in movement at downtown department store lunch counters.

After weeks of demonstrations, when the sit-ins failed to force down racial barriers at the luncheon areas, the students initiated a boy-cott of all downtown businesses. The entire African American com-munity joined in and withheld its purchasing power from the primary downtown shopping area. Many of the students were arrested and jailed as sit-ins continued. But the movement only grew.

For all of us at the newspaper, the student sit-ins and the boycott were a long and gripping news story. It accelerated when Vanderbilt University Divinity School expelled James Lawson for advising the stu-dent sit-in demonstrators whose nonviolent actions were considered "crimes of trespass." By the time the school's board of trust reversed the expulsion, Lawson had enrolled in Boston University, where he earned his Ph.D.

The boycott and the sit-ins together paralyzed the Nashville econ-omy in the spring of 1960. A defining moment came early on the morn-ing of April 9, when a bomb rocked the home of Z. Alexander Looby, a highly regarded City Council member and a lawyer for the movement. Looby and his wife escaped injury—but the explosion blasted the conscience of the entire community.

That morning a mass march from Tennessee State campus to City Hall resulted in a confrontation between the protesters and Mayor Ben West. In an exchange with Diane Nash, a Fisk student, the mayor openly expressed the view that the merchants' position was morally indefensible.

That made headlines next morning—as the ongoing racial conflict had made news over several months. Within a few weeks of the bombing, the department store owners capitulated and the lunch counters were integrated. Once more, the intent of a bomber backfired.

Our news staff was convinced that the paper had helped alter community attitudes and create a climate in which peaceful change could take place.

Then, suddenly, it all changed for us. Our editor, Coleman Harwell, resigned when a new publisher took over control of the paper. Ed Ball, a veteran executive from the Associated Press, became the new editor—and the paper's effective and thorough reportage on the civil rights conflict ended.

No more was the civil rights struggle a priority at the paper. No more would *Tennessean* staff report about racial conflict in other communities. No longer would the civil rights controversies in our town receive significant play. And no longer would our editorials regularly urge community acceptance of desegregation.

The Tennessean, we were told, was out of step with its readers. That decision forced a "stay or go" decision on some of our staff members. Within a few months, the reportorial ranks lost talented journalists. Halberstam and Tom Wicker went off to the *New York Times.* Westfeldt spent six months in government service writing the 1960 U.S. Civil Rights Commission report in Washington, then joined *NBC News* in New York where he produced the Huntley-Brinkley report. Later, Fred Graham followed Halberstam and Wicker to the *New York Times* where he covered the U.S. Supreme Court.

&

I departed in mid-1960 to join the political campaign of John F. Kennedy as the administrative assistant to Robert Kennedy, the campaign director.

After the election I spent a year in the U.S. Department of Justice as Attorney General Kennedy's administrative assistant. My work there included duties in the field of civil rights.

The most difficult moment for me came after the Freedom Riders' trip through the South on Greyhound buses met with bloody violence in June 1961 in Anniston, Alabama. I was sent south by the attorney general to assist the Freedom Riders.

The story has been told elsewhere of how I failed in the assignment. After I had received a pledge from the Governor of Alabama that he would provide state police protection, a second wave of Freedom Riders were met at the Montgomery, Alabama, bus station and assaulted by a mob. Those who were injured included some who had been part of the Nashville sit-in movement. Among them was John Lewis, now a U.S. Congressman from Atlanta.

As I attempted to help two of the young women under attack by the mob, I was injured and hospitalized.

Back at *The Tennessean* the policies of Ed Ball, who had briefly been my editor, proved less than successful, and early in 1962 he resigned. I was invited back to replace him by Amon Evans, who had become the newspaper's new publisher. I accepted on the spot.

It was with great satisfaction on my return as editor to direct, with the support of the newspaper's new publisher, that *The Tennessean*'s former policies of aggressively covering the news—including developments in the field of civil rights, at home and across the South—would be renewed.

From the Freedom Summer to the Edmund Pettus Bridge, *Tennessean* reporters were sent to cover the events as change continued to envelop the region and my hometown. The Nashville sit-ins moved from department store lunch counters to restaurants and the movie houses with their third balconies. Our reporters covered every event. Civil rights proved to be a news story worth continuous coverage.

From time to time, the generational rebirths of the Klan required investigation. During one eighteen-month period in the 1970s, Jerry Thompson, a brave staff member, gave up his city editor's job to infiltrate the Klavern of David Duke and expose the depth of his racist philosophy.

As in other cities where the media worked hard to feel the pulse of the total community—Atlanta, Little Rock, Louisville, and a few smaller towns—there were complaints, protests, occasional threats, and cancellations of subscriptions and advertising from those opposing change. The South, however, under pressure, was in transition.

As the injustice of the system of segregation became more obvious as a result of media attention, more Southerners gradually came to the view that overt racist policies would ultimately decimate the region's economic viability, destabilize its comity, and defile its honor.

Covering the news was one thing. Opening the newsroom to talented journalists who were not white was a step that was long overdue.

When I returned to the paper as editor in 1962 there was no full-time reporter who was a minority. William Reed, a native of the town, worked part time, narrowly covering news in the African American section of town. He had no desk in the newsroom, no fringe benefits, and no respect from many of his peers. He held a full-time job with the U.S. Postal Service.

I asked Reed to give up the job as a postal clerk and come to work full time as *The Tennessean*'s religion news editor. He seemed reluctant. In those days, there was a feature in our paper each Monday in which the religion news editor reported on the service and sermon at a church he had visited. It was a popular column both with readers and the city's pastors. Reed, before accepting my offer, asked if I intended for him to continue with that feature if he took the job. I did, of course. He understood immediately that it would be the newspaper's way of integrating at least one white church many Sundays during the year. He smiled at the thought. A week later he accepted my offer—with a caveat.

"I'm not going to give up the clerk's job at the Postal Service," he said. Instead, he explained, he would arrange his schedule so that he could be faithful, full time, to both positions.

I argued with him, but he was adamant. "To tell you the truth," he said, "with your ideas I can't be sure how long you will be around here as editor. I may need something to fall back on."

Bill Reed was the first in a stream of people of color who were recruited to work as reporters, photojournalists, and editors at the newspaper. He went on to become the first African American to serve as President of the National Religion News Writers Association. He was still at work, integrating churches on Sundays, when the paper was sold to the Gannett Company in 1979. That company's policy of affirmative action enhanced our paper's recruiting of minorities.

In 1984, Reed retired. At a celebration in his honor he recounted our conversation. He pointed to me across the room. "I thought he would be gone from here long before I was," he said.

In 1991, I retired as editor, publisher, and chairman of the paper, and a decade later still struggle to understand the phenomenon of racial intolerance that was so dominant in my region for so many years. The dregs of it still haunts the South and nation.

From 1619, when the first African slaves were thrust onto the continent at Jamestown, Virginia, the sight of colored pigmentation of human flesh has afflicted too many members of the white race with a rare virus that makes amnesiacs of too many of us. The sickness wipes out memory and blots out appreciation for the nation's most revered legacies—the patriotic commitment to equality and the religious commitment to love of neighbor.

The virus lives. Issues such as racial profiling, police brutality, pink lining, affirmative action, and voter disenfranchisement continue to challenge journalists to explore and expose issues more subtle than the blatant segregation that once provoked street demonstrations and evoked the strains of "We Shall Overcome." Too many across the nation do not understand why.

There was a time when I listened to that anthem and wondered whether "they" would, indeed, ever overcome. Now I wonder whether we all will.

John Seigenthaler, Sr.'s career as an award-winning journalist for The Tennessean *began in 1949. At his retirement forty-three years later, he was editor, publisher, and CEO of the paper.*

In 1982, Seigenthaler became founding editorial director of USA Today *and held that position for a decade before leaving to create the First Amendment Center at Vanderbilt University in 1991.*

A former president of the American Society of Newspaper Editors, Seigenthaler serves as board member and advisor to various public and pri-

vate organizations and universities; is chairman emeritus of The Tennessean; *and has been honored at Middle Tennessee State University with an endowed chair in his name.*

Currently host of "A Word on Words," a weekly book review program distributed through Southern Public Television Network, Seigenthaler is married to the former Dolores Watson, a professional singer. Their son, John Seigenthaler of New York City, is weekend anchor for NBC-TV.

© Jon Rou

Talking White

KIMBERLY SPRINGER

SOMETIMES I AM jealous of biracial people.

"Ah ha!" everyone yelps, "Finally, someone admits it!"

Well, there is, of course, a catch: my feelings of envy are not rooted in self-hatred, internalized racism, or pining for any illusions of privilege that might come along with the "right" hair or skin tone. Rather, I am jealous that biracial folks in the United States are pardoned their apparent confusion when it comes to white and black culture.

Speaking as an outsider to the struggles of biracial people, I can only guess what kinds of negotiations go on in daily life as they try to register on some mythical scale of black authenticity.

As an African American, feminist, post–civil rights, Generation X, Boho, affirmative action beneficiary, however, I am rarely allowed any excuse for my confusion or frustration as I try to connect the many strands of my life that are rooted in being pushed to succeed—no, *excel*—in a white-dominated society, while making sure I "stay black."

For me, race has always been constructed, never defining my essence, yet defining *me* completely. I grew up assimilating into white culture, not particularly caring to hear the same story about Harriet Tubman for Black History Month. My goal, as it was defined for me by my position as a "gifted and talented" black girl in an incredibly white high school, was to excel *in spite of* my race, never *because of* it. I was to do everything twice as well as the white kids, because they expected me to fail.

Yet, as I stand today with a freshly bestowed doctorate degree, I am trying to come to terms with the costs of that assimilation and of my position as a black feminist in a culture of "posts": post-feminist, post–civil rights, postmodern. I allude to the costs that are rarely spoken of in black communities, but always understood. It is like the black version of "the problem that has no name."

I cannot name it because I have rarely heard others speak plainly about it. Several works of fiction by black women, such as Andrea Lee's *Sarah Phillips,* Kim McLarin's *Taming It Down,* and Veronica Chamber's *Mama's Girl,* have alluded to the dissonance that black people feel when they are, in a sense, caught between black and white culture. When they enjoy old-school slow jams, but can just as easily get, like, totally stoked listening to Led Zeppelin. When they have an affinity for the *Tom Joyner Morning Show,* but also pledge loyally to their public radio station because they cannot imagine the commute to work without National Public Radio. When they love seeing African print cloth on a brother or sister but, quite frankly, feel like a cultural tourist when they attempt to wear mud cloth.

I used to relate the circumstances of my birth as some sort of badge of black authenticity when I felt my blackness threatened. Born in 1970, I lived the first two years of my life in East St. Louis, Illinois, which was, in the media and most likely in reality, a more-than-rough-and-tumble sister city to St. Louis, Missouri. It was more than the other side of the tracks: it was across the tracks, across the Eades Bridge, *and* across the river. The city boasts the race riot of 1917, a failing infrastructure, out-of-sight unemployment (spurred by the mass exit of major employers such as Sears, J. C. Penney, and Kmart), extreme poverty, and a general hopelessness that overshadows a history of black pride and self-determination.

Yet, to my young mind, East St. Louis was "down South," where my grandmother Teresa carried butterscotch and peppermints in her purse and loved me more than anyone in the whole wide world—or so she had a way of making all of her grandbabies think and feel. It was the home of my cousin Trina, my favorite Uncle Sam, my play-grand-mother Miss Harris, a summer friend named "Pinky," and some of the best homemade ice cream on the planet—the stuff worth sitting through a long, hot sermon for. I could not understand why my parents had left this place where I felt cherished just for being me. As I understand it now, though, they continued a fairly typical pattern of migration begun by my Mississippi-born and -bred grandparents. They moved from the South to the North in search of better employment opportunities for themselves and better educational opportunities for me, their only child.

In Grand Rapids, Michigan, my home until I graduated from high school, life was whiter than white, but I had no idea because it was all I knew. Spending my formative years in a predominately Dutch, Christian Reformed city of more than 500,000, I had no idea that "Van Dyke" and "Vanderveen" were not as common surnames in other cites as were "Smith" and "Jones."

It was in this place that a grand experiment was carried out, with me as the lab rat. Question: if you take a girl out of the ghetto, do you take the ghetto out of the girl?

The most common test of this experiment was "The Black Authenticity Aptitude Test." I am sure this aptitude test has been administered by BATS—the Black Authenticity Testing Squad—to many an unwilling subject. I took it frequently and often failed. The one section I could never seem to pass was the Talks White/Talks Black one. My test always came back stamped "talks white" and I was therefore cast out of the inner circle of blackness.

This construct of how black and white people are supposed to talk has never been used as a compliment. Accusing someone of talking white lacks the historical specificity of calling someone an "Uncle Tom," but it highlights how race is constructed within black communities and how we use it against one another.

Talking white has won me many a threatened ass whupping. The first person to wield this taunt was two years older than me. Tricia

Grady was a bully. I can still see her face, all contorted and angry, saying, "You think you're special 'cause you talk white!"

As a fourth grader, I had no idea that I had mastered any languages
other than English. Tricia's big ol' face, with two pigtails sticking out
akimbo from the sides of her head like a bull's or Satan's horns, did not
convince me that this other "white" language I'd learned was a good
thing to have picked up. I guess my shaking reply of "Nuh-uh" must've
been spoken in sufficiently black English because the promised butt-
kicking never did manifest itself. I breathed a whitey sigh of relief when
Tricia actually managed to graduate from Mulick Park Elementary's
sixth grade.

Similarly, in City Middle/High School two girls who were several
years older than I decided that I did not talk black and threatened a
righteous ass-whupping. Marcia and Dee added to my list of sins
against blackness—"acting white."

What was it that tipped them off? Were New Wave hits by Duran
Duran escaping my lips as I searched for my math book in my locker?
Had half of my ass fallen off on my way to class, making me walk with
a stereotypically flat, white one? I guess I didn't speak as if I were from
the ghetto, or I didn't wear clothes that were appropriately black.

Yet even at thirteen, I had sense enough to think, "What the hell
does it mean to *talk* black or to *act* black?" How does one explain the
social construction of race when one has not even heard of the concept?

I could barely understand the political ideas behind talking ani-
mals in George Orwell's *Animal Farm*. How could I explain to two bullies that their ideas of race were developed by a history of racism and
the economic imperatives of slavery? Besides, I had a super-drippy Jheri
Curl—how could I not know I was black with all that curl activator
dripping onto my upturned Izod collar?

Since my efforts to diffuse the bullies' hostility were useless, I did
what anyone who wanted to keep their face intact would do: I avoided
these mean, angry devils as long as I could. Then, just as I realized
there weren't enough stairwells in the school to use as detours until my
two tormentors graduated, my friend Christa, unbeknownst to me,
came to my rescue. It happened when she got into a conversation with
Marcia and Dee about me.

"What's her problem? Why she act white?" they asked.

Sensitive to my torment, Christa told them that my father was a *white* man. For a split second, even *I* believed her lie.

"Oh! That's why I talk white," I thought. "Wait . . . *what?!?*"

But Christa must've been convincing, because after she offered that explanation, Marcia and Dee stopped picking on me. It was as if I'd been granted a special dispensation from Our Lady of Assimilation. If my father was white, of course, I talked and acted white. I was merely confused and, clearly, not expected to know how to be authentically black.

I reflect on Tricia's anger and accusation that I was guilty of the heinous crime of talking white. What did it mean that Tricia picked me, out of all the other black girls going to school with a bunch of white kids, to make my recess a living hell? What did it mean that black children pick a construct of race as their weapon against other black children?

The only explanations I can offer are more sympathetic than I sometimes care to be. The spiteful inner child in me hopes that those black girls who chose me as their psychic punching bag are living highly unsuccessful lives, while my white-talking, white-acting self has gone on to make something of myself. And then I realize that my vengeful thoughts hold, at least, the beginnings of some understanding of their behavior.

More than race, class was at the crux of their accusations. Though they knew nothing of my working-class home life, these girls assumed that because I had reached a certain level of assimilation in my speech and the pop culture I indulged in, I aspired to something "better."

Writer Rosemary Bray faced similar issues. In her memoir *Unafraid of the Dark*, Bray wonders about the price of assimilation and success in African American communities. "Was I really better than my parents and brothers and sister, or was I better at playing the game of being absorbed into the elite?" she asks. In adolescent logic: my tormentors thought that *I* thought that I was better than them.

Really, I wasn't stud'in' them, and perhaps that was also a part of their behavior toward me: I didn't hang out with that many black kids because, in our schools, there *weren't* that many black kids. Like most kids, I chose my close friends by what we had in common, where we lived, whom I took the public bus to and from school with. Living in a fairly integrated neighborhood, I did not seek out white friends over black ones, but I can see how it might have appeared that way. These girls at school saw nothing of my interactions with my black friends in the neighborhood, at the local park, at New Hope Baptist Church, or anywhere else for that matter. Dare I say, some of my best friends . . .?

Saying "them" instead of "dem" was at one time called "talking proper." I can still hear relatives at family reunions exclaiming to my parents, "Ooh, she talk so *proper*!" That was not an accusation of black inauthenticity, but a compliment to my parents for raising a daughter who was polite and spoke "good English." For a certain generation, talking proper signified that one might be able to make something of one's self and, therefore, achieve something for the race.

In the shift from being praised for talking proper to being derided for talking white, we see a shift in black folks' attitudes—from being seen as doing something good for the community as a whole to merely selling out in one's own self-interest.

I'd somewhat forgotten about my childhood angst over talking white until my mid-twenties. It was winter break and I'd just spent a week with my parents in Michigan. I was ready to head back, not so much because I gave a damn about school, but because it was about forty degrees warmer in Atlanta, where I was in graduate school.

Then, too, my relationship with my father has always been tenuous and fraught with opposition. His bipolar disorder. My conflicted desire to be the "good daughter." His chauvinism and my feminism. Needless to say, by the end of the trip, the fur and mistletoe were flying.

My father had one last request before I left. Would I please re-record the message on the answering machine?

Now you have to understand that, in the past, when I've gone to visit my parents, it's as if I was wearing a bow and a note that read, "Surprise! Your annual visit from your personal assistant is here! Typing, calling, answering the phone—your wish is her command."

Unfortunately, though, some feminist 'tude and my own work to do, instigated a minor rebellion against my annual service visit. I insisted on knowing *why* he wanted me to re-record the message.

"Because I want it to sound professional," my father explained, stopping himself just short of, "Because I told you so."

"What do you mean, '*professional*'?" I asked, more suspicious than rebellious.

With an exasperated sigh, he said, "I want it to sound right."

Maybe I was having flashbacks because I could've sworn I heard him say, "I want it to sound *white*." And even if that's not what he said, that's what he meant.

I refused. I would not perform whiteness for my parent's answering machine. Then, feeling a little bad, I was on the verge of relenting when I was instructed to end the message with, "Have a blessed day." As a card-carrying backslider who was hypervigilant about religious proselytizing, I found this highly offensive.

At the end of my visit, my father and I grudgingly kissed one another on the cheek and I stalked off to the airport, bitter that even my own father thought I talked white.

For me, this and similar conversations with family are the back-handed ways in which praise and criticism are delivered. On the one hand, my family is proud that I have succeeded in a racist and sexist society that would much rather see black women taking care of white children than their own. My way of speaking and acting presumably white are just that to them: a performance that I give in order to succeed on their terms or, as Bray put it, to be absorbed into their elite.

Yet, on the other hand, my way of being in the world is seen as a telltale sign that I am not black enough—that somehow I failed in my mission to infiltrate white culture. I got the goods (education, job, status), but I came back having gone native (with white dialect, taste in music, and a diminished appreciation for chitlins).

I have since learned not to care what others think of me. But other blacks, some of whom I call kin, remind me of my mistreatment when I encounter young brothers and sisters in my position. There they sit, eagerly asking me questions about college and places I've lived, and I realize that part of my purpose in life is to encourage them on their path to self-fulfillment and community building. Still, I wonder about the hurts they've experienced along the way and what lies ahead for them as we, an increasingly economically divided black community, continue to find ways to pull one another down.

I am not hopeless, but perhaps a bit less enthusiastic about blacks treating one another with more kindness and re-establishing our community ties. Yet I am willing to work for this vision. Part of what motivates me is remembering going down South in the summer and being among black people who cared about one another. I am motivated by the knowledge that, in spite of being seen as assimilated and loving whiteness, my love for black people, history, and culture is greater than that of those who shoot one another in the street over some East Coast/West Coast rapper bullshit, or those who call themselves black but sell drugs to someone's mother, father, or child.

I know when I return home to visit my parents and extended family that I do not talk white; to the contrary, something in me melts, relaxes, and shifts. The way that I communicate with my mother when we are having our ritual mother/daughter talk is certainly not "white." But, it's not "black" either. Instead, it is woman-to-woman, love-to-love.

Kimberly Springer, *thirty-one, teaches at Portland State University in Oregon. After graduating from the University of Michigan, Springer received her Ph.D. in 1999 from Emory University's Institute for Women's Studies. A banner year for Springer, 1999 also saw the publishing of her first book,* Still Lifting, Still Climbing: Contemporary African American Women's Activism *(New York University Press, 1999).*

Springer, an independent radio producer and founder of Colored Public Radio, is currently writing Living for the Revolution: Black Feminist Organizations, 1968–1980 *(forthcoming, Duke University Press).*

© Natalie Angier, photo by Gary Orloff

Central Park Samaritan

Natalie Angier

My friends and I were in Central Park on a splendid weekend afternoon in August of 1970, down for the day from our cruddy Bronx neighborhood and now sprawled on the grass of Sheep Meadow, eating hot dogs and potato chips and arguing loudly. We ranged in age from twelve to sixteen, and we were a multicultural jambalaya: there was Ann, a surly, freckle-faced Irish girl who eventually would come out as a lesbian; David, a Greek boy with a Greek god's beauty and a Socratic taste for other males; Ritchie, a lithe and long-lashed Puerto Rican for whom I quietly, urgently yearned; Harold, tall and black and self-possessed, who could be as sweet as morning one moment, distant and sarcastic the next; and me, half-WASP, half-Jew, abrim with revolutionary vinegar. We all considered ourselves avant-garde, street-hard, and spit-polished. We liked the Rolling Stones, Frank Zappa, J. R. R. Tolkien, and the Joshua Light Show. We smoked grass and cigarettes, and popped amphetamines when we could get them. When we couldn't, we hyperventilated until we saw light shows of our own.

Oh, we were hip all right, and we agreed on many things—with one big exception. I was my mother's daughter, which meant I was a budding radical feminist, while my friends had nothing but scorn for the movement they derided as "women's lip." So that day in Central Park, we were squabbling about feminism, four against one. As I struggled to articulate the need for a Women's Rights Movement, I felt flustered, hostile, and betrayed. Even Ann, my best friend and fellow non-fellow, was sneering at the very idea that women and girls had any valid complaints. As far as she was concerned, most women were spoiled rotten, and those who weren't were "flakes" or "bitches."

I was about to give up, or maybe burst into tears, when I noticed that a black man in his early twenties was standing by our blanket and listening to the discussion. Finally, he knelt down and began talking.

"She's got a point," he said to the heckling quartet. "Women have a raw deal in this society. They don't get paid as much as men do for the same work; they're hassled when they walk down the street; they're told that women shouldn't be doctors or lawyers or anything but housewives. Do you really believe that women are inferior? Do you really think that your friend here is inferior to you?" He jerked his chin toward David, who'd been the noisiest of my adversaries.

David's cheeks turned flamingo pink. He was too embarrassed to speak, as were the others. For a few magic moments, the young man continued to defend the women's movement, with a thoughtfulness and eloquence that put my prior sputterings to shame. Then, without telling us his name or why he cared enough to join the debate in the first place, he stood up and waved good-bye.

My hero. My black white knight in shining armor. Three decades later, and I still feel a swell of gratitude when I remember the stranger who came to my rescue. He had just the right mix of credentials to trounce my critics. He was older than any of us and he was male, which gave him not only the natural authority that accords to men, but also a presumed disinterest and objectivity—he had nothing to gain personally should feminism succeed.

At the same time, he was black, which meant he knew about oppression. He wasn't being patronizing. He wasn't stepping down from a place of privilege and presumption to lend a small, snarling girl a hand. As he saw it, and spoke it, the women's liberation movement was like the Black Power Movement, or like the nascent American Indian Movement, an expression of the innate human thirst for freedom, justice, and respect. How can you mock this desire in any one of us, without making a mockery of us all?

The civil rights movement and feminism have a long history of collusion and symbiosis. In the nineteenth century, Elizabeth Cady Stanton, Susan B. Anthony, and other leaders of the early women's rights movement began their radical careers agitating against slavery. Likewise, my nameless Central Park redeemer had a luminous progenitor: Frederick Douglass. At the first Women's Rights Conference, held in Seneca Falls in July 1848, Elizabeth Cady Stanton presented her Declaration of Sentiments, modeled on the Declaration of Independence. In the Sentiments, she laid out a dozen resolutions. Among them were allowing women the right to divorce their husbands, to keep their own property, and, above all, to vote. The mostly female audience gathered at Seneca Falls were unanimous in their support of eleven of those resolutions. But they balked at the outrageous notion of women in the voting booth, and even Stanton's heartfelt pleas did not sway them. Only when Frederick Douglass, a former slave and one of the nation's most brilliant orators, stood up to argue in favor of female suffrage did their skepticism soften. "Suffrage is the power to choose rulers and make laws," Douglass insisted, "and the right by which all others are secured." The resolution passed at Seneca Falls with a bare majority, and the long, bruising battle for women's suffrage had begun.

A century later, the modern feminist movement was inspired by the Civil Rights Movement of the 1950s and 1960s. Jim Crow laws, men's-only universities—it all looked like the same sorry business: a duct-taped, pale male parcel of social control, economic marginalization, de facto disenfranchisement, and cleverly cloaked purdah.

When I was fourteen and, as a result of my parents' separation, unhappily transplanted to Michigan, I briefly dated a guy named Dean Hoover, for the sole reason that he was gorgeous, his physique photographable. As for the rest of him, well, let's just say he was laughable.

He would talk idly on a Saturday night of rounding up his friends to go "beat up some niggers"—though I'm pretty sure he never carried through on the plan. He also insisted to me that men were in every way superior to women, that they were stronger, braver, and smarter—

this from a guy who was twenty and still in high school (not to mention courting a fourteen-year-old!). Dean's sexism and racism were so extreme and blatant that I could mock them, but nevertheless they seemed to me as inseparable and comfortable together as peanut butter and jelly smeared between two slices of gummy white bread.

Oh, I know that it's quite possible to be a selective radical. Stanton and Anthony eventually made the terrible mistake of distancing themselves from black activists. They held a misguided belief that it was a zero-sum game, that there was only so much social justice to go around, and that whatever good accrued to African Americans would be at the expense of women's rights.

Eldridge Cleaver famously and idiotically said that the only position a woman should take is prone. But in my mind, and in the part of my soul that refuses to be iced no matter how many years of Reagan, Bush, the DLC, and Bush recrudescent I've endured, sexism and racism remain alive and well, two sides of the same wicked coin of the realm. Yep, I really believe that. I won't get into a competition over who is more "oppressed," or who has a greater right to reparations, affirmative action, a pissy feeling of disgruntlement. I remember a discussion I had with a friend of mine in college, Herb Jordan, a like-minded leftist. Herb was saying something about how he couldn't imagine what it would be like to be a woman in our society, that it must be really terrible. My eyes practically gogged out of my skull.

"Herb, what are you saying?" I said. "You're *black*, for crying out loud! Do you mean to tell me that you think it's harder to be a woman than to be black?"

Yes, in fact he did. And not long after, I asked a bunch of white-guy friends of mine whether they'd rather be black men or white women, and they all said, without hesitation, black men. At which point I fell into a funk, wondering what men must think of women that the prospect of being one fills them with horror. Lord, do what you please! Put me at risk of being turned into a human colander by the police because I'm reaching for my cell phone. Anything, anything but the dread Gynomorph Machine!

All of which tells me there's plenty of work to go around. The struggle for social justice and universal human rights has just begun— is beginning anew every day. Any one of us can only do so much. I'm a feminist who spends a lot of time thinking and writing about women's place in the world, how it might have evolved, and where women might go next if they keep hammering away. But mutiny is mutiny, and hammers work no matter who holds the handle. Just as progress in understanding the nefarious ways of one virus can help in fighting all viral diseases, so I believe that going after sexism indirectly benefits other quests for parity and fairness. Let's face it: the odds against success for any of us are overwhelming. Women make progress for a while, but then people stop paying attention. The next thing you know, the number of women being given tenure at major universities begins to flatten out, and then to drop. There are no more women running big companies or big newspapers today than there were twenty years ago. There is still no day care for working women, and women risk impoverishment because they take time out of their careers to do something self-indulgent and strictly personal—like raising the children who will be the next generation of taxpayers.

By the same token—or tokenism—African Americans make economic strides, but they still can't get a toehold on real security or wealth. Blacks and whites earning the same annual income nevertheless show a chasmic gap in assets, with whites having seven times the net worth of their black peers. Even in my relatively well-off patch of Maryland, Montgomery County, African American babies are four times more likely to die than are white babies. Our prisons remain disproportionately black, and we just keep building more of them. Glad we got that little social adenoma under control!

Not only are statistics stacked against us, but I see the same devious tactics applied against both women and minorities. Science is always a good one. In the nineteenth century, phrenologists measured skulls and declared blacks to be barely past Cro-Magnon, while gynecologists warned women that the uterus competed with the brain for blood, energy, even phosphates, and that the woman who attended college risked nothing less than an atrophied womb.

Today, a certain breed of neo-Darwinists called evolutionary psychologists argue that women are "naturally" less inclined to ambition, sustained creativity, and achievement than men are. Other self-styled evolutionary thinkers insist that Africans are less intelligent than Europeans and Asians because they are designed to invest in "quantity" of offspring rather than "quality." To both set of assertions the same response can apply: you have virtually no data to support your claims, and alternative explanations can explain every pattern you describe. Besides, your track records are terrible! Have you no humility, sirs?

Another weapon used to great effect against both women and blacks is the familiar *Lupus ovinus*, also known as the wolf in sheep's clothing. These dangerous chimeras include women who call themselves feminists but zealously fight against feminism's goals, and African Americans who claim the mantle of Martin Luther King, Jr., in arguing against affirmative action, or indeed, any social activism at all. Most are employed by conservative "think tanks" like the American Enterprise Institute and the Hoover Institute, although they occasionally end up in the Supreme Court and Republican administrations, and they invariably find fame far beyond the merits of their writing or cognitive talents. Op-ed pages and television talk show slots are at their disposal, for nothing is sexier than treachery, catfights, and hissy fits. Who better to say that a member of a "special interest group" is playing the victimology card, is in fact crying wolf, than the woolly wolf itself?

But this is a crude old trick of autocracy, the recruiting of one subordinate to keep the others in line. The palace fool comes from pariah stock. And just as I think of the Women's Movement and the Civil Rights Movement as natural symbionts, so the obverse applies. People like Christina Hoff Sommers and Clarence Thomas share a feeding style and cultural niche: they are the parasitic beneficiaries of the social agitators they disdain. Where is the lindane when you really need it?

In sum, I am a political dinosaur, parked forever in a Jurassic utopia, who can't help but think of blacks as my potential allies, my comrades, and my friends. True, I don't have many real black friends, but then, I don't have many girlfriends, either. That doesn't stop me from being a feminist committed to the old-fashioned principle of sisterhood. And time, and distance, and improbability don't stop me from hoping that some day I'll come across my Central Park samaritan again, and that he'll still be singing battle hymns, and that, if I asked, he'd sing one for me.

Pulitzer Prize–winner **Natalie Angier** *was born in 1958 and grew up in the Bronx and in Michigan. She studied English literature, physics, and* *astronomy at Barnard College and was a staff member at* Discover *magazine before joining the* New York Times *in 1990. She won the Pulitzer Prize for reporting as a science writer in 1991.*

With the publication in 1999 of her latest work, Woman: An Intimate Geography *(Houghton Mifflin, 1999), Angier peeled back centuries of layers of gender-based stereotypes in a joyful, irreverent, yet thoughtful romp through female anatomy and physiology. Enthusiastically received by critics as a "must read,"* Woman *continued the widespread acclaim Angier received for her previous books,* The Beauty of the Beastly *(Mariner Books, 1996) and* Natural Obsessions *(Houghton Mifflin, 1999).*

Angier lives in Takoma Park, Maryland, with her husband Rick Weiss, a science reporter for the Washington Post, *and their daughter Katherine.*

© Marcia Yapp

It All Started with My Parents

Lucy Gibson

Mommy (querulously): "Why are you opposed to Negroes
having equal rights?"
Daddy: "It doesn't make sense. They're lower on the
evolutionary scale."
Mommy (shocked): "What? How can you say that?! What
proof do you have?"
Daddy: "Well—uh—just look at 'em!"

> (Dialogue between my parents when I was
> around eight years old, circa 1957.)

IT ALL STARTED with my parents. As a little girl in Appleton, Wisconsin,
I loved both my mother and my father, but my dad sometimes said
things that hurt my feelings. Eventually I started to take sides between
them: I got the message that my father didn't think much of me because
I was a girl. He said that girls weren't as smart as boys, that girls could
parrot facts and get good grades in school, but as they got older, their

abilities would not match those of males. Males, on the other hand, could really *think*. He said that women only went to college to get an M-R-S degree, and all they really wanted was a meal ticket. In short, he was contemptuous of females—their intelligence, their abilities, their right to respect, their aspirations, their integrity, their frailty.

His attitude wasn't lost on me. The first time I remember being angry about it, I was about seven. I knew I was a real person, just as good as my brothers, and I knew I never would accept his put-downs. Or so I thought.

My dad had contempt not only for women, but also for people he considered "lower races," particularly black people. Oddly, both my parents inculcated in us children the importance of equality, regardless of a person's class, and the importance of being honest, and treating people fairly and equally. Yet paradoxically, my father made a lot of specific exceptions to the principles that he espoused in general. He believed that whites were mentally superior to other races, and men to women. He particularly disliked and mistrusted black people.

My mother, on the contrary, believed strongly in the equality of the races, so this was one of the subjects they argued about.

Growing up listening to their arguments, I was constantly presented with the "race question." It wasn't hard for me to decide which side I was on. My father's prejudices felt hurtful to me, and besides, they didn't fit with my parents' other teachings.

Although it seemed no people of color lived in the Appleton area, I was often conscious of the issue of race. Besides my parents' regular arguments, black people were in the movies occasionally, and one day some white people brought the issue out in public on the street. It was the late 1950s, in front of Woolworth's dime store in downtown Appleton, and I was about nine.

Picketers were standing in front of the store, asking people to sign petitions to the company to allow Negroes to be seated at their lunch counters in the South. My mother stepped right up and signed gladly. My father hung back, muttering, "I'm not signing anything!" It surprised me that his demeanor wasn't belligerent, but shamefaced and afraid.

During my high school years, I became aware of the Civil Rights Movement from articles in the newspaper. The reports made me sympathetic to a movement that sounded noble and justified, in spite of the paper's attempts at objectivity. I was impressed by the courage of the people involved, and hoped for their success. It never crossed my mind that I might do anything to support them.

I was truly a member of the silent majority in those days. I was afraid to make a peep about what I saw as wrong in society. I watched TV and read the newspapers, hoping to see other people doing good things to counter the evils of the world. I knew *I* couldn't do anything!

Today, I see my youthful repression as a kind of moral cowardice force-fed to me by my parents and society because I was a girl. In the 1950s and '60s when I was a child and teenager, my generation wasn't aware of feminism; passivity was the only acceptable role for me. I was an *angry* passive young woman—but I scarcely realized how angry I was, let alone why. At this point, anger did not give me strength or focus. Given my father's disapproval, my bad case of acne, and the social ambience of the 1950s and '60s, by the age of eighteen I was terribly shy and socially backward.

After graduating from high school, I spent my first year of college at Lawrence, a small liberal arts school in Appleton. With no better idea of what to do with myself, and finding music the brightest spot in my life, I took the advice of my church choir director and got a work-study/grant/loan package for the freshman year as a music major, after prevailing on my dad to fill out the financial aid information about his income.

Lawrence's rule for freshmen required me to live on campus. It wasn't easy for a person so socially inept. I was afraid, yet overjoyed to get away from home. One of the things I wondered about was the possibility of meeting black people in real life for the first time. I wrote to the admissions office and asked if it would be possible for me to room with a Negro, since I had never met any Negroes. Lo and behold, they accommodated me and teamed me up with Rosalyn, who was from Florida. They gave us each other's address so that we could get acquainted by letter before meeting in the fall.

We exchanged letters, but I didn't feel any rapport with Rosalyn. She told me green was her favorite color, and one of her favorite possessions was a green alabaster egg. What was she talking about? That was trivia to me. I couldn't relate. Full of my own sense of priorities, I had no social graces and was too immature to know enough to be patient in getting to know someone. (And besides, *my* favorite colors were . . . !)

Rosalyn told me that she sewed her own clothes and *Vogue* was her favorite magazine. That was the first time I had heard of *Vogue*. I had no concept of style and didn't like sewing. Moreover, I had been taught a certain contempt for concern about appearances even though I was neurotic about my own appearance. I didn't think it was proper to care about clothes and fashion; I thought of fashion and fashion magazines as ignoble.

Then Rosalyn wrote and said that she needed to come north early, and she wanted to know if she could come and stay at my family's house for a week or two before the dorms would open up. I was completely thrown off balance. The concept was ridiculous.

Aside from my Dad's attitude, there was our house. Dad bought us a house in Menasha, a paper mill town about five miles from Appleton, in the summer of 1959. The first house our family owned, it was tiny, a veritable shack. The older half appeared to have been made from old railroad ties and other scrap lumber, and my dad added on the newer half himself, with some help from my mom and us kids. The whole thing was uncomfortable, with little privacy: a barracks-style bedroom for my three brothers, with only curtains separating it from the living and dining areas, and unfinished openings between the old and new halves of the house. The linoleum in the dining room, in the newer part, was cracked along the plywood floor seams, and the linoleum in the kitchen, in the older part, was completely worn through to the floor boards. My own tiny bedroom had no closet, but was crowded with a homemade plywood wardrobe, and the ceilings were not gypsum board, but some kind of thick paperboard that had warped from ceiling leaks, until there was a gap in it that I imagined spiders from the rafters would drop through at night.

It was a source of great embarrassment to me and my brothers that the older half of the house was sided with white asbestos shingle, while the new addition was covered by brown *faux*-brick roll roofing made of tar paper, with plastic sheeting sticking out of its edges. (The plastic was the vapor barrier that Dad had scientifically devised to enhance the insulation.) As if the tar paper and plastic weren't bad enough in themselves, my Mom, in a fit of homemaking zeal, had decided to make the whole house the same color, so she painted over both tar paper and asbestos shingle with a shade of hot pink.

For years, my shame at my appearance was paralleled by my shame about our house. My younger brother, more outgoing than I, actually had friends. They told him that our house was known as "the pink ice shanty."

In relation to Rosalyn, my shame about the house was also paralleled by my shame about my dad's racism. What to tell Rosalyn? I couldn't tell her about the racism! It seemed less embarrassing to admit to a stranger that the house was completely inadequate for guests—which it was—than that my father wouldn't allow her to stay with us for any other reason. Even had she been white, he wouldn't have allowed her to stay. He didn't trust strangers, and he had no respect for kids, especially girls. For some acquaintance of mine to ask to put up in our house was beyond the pale entirely. But had it not been for those factors, Rosalyn's blackness would have been the clincher.

I steeled myself to ask him if she could stay. He turned me down. Unwilling to admit to her that we couldn't or wouldn't provide her with hospitality because of what she was, I told her the inadequacies of the house. I kept the description subdued, not wanting to detail the condition of the siding, the flooring, etc. I just told her the house was very small, and the only place for her to sleep would have been on a small cot wedged between my bed and the wall of my room.

Looking back, I wish I had had the gumption—and the words—to come out and tell her, "You can't stay at our house because my father is a racist." That would have put the onus on him and taken it off of me, but I felt the family tie and the family shame, and I took it on myself.

I'm pretty sure Rosalyn thought up this request as a test, and assumed, from my response, that I came from a racist family. When we met, I felt she didn't like me, but the truth was that I also didn't feel anything in common with her. I think I wanted to talk about race and racism and the Civil Rights Movement, but Rosalyn seemed to be only interested in clothes and *Vogue*. Somehow she wasn't on the wavelength I expected, or wanted.

Whatever she felt when we first met, it wasn't long before it was clear that she disliked me, and she began to make life hard for me in the dorm room. She would come in late at night, just as I was going to sleep on my side of the room, turn on the overhead light, and put on loud music. At first, I asked her to turn off the music and use a lower light, but she refused, and I stopped asking. I developed passive avoidance behaviors. I don't remember that we ever talked directly about what was wrong between us. I guess she couldn't bring it up any better than I could, although she occasionally made oblique comments about "Europeans." She just seemed angry, and tried to somehow dominate me or get rid of me. I was mortified, knowing I had chosen to live with her, and finding that, as enlightened as I wanted to be, I couldn't even talk to, let alone get along with, this black person.

I finally requested a change of roommate. I moved in with a quiet, unassuming little white girl who was, if possible, less prepossessing than myself, although a lot more optimistic and not as pimply. After that, I was able to get some sleep.

The last I saw of Rosalyn, she was hanging out with beatniks on campus, wearing dark stockings and *Vogue*-style shifts (which looked great on her tall, slender figure), and working on theater projects. Since she grew up in Florida in the 1950s and '60s, I'm sure she was well-acquainted with racial oppression, but my theory is that she saw high fashion and the theater as worlds where race wouldn't make such a difference.

Some time after I moved into a different room, a young woman named Sue Nordeen, a much more forceful person than I, took me to another floor to meet another black girl, a scholarship student from the South named Berni, and a wealthy East Coast white girl named Sarah. I don't remember exactly how or why we were introduced to each other, but I do remember that we hit it off immediately. Nordeen (as we called her) and Berni both behaved rather protectively toward me. I think they saw me as weak and vulnerable, and their instincts were to protect and be kind. I'm glad they did. I needed some kindness.

That year was very difficult for me, but so it was for many of the girls who were newly away from home. Berni and Sarah each had their own emotional stresses, but somehow, the three of us together managed to fill Sarah's dorm room, our most common meeting place, with belly laughs. We constantly found reason to satirize the world around us, and somehow, among us three, there was some understanding.

That experience was redeeming for me. It showed me that I could have friends in the wider world, away from my family. It made me feel that I had some strengths that were appreciated by other people who seemed intelligent. Also, it allowed me to think that it wasn't all just my fault that I hadn't gotten along with Rosalyn; maybe it wasn't my being racist that had made it a bad relationship. But I was still ashamed of the possibility that it was my fault.

Sarah asked me once, "Yeah, but didn't they give you Rosalyn as a roommate because you asked for a Negro roommate? I heard they only gave Negro roommates to white students who requested them."

"No," I replied. "I didn't ask for a Negro roommate."

I was afraid that there might be something wrong with my asking for a Negro roommate. Maybe it showed that I was discriminating in a sense. Maybe it showed that I was singling out Negroes. Anyway, it was a failure on my part. So I denied I had done it.

I had some assumptions about black people that were rather dashed at Lawrence. I had thought of black people as heroes, and assumed that they, especially those going to college, would all be very noble and intelligent and also easy to talk to. Much to my chagrin, I found that the few black students at Lawrence were not particularly easy for *me* to talk to. (But then, almost no one was easy for me to talk to, so what did I expect?)

I also found, to my surprise, that the female students were not more friendly than the male students. I had had a close emotional relationship with my mother, and had somehow extended that to the assumption that it should always be easy for women to develop empathy with each other. However, the black women students at Lawrence, with the exception of Berni, were not particularly friendly to me. Neither were the men, but I hadn't expected it of them, so I wasn't surprised.

Berni characteristically stands up for underdogs. I was emotionally crippled in many ways when I arrived at Lawrence, and her attitude gave me more strength. A few people in my life, including my younger brother Bill, and Berni, in some sense saved my sanity at stressful periods. I'm grateful for her empathy and kindness, which are sometimes laced with intense anger, usually against the cruelties people wreak on the vulnerable. She has a strong sense of justice, which she got from her mother, who raised her and a sister through very hard times. Her point of view has been important to me personally, in helping me break out of an ingrained sense of helplessness and lack of entitlement.

Besides that, I think the opportunity to be friends with a black woman was important because it stopped me from wondering if such a thing were possible. It helped me set aside some of the self-doubt I experienced with Rosalyn. It felt like a privilege to my bruised and lonely soul to find real friendship with other young women, both Berni and Sarah, and it was a double privilege to have that relationship with a black woman.

Thanks to Berni, I had a clearer focus as I continued experiencing the effects of race in America. She became a kind of mythic hero whose friendship strengthened me in my psychological battle against the emotional ogre on my back, my father.

My father's attitude toward me brought me down severely for a long time. There came a point in my life when I decided to disown him in my own mind. It was occasioned by a letter he sent me in which he used the phrase "pullulating excrescences" as a description of black people. I usually didn't say anything to him about his scurrilous expressions toward people who didn't qualify for his approval. This time, however, I had gently responded to a letter that insulted gays and black people, by asking him please not to use such bad language toward them, since some of those people were my friends and I thought well of them.

His response was slap-in-the-face provocative, and in despair, I decided I had had it. I didn't tell him I was disowning him. I didn't want the argument, the anger, the stress of confronting him with it. That would be playing into his game. I just decided for myself and to myself that he was not my father. His beliefs would not affect how I would live my life.

The day I made that decision, I saw a black man walking down the other side of the street, and was surprised to realize that I felt calm toward him. I no longer felt a kind of guilty conflict at his very existence, something I hadn't realized was happening to me until it stopped. I didn't stop caring about race or racial injustice. I just stopped feeling that I had to take so much responsibility for my father's attitude. What a relief!

Although that decision helped me, I still knew he was my father. I remained interested in the possibility of redemption for him, for people like him, and for myself in relation to people like him. My decision to disown him wasn't really a way of ignoring his existence. It was just a step on my journey to change the world inside my own mind. About the same time I made this decision, I ran across an essay by Richard Wright that gave me a startling insight about my father.

My father came from Germany with his family when he was about twelve, around 1926. His family were peasants, and they fled the chaotic economic conditions in Germany, as well as their own low social status. Looking back at comments I heard from my father and grandfather over the years, I eventually came to better understand my father's bitter, angry, and cynical world view. I believe it originated with the bitterness his whole family and class felt over being inferiors in German society in the early part of the century, as well as with Dad's experience of being a despised immigrant. He spoke little English when he came, and was harassed at school because of that and his clothing, which was in a style strange to the American children. In WWII, he was not allowed to enter officer's training because he was German-born.

Ironically, though, here in the States, Dad got a master's degree and gained the status of a college teacher, a very respectable position from the point of view of German culture, and from that position, he continued to express his bitterness and cynicism partly by finding others to take the lower status his family had come here to escape. His bitterness, anger, and cynicism were, I believe, part of his culture, defense mechanisms closely held for self-protection, which he did not give up when he moved into an outwardly better situation.

Seeing my father's attitudes as partly a reaction to oppression was an insight that first hit me when I read "How Bigger Was Born," Richard Wright's 1940 introductory essay to his book *Native Son*. Wright had intuited that Nazis in Germany, Russian revolutionists, and American Negroes all had something in common. "How Bigger Was Born" tells of Wright's desire, in *Native Son,* to illustrate the essence of the desperately rebellious characters he had experienced among black people from his youth, and later had recognized in other cultures as well. To quote a little from Wright's essay:

I read every account of the Fascist movement in Germany I could lay my hands on, and from page to page I encountered and recognized familiar emotional patterns . . .

But more than anything else, as a writer, I was fascinated by the similarity of the emotional tensions of Bigger in America and Bigger in Nazi Germany and Bigger in old Russia. All Bigger Thomases, white and black, felt tense, afraid, nervous, hysterical, and restless. From far away Nazi Germany and old Russia had come to me items of knowledge that told me that certain modern experiences were creating types of personalities whose existence ignored racial and national lines of demarcation, that these personalities carried with them a more universal drama-element than anything I'd ever encountered before; that these personalities were mainly imposed upon men and women living in a world whose fundamental assumptions could no longer be taken for granted: a world ridden with national and class strife; a world whose metaphysical meanings had vanished; a world in which God no longer existed as a daily focal point of men's lives . . .

From these items I drew my first political conclusions about Bigger: I felt that Bigger, an American product, a native son of this land, carried within him the potentialities of either Communism or Fascism.

I understood what Wright meant when I thought of my father. Although he was not a "Bigger" overtly, because he was not overtly self-destructive and rebellious against the established order, nevertheless he turned his anger and rebellion inward against his own family and community, in some ways against himself, and against others whom he could scapegoat. I think he couldn't give up those feelings, because they were defense mechanisms. He actually identified with Nazism to some extent, and I think that was because it expressed and validated his anger, identified his kind of people as superior, and allowed him to identify with the oppressors as a form of self-defense. My father had in a sense gone over to the enemy.

His rebellion was against facile optimism, positive thinking, kindness, ideas of equality. He knew those things to be dangerous, as an abused child knows it to be dangerous to assert his right not to be abused—and as an abused child comes to identify with the abuser, out of fear, rather than with other victims of abuse.

Wright's insight was welcome to me in three ways. First, although I had been trying to analyze my father all my life, this was the first time I felt I had found a plausible kind of explanation for why he was the way he was. Being able to define him made me able to feel a little distance from his insanity.

Second, it enabled me to have some respect for my father for being at least human, and therefore to relax some of the anger I held against him. I was happy to learn that my father might not be completely separate from the rest of the human race by reason of his Germanness or his whiteness, or even his racism.

And third, it was a relief to me to find that Richard Wright, the great black author (whose writing I very much admired), could see my father and people like him as human beings on equal terms with his fearsome protagonist, Bigger Thomas, and with, by extension, himself. I felt that Wright had not only enlightened me about my father, but had also offered a kind of acceptance of myself, by naming me a member of the same human race.

This was a kind of breakthrough for me. It represented acceptance from black people, something I had wanted, but couldn't manufacture for myself. Richard Wright gave it to me through his universalist perspective, which I instinctively felt to be correct in light of my experience of my father.

This sharing of humanity came through a negative vision: the squelching of humanity resulting in a kind of monstrosity. The vision of the human being in this situation carries, in a sense, its own compassion and forgiveness. It carries a recognition that the evil we see in Nazis, racists, and social psychopaths is something that may arise when humanity is too much wounded, oppressed, or warped. Negative as that vision may sound, still, it tells us something about what human beings need to be fully human—the same concern that arose for the concentration camp victims of WWII.

My father died recently. Although I felt estranged from him, in the process of his decline I came to remember that there were good qualities he gave me, and good things he did for me. He was aware of the repressive power of racism, although his consciousness of it was vague. He took the wrong turn in figuring out how to deal with it, letting fear and prejudice guide him. Without feeling the least bit comfortable with his bigotry, at least I can recognize that my father's weaknesses illustrated, rather than negated, his humanity.

I've worked many years to get the ogre off my back, and have had some success, thanks to black and white friends and role models, both people I know personally and authors and heroes I've never met. Looking back, I see that the freedom of my current world view was hard won: I had to fight through a lot of garbage to get to it. I know many other white people haven't achieved this freedom, and many black people are very broken down by the burden of racism they've carried in their lives. I want this to change. It's a journey that's not over at all for me, or any of us.

I started this story thinking it was about my life experience of race in our society. It has turned out to be largely a story of my relationship with my father. My relationship with my mother supported me powerfully throughout my life, even after she died. My father, on the contrary, broke me down. But paradoxically, if it weren't for him, I might not have cared so much about racial and other forms of bigotry and discrimination. My mother made me a human being. My father made me a militant.

Thanks, Mom and Dad. It all started with you.

Lucy Gibson has a B.S. in mechanical engineering from the University of Wisconsin and owns Inspirations Illustrated, a patent drafting business. Gibson has been involved in grassroots political activism in Madison, Wisconsin, as well as in farm communities in the U.S. South and in Central America.

II. Fear and Longing

© Dr. Julianne Malveaux

Race, Rage, and the Ace of Spades

JULIANNE MALVEAUX

I'M SITTING ON a panel, trying to get a word in edgewise. Four white men are stepping all over my lines, courteously (if gruffly) yielding to each other, but treating me as if I am invisible. My attempts at interruption are unheard, my throat clearing, hand raising have no effect.

"Can't a black woman get a word in edgewise?" I finally shout out.

"Don't play the race card with me," sneers the white boy of the moment.

Ordinarily we are told to "play the hand we are dealt" in life. The twenty-first century message, though, is that if life deals us the race card, we aren't supposed to play it. Simply hold it, suppress it, swallow it.

If we believe the myth of the level playing field, the race card should have no more influence, and no less, than any other card. My life experience suggests, instead, that almost any card, in almost any circumstance, can trump the race card. And so I find the level-playing-field crowd deliberately myopic. They've stacked the deck and then told black folks that we can't play the cards we have.

I don't know exactly when white folks started telling black folks, with all undue derision, "Don't play the race card." Perhaps the term "race card" was introduced at the moment when affirmative-action critics started whining "reverse discrimination," even though there is overwhelming numerical evidence that whites still hold more than their share of elite jobs, contract opportunities, and seats in university classrooms. The same folks who don't want to hear about a race card used the race card to their advantage when they excluded African Americans from a set of opportunities. Indeed, the race card was rendered powerless against any other card in 1857 when the Supreme Court declared in *Dred Scott v. Sandford* that black folks had no rights that whites were bound to respect.

The signs don't say white or colored any more. Dred Scott may now be Congressman or State Assemblyman Dred Scott, and be nearly forty times more likely to be investigated than his or her white counterparts. Runaway slave Dred may now be called Amadou Diallo, a twentieth-century black man who learned that he had no rights—not even the right to carry a wallet—that reckless white police officers were bound to respect. Because the signs don't say white or colored, and because so many don't want to "play the race card," the killing of Amadou Diallo turned out to be a procedurally correct killing, not an awful and irrational show of force, a modern-day lynching.

Whenever I hear the phrase "playing the race card," though, I have a vision of a bunch of raucous folks sitting around a table, playing bid whist. At the beginning, the play is always a bit subdued as people try to size up the hands of both their partners and opponents. As the books pile up and the odds become clearer, big-time trash talking is as much a contest as whist. Eventually, as the number of cards in a hand dwindles, the trash talking crescendos.

I've sat at whist tables where players' necks have nearly swiveled 360 degrees, they've talked so much trash. I've seen people stand up and throw cards on the table, spit on them, and paste them to their heads. This is especially true if a team can take all the books in hand, called a "Boston." It is a feat that can only be achieved by a combination of the luck of the deal and the skill of manipulation and counting.

Trash talk tends to get wild. Some people choo-choo like a train to indicate that the train is coming to Boston. "Hartford!" near-winners shout, as they pick up the next to last trick. "Providence!" others holler, indicating that Boston is just around the bend.

Trash-talking players don't simply place cards on the table. They throw them, snap them, or sometimes coyly draw them across the table before turning them up. When aces show up, especially aces of trump, they often get a special welcome.

What do you do with the Ace of Spades? You slam it, slap it, thwack it on the table.

The Ace of Spades is a powerful card, the greatest spade of all. But even the best spade can be trumped in a society that believes in Dred Scott, that adheres to the notion that a black man has no rights whites are bound to respect.

When the Ace of Spades is trumped, it is a reminder that even the "best black" is too often perceived as not good enough to play in the big leagues. Should the holder of the Ace of Spades, then, play the race card?

She must, if it is one of the cards that is dealt.

I live off Fourteenth Street in Washington, D.C. Once upon a time this Shaw area might have been called "the hood," but now it is gentrifying. Fresh Fields is coming. The Fourteenth and U Street corridor is thriving with nightclubs and restaurants that cater to the under-thirty set. Thanks to a $5,000 tax credit for first-time D.C. buyers, young white suburbanites are hungrily looking at my neighborhood as a new frontier for urban pioneers. While the logic of the tax credit is compelling, there is something implicitly unfair about rewarding people to come to a neighborhood and run property values up without rewarding those pillars of the community who stayed through blight and turmoil. Some of those community stalwarts are elderly, retired, and challenged to pay property taxes that are rising thanks to urban renaissance. Need I say that the stalwarts are often African American? Does race matter here, or am I again playing the race card? My new white neighbors are hostile to an old black church, which has been in the neighborhood for more than a century, because its Sunday parking places a burden on the neighborhood. Is it race, or a property fight? Or does the property fight have racial dimensions?

Many African Americans in Washington, D.C., believe in something called "the Plan." It's a "conspiracy" to reduce this majority-black city to a majority-white one through gentrification, neighborhood transformation, different policies of housing lending, and the support from City Hall for white-owned rather than black-owned businesses. Though aspects of "the Plan" can't be proven, those who believe in it point to the fact that the D.C. City Council, in this majority-black city, is majority white, by a 7-6 margin, and that race often rears its ugly head in Council battles, especially around issues of poverty and education. Though votes don't often split along 7-6 lines, coded racial language is sometimes used in discussions. Even attempts to have "race-neutral" conversations are tinged with race in some contexts. How, after all, can you be race neutral in a city where the majority is being governed by a minority? But when activists frontally deal with the issue of race, those accused of a perceived bias often whine that "race has been injected." In other words, don't play the race card.

Once a white man tried to break into my house. He came armed with a screwdriver and was fiddling with my front door as I entered the back door and heard the rattle. I rushed to the front, baseball bat in hand, opened the door, threatened him, and called him every kind of motor scooter I could. I followed him down the street, and he entered an apartment three houses down. I telephoned my neighbor and demanded the identity of the would-be robber. I was told a "mistake" was made and that I should "get over it."

I called the police, who came and were persuaded by the clean-cut white man who no longer had a screwdriver that he had attempted to enter my home "by mistake." First he said he was looking for his girlfriend. Then he said he had mistaken the numbers on the front door, though the numbers were very different. Then he said that since he didn't get in, it ought not be a big deal. The police concurred and asked him to "apologize," which he did reluctantly. They didn't take a report, nor did they make an arrest, although I felt that a charge of attempted burglary might be appropriate.

Need I ask whether two police officers would have engaged in polite chitchat if a black man had attempted entry into a white woman's home? I can't ask the question if I can't play the race card. But the race card is prominent in the hand I've been dealt, and the trump card is a big part of the white boy's hand. Not only did he get away with attempted burglary, but later he used the fact that I chased him down the street with a baseball bat (good thing I believe in gun control) to bear witness to my "hot" temper.

❧

Early March. The calendar said winter, but the temperature said spring. I'd been stuck at my office computer all day, taking phone calls, writing, taking meetings. At 6:15, with the temperature still well above sixty degrees, I decided to take a walk through my gentrifying neighborhood, just to get some air.

There was a touch of wind. I was enjoying my walk, enjoying the breeze. I walked down to K Street, and had turned around and was headed back when I noticed that a white woman, a neighbor, was walking near me. We began to walk in companionable lockstep, making empty small talk.

I was content, and contentment doesn't settle easy on my restless, edgy spirit. Too often, contentment and joy are fleeting feelings lurched back into reality when I've got to play the hand I'm dealt. Most of the time, ebonically speaking, I don't have no trump cards. From time to time, I get the Ace of Spades, one of the baddest Aces in the bunch, especially in a no-trump game.

The walk was pleasant and I had not even had to go into my pack of cards just yet. But when we crossed O Street, there was a black man, spread-eagled against a police car, and my pace slowed because one never knows when a brother needs a witness. Not that witnesses would have helped Amadou Diallo or Patrick Dorismond, recent unfortunate victims of lawless New York City cops. Still, it was habit that I stopped and watched to make sure nobody's rights were being violated.

The woman walking with me slowed her pace, too. We had not exchanged names, but she seemed as curious as I was about the black man who had his legs wide apart, his arms resting on the police car. There were two police cars just for this one man, who seemed disheveled but not disorderly.

This was the element, she said, that we needed to rid from the neighborhood. My neck nearly snapped as I turned to her, about to say something. Her face was guileless, so I checked my anger for a moment, and asked aloud what "element" she meant. She nearly spit her answer when she spoke of the unsightly homeless men who hung out on the streets, often panhandling. She added, just in case I was wondering, that she was as disgusted with homeless white men as she was with homeless black men.

I wasn't planning to invite the homeless man leaning on the police car into my home anytime soon (although my tendency to play social worker is a bad joke among some of my friends). But I'm less inclined to be angry at his "element" than I am at the series of social policies that have encouraged homelessness in so many of our cities. The data on the shrinking availability of affordable housing are staggering. There are more than ten million Americans who, in the middle of economic expansion, still earn a minimum wage that Congress was reluctant to increase in the spring of 2000. With housing costs rising, is there any wonder that our city is plagued with homelessness? They are people, not an element.

The contentment of a wind-kissed night was suddenly dissipated, the companionable walk suddenly turned sour. I didn't really feel like debating the "element" with this random white woman, and didn't feel like battling over social policy issues as we drifted within a few blocks of my home. But I said a few things, harsh and edgy, about attitudes like hers. And she said a few things about the quality of life in the neighborhood. I told her that quality of life is the excuse New York Mayor Rudolph Giuliani used to have his Gestapo-like police force with their zero tolerance for crime round up tens of thousands of people, disproportionately people of color. It's not all race, my neighbor said. Here we go again. Don't play the race card.

Even in moments of contentment, the race card rears its ugly head. An afternoon drive can turn into an ugly confrontation when the police pull us over for no reason at all. A morning of shopping turns into a series of swallowed slights when we are followed, waited on out of turn, and have our credit card checked three or four times. And this is just the little stuff, the minutiae that can either merely irritate or set one off, especially if one has hot-tempered radar that is often described as searching for slights. I didn't have to look hard, though, to find a white boy with a screwdriver trying to break into my home, and a police officer too willing to invoke the Dred Scott decision on me.

Even in moments of contentment, the calculations I call "the racial calculus" are grinding at the back of my brain. Did the maitre d' at a favorite restaurant seat me out of turn because he forgot I was standing there, or because I am black? Am I annoyed enough about it to complain? To leave? Or will I sit and silently seethe, leaving a tiny tip to communicate my displeasure? Black folks used to say nothing about slights like this, because they were relieved to be seated at all.

I remember once traveling with an older relative who elbowed me whenever I complained about racist minutiae. Her message was "don't play the race card." Don't call attention to yourself—you pay a price for playing it. But don't we also pay a price for not playing it?

The small stuff is important. It is the minutiae that has a negative effect on quality of life. But the small stuff muddies the waters, and often occupies too much of our time. We can catalog racial slights and repeat them until they become mythology. The white boy with the screwdriver, the white man who thought the executive sister was a secretary, the doctor who was pulled over and made to hit the floor because the police officer had too many limitations to see past racial profiling.

Beyond the minutiae, there are assaults on affirmative action, the poverty that exists amidst prosperity, the crowding of our jails, the erosion in the quality of public education, the inability of Congress to condemn its own Klan (Conservative Citizen's Council) members, the Confederate flags still flying in parts of the South, the Rebel mentality prevailing in parts of the North, Midwest, and West.

The litany is long and more compelling than the mythology of minutiae. But we continue to catalog the minutiae because they hit us where we live, because the minutiae make Dred Scott real. They remind us that we aren't the only ones who play the race card; often we simply call attention to it. Don't tell me white folks aren't playing some kind of race card with racial profiling. Workplace racial hazing and other race-based actions persist, despite progress.

❧

My racial rage is never more acute than around July 4, when my neighbors and friends pull out the fireworks and celebrate our nation's birthday. The flags fly and people pledge allegiance to "one nation, indivisible." But for African Americans the nation is all too divisible.

The data tell us that there are two Americas. Yes, there is a blurring of the lines, the existence of a large and vibrant black middle class, a growth in the number of African American millionaires who dominate sports and popular music. But aggregately, African Americans earn about 60 percent of what whites earn and have just 10 percent of the wealth. Two Americas, not one nation "indivisible."

The Fourth of July celebration sticks in my craw and the only thing that makes me swallow my bile is a session with the Ace of Spades, a moment to read Frederick Douglass's masterful speech, "The Meaning of the Fourth of July to the Negro." Douglas said the Fourth is "not a celebration, but a sham," and in this city of history and monuments, the sham is all too obvious.

Just as there are two Americas, there are two Districts of Columbia. Ward Three has the city's highest per capita income; Ward Eight has the lowest. Ward Three has clean streets, frequent garbage pickup, activist, if over-employed, citizens. Ward Eight is on the mend, but its blight is as disheartening as the number of jobless men and women on the streets in the middle of the day. Mostly white Ward Three has political and economic muscle; mostly black and poor Ward Eight is treated like a stepchild of the city.

You can walk around Ward Eight for hours and never see a white person. You can do the same in parts of Ward Three and see black folks sprinkled like "flies in the buttermilk."

Two Districts of Columbia, two different realities. No wonder my neighbor sees an "element" and I see a man. No wonder some of our District's residents see benign neighborhood improvement in actions that others see as steps triggering their removal. Some see rising property values; others see "the Plan." No wonder, among our majority-white city council, some say race, but don't see it, while others see race, but feel they can't say it. These two Districts coexist uneasily in the shadow of our national monuments. No wonder my hand quivers with uncertainty when I go to pledge to "one nation." No wonder I find a paradox in African American patriotism.

We built this country, but it doesn't value us equally. Our dads and brothers and uncles fought in wars, only to come home to fight for their rights. When we hear people singing about "bombs bursting in air," are we visualizing gunfire in Vietnam or in South Central Los Angeles? Patriotism? Please.

When I say I am not patriotic, well-meaning whites often ask me to "love it or leave it." That's when my latent sense of ownership sets in. Why should I leave? Black folks built this country. It's not love it or leave it, but improve it or lose it!

Our nation's continuing commitment to Dred Scott, our continuing need to trump the Ace of Spades, our myopia about race matters, is like a filth that blights the monuments that gleam at night. It is a cloud you can almost see when a plane makes that special landing, circling south so the Washington Monument stands out in the distance. It is a patriotic symbol to some, but a broken promise to others. It gleams majestic, pristine white against a navy night sky, a promise or a challenge, depending on perspective. Against my will, the riveting sight often elicits twinges of patriotism.

According to polls and other measures, perspective often differs sharply by race. A February 2000 Gallup poll says that the majority of whites (74 percent in a recent study) think that there is no difference in the way that white people and African Americans are treated. Not surprisingly, less than half as many African Americans concur. Not only is there a racial gap in perception, but the gap is growing.

African Americans are being played when white conservatives distort Dr. King's dream and excessively quote his "I Have a Dream" speech in which he said that he looked forward to the day when Americans are judged not by the color of their skin, but by the content of their character.

Dr. King also said that our nation needs to cash the check on the debt it owes African Americans. When we fail to play the hand we're dealt, a hand that includes the race card, we say we're prepared to file the uncashed check under "get over it," and to accept that our spades are always trumped.

If life is a card game, though, we must play the race card. To be sure, we have to be tactical, knowing when to hold 'em and when to fold 'em.

We hold them on South Carolina, on the assault on affirmative action, on the struggle for economic justice. Sometimes we fold them on the minutiae. But when the minutiae become egregious (as when a racially profiled young black man was asked to take off his shirt at Eddie Bauer, go home, and return with the receipt), economically harmful (such as the employment discrimination suits at Coca-Cola and Texaco), or physically threatening (as in the Rochester, New York, case in which a young black girl was killed because of the racially-based zoning of buses), there is no folding the hand.

The cards are stacked, but from time to time, the concept of "just us" yields to the Ace of Spades. So spit on that race card and wear it on your head, just like the winner in a bid whist game. Stand on the chair and thwack that card down on the table, just like the team that just ran a Boston.

Dred Scott says the Ace of Spades is trumped sometimes, maybe most of the time.

Not every time.

Julianne Malveaux, Ph.D., *earned her doctorate in Economics at Massachusetts Institute of Technology. An economist, writer, and syndicated columnist, she is one of the most provocative, progressive, and iconoclastic public intellectuals in the country. Since 1990, her weekly column has appeared nationally in over twenty newspapers through the King Features Syndicate. She has written for numerous popular publications, and is a regular contributor to* Essence, Ms., USA Today, *and the* San Francisco Sun Reporter.

© David Bradley

To Make Them Stand in Fear

DAVID BRADLEY

ONCE UPON A time I made good money during what was then called Black History Month. Each February, I could be found on several college campuses—usually lily-white ones—leading class discussions, delivering a reading of my fiction, or lecturing on some black historical topic.

The beginning of the end of this came in 1987, at a generic university that I call Charolais State at Goodplacetoraisekids City. There, in an undergraduate literature seminar, I described an incident that had taken place in 1934, near a town called Greenwood, Florida.

A black man named Claude Neal was accused of raping and killing a white woman, Lola Cannidy. The sheriff arrested Neal and hid him in a jail on the other side of the state line; however, some Greenwood Good Ole Boys, who called themselves the Committee of Six, penetrated this ruse, went over in the wee hours of the morning, persuaded the jailer to release Neal to them, took him back to Florida, and hid him in a swamp.

111

At noon the Committee made an announcement, broadcast on local radio, that at sundown, Neal would be taken to the Cannidy farm, where Lola's father would castrate him. Then he would be escorted to the pig pen where Lola's body had been found and killed. The announcement concluded—and I quote—"All white folks are invited to the party."

Soon white folks did start arriving at the Cannidy farm, equipped with picnic hampers, guns, and moonshine liquor. Eventually, eight thousand gathered—men, women, children, babes-in-arms. Some, impatient, went to Neal's cabin and burned it. Others were content lighting bonfires. A state senator tried to distract them with a speech, to no avail.

Meanwhile, back at the swamp, the Committee of Six, learning that these rednecks were liquored-up and riled, feared their agenda would produce a frenzy and somebody might get hurt. So they decided to torture Neal in private, and just kill him in public.

So they beat Claude Neal and branded him. They cut his testicles off and made him eat them. They cut his penis off and made him eat that. Then they put a noose around his neck and asked him if he wanted to confess. When he declined, they threw the rope end over a tree limb and slowly hauled him up until strangulation produced unconsciousness. Then they revived him and asked again. Eventually he confessed.

He also died.

This left the Committee with a problem. They'd invited folks to a lynching. When their guests learned they'd had all the fun themselves, they'd be lucky if they didn't end up standing—or hanging—in for Neal.

But the Committee had an idea. They tied Neal's body to the back bumper of a car and drove slowly past the Cannidy farm, letting the body flop around, in an imitation of life. They planned to cut the rope and speed away before the mob discovered the guest of honor had departed prematurely. Unfortunately, the mob saw them coming. Fortunately, one of Lola's female relations ran out of the kitchen with a butcher knife and stabbed the body through the heart; the mob thought *she'd* spoiled the entertainment.

Nobody could really blame her, so the mob took their disappointment out on the body. They kicked it and spit on it and said all manner of evil against it. They couldn't urinate or defecate on it, there being ladies present, but they shot it fifty times, and ran over it six times with cars.

After that the Committee took charge of the body, hauled it to the county seat, and hung it from a lamppost in the courthouse square. Everybody was satisfied except old man Cannidy, who said the Committee "done him wrong" by not letting him do the castrating.

I'd told that story many times during many Black History Months, as a dramatic introduction to an important, albeit undramatic, argument: that, though in the past, methodological and personal biases of American historians had conspired to both conceal critical truths and prevent their later discovery using traditional historical methods, it was yet possible to discover some truth using non-traditional methods.

One such method was based on a theory of the French thinker, Michel Foucault, who held that a literary text was not the expression of an individual writer, but of an entire society. According to Foucault, every writer was, in a sense, society's scribe. This suggested that one could assemble a group of roughly contemporaneous texts from a given society, "read" the amalgam using the tools of literary criticism, and discover meanings the author had, intentionally or unintentionally, encoded in the text. In this case, however, the "author" would be a society, and the meanings discovered would be the encodings of a common, social mind—a structure akin to what is sometimes termed the *zeitgeist*.

Though arguably not as valid as traditional historical analysis based on documentary and material evidence, this technique is useful when documents or artifacts are unreliable or unavailable—precisely the problem that compelled the creation of what was originally called Negro History.

Usually, I advanced my argument by moving from the description of the Claude Neal lynching to a description of how my own understanding of lynching sprang, not from history courses, but from an independent study of Southern novels I'd undertaken as an undergraduate. Then I'd noticed that lynching—or the threat of lynching—was a trope common to such works, whether artistically high-toned or low.

These fictive lynchings had similar plot elements (black male, white female, white males, rope, tree), motivations (outrage at some unwanted sexual advance made by the black male toward the white female—or, alternatively, the killing of a white male by a black male), overt action (the white males joining to protect or avenge the outrage), and quasi-Gothic symbolism (white female as right social order, black male as threat to same, white males as successful defenders thereof). The lynching itself was described as a quasi-religious ritual of reaffirmed decency. It seemed these novels offered insight into what historian W. J. Cash called "the mind of the South"; it appeared Southern writers had provided a cathartic cultural experience through which a lost sense of social dominance might be regained. Insight into what I came to call the American Mind came when I read—also outside of class—Owen Wister's *The Virginian*.

The Virginian is not a Southern novel. It is the prototypical Western, the source of all the conventions of Saturday serials and TV horse operas: dialogue like "smile when you call me that"; action like the runaway stage coach; characters like the East Coast tenderfoot, the New England schoolmarm, and the strong-but-silent cowboy hero. Though Wister's novel is set in Wyoming in 1885, the hero hails from Ole Virginia, and is called "the Virginian"—hence the title. In addition to shooting the rattlesnake before it bites the tenderfoot and wooing the schoolmarm, the Virginian directs a lynching. But the lynchee was a white man—not an alleged rapist, but a confessed horse thief. There was no dramatic pageantry; Wister kept the event offstage.

I was struck by the contrast between Wister's lynching and those depicted in the Southern novels—notably Joel Chandler Harris's *Gabriel Tolliver*, which was published the same year, 1902, and which, though subtitled *A Story of Reconstruction*, could have been sub-subtitled *Uncle Remus Gets His Black Butt Lynched*. Both were historical novels set in the not-so-distant past. Both heroes were proud Southern men—the Virginian fought for the South during the Civil War, and had typical Southern attitudes towards blacks. Both novels were hugely popular. And, of course, both depicted lynching. But in *Gabriel Tolliver*, lynching was a noble, affirmative action. In *The Virginian*, it was a necessary chore. The Virginian said, "If I had to, I'd have to"—which isn't "A man's gotta do what a man's gotta do," but is close enough.

Having brought students this far through a narrative of personal experience, I'd shift to academic mode, introduce Foucaultian theory, and suggest that at the turn of the twentieth century lynching was not only an historical fact, but also a source of deep conflict in the American Mind. Then I'd challenge them to find any but the most covert reference to lynching, much less to conflict, in historical documents of the period.

Usually I pushed my point no further. At Charolais I didn't even push it that far. Instead, I went off on a personal tangent in the course of which I spoke of another text I'd encountered as an undergraduate, called *One Hundred Years of Lynchings*.

This wasn't fiction, but a collection of newspaper accounts compiled by a researcher, Ralph Ginzberg. At first I'd perused it in the same detached manner as I'd analyzed Southern novels and *The Virginian*, calmly noting how elements I'd isolated in the fiction were expressed in these actual accounts, with academically amusing differences.

The theme of a black man accused of "outraging" a white woman remained common, but in fact the outrage was sometimes merely verbal; in 1916, in Hartwell, Georgia, for example, two black men were lynched for saying, "Hello, sweetheart," to a white girl. The theme of mutilation, by contrast, seemed more shocking rendered in journalistic prose, as in the account of how Charles Fisher, accused of kissing a white farmer's daughter, had his lips off cut and was "mutilated . . . in other ways below the belt."

And while in fiction the lynchings seemed to be celebrations in the sense of ritual, in fact they seemed like celebrations in the sense of picnic. The events were often publicly announced and attended by large crowds. Pieces of the corpse were often hacked off and hawked as souvenirs. Photographers took pictures of the corpse, of people posing with it. Those photographs were often made up as postcards to be sent to distant friends.

That last detail arrested me, for at this same time, certain works of literature, because of their frank depictions of physical love, could only be sent through the U.S. mails in the proverbial plain brown wrappers. Yet the same post office would deliver graphic depictions of naked hate—and at a cheaper rate. To say that I was shocked would be understatement; more accurately I went into shock. In that state I became fascinated by lynching—some would say *morbidly* fascinated. One psychiatrist did say I was dangerously obsessed.

In fact, my intellectual engagement probably prevented me from doing something physically destructive or self-destructive—a risk run by any black American who studies American history. American history can drive you crazy if you're not careful—and even if you are.

The less said about what happened in that class at Charolais, the better. Suffice it to say that my flying off on a personal tangent led to other departures, and I resolved to never again speak publicly of lynching if I could help it.

I couldn't help it.

That evening, during the Q & A session after my lecture, a black male student who had been in that class asked me to comment on an incident that had taken place in Queens County, New York, on Friday, December 19, 1986.

That evening four men—Curtis Sylvester, Cedric Sandiford, Timothy Grimes, and Michael Griffith—were westbound on an expressway called the Belt Parkway, bound for the neighboring borough of Brooklyn. Their car broke down, leaving them stranded in a neighborhood called Howard Beach, which was ninety-eight percent white. Sylvester, Sandiford, Grimes, and Griffith were not. A mob of drunken, sex-crazed white male youths, armed with tire irons, tree branches, and a baseball bat, undertook to run them out of town. I will cut past the chase to the dénouement: Sylvester, Sandiford, and Grimes made it out of Howard Beach alive. Griffith did not.

The student actually had two questions. First, had what happened been a lynching? Second, could a lynching happen in Goodplacetoraisekids City? To answer effectively I had to take the audience through some of what I'd learned about lynching during my shocked obsession. I also had to take myself back through it—it was not a sentimental journey.

Now, alas, it is necessary to take that trip again. Not only because lynching is a significant historical phenomenon—although it is; the official total of lynched black people is 3,446, which is an average of one lynching every nine days for the eighty-six years during which records were kept—but also because incidents exhibiting lynching characteristics still occur with obscene regularity in contemporary America, suggesting that the idea of lynching has become deeply encoded in American culture.

In 1997, near a town called Independence, Virginia, two white men kidnapped a black man named Garnett Paul Johnson, hung him on a cross, soaked him with gasoline, burned him to death, and then beheaded the body with a dull ax. A year later, near a town called Jasper, Texas, three white men kidnapped a black man named James Byrd, Jr., spray-painted him white, chained him to the bumper of a pickup, and dragged him until his body parts were distributed along two miles of country road.

Public responses reveal a schism in the contemporary American Mind. Most Americans—and the majority of white Americans—insist these incidents are isolated and the pathology that produces them is restricted to the perpetrators, or to small groups at the fringe of society, like the white supremacist cultures that grow like bacteria in the agar of our prisons. But some Americans—and the majority of black Americans—fear these incidents are somehow connected; that the motivating pathology is epidemic in, if not endemic to, American society as a whole. In other words, some Americans think lynching is History, others, Current Events . . . and still others that lynching is coming back into fashion.

Be the truth as it may, no society can prosper while plagued by such a fundamental disagreement, for such disagreement renders it vulnerable to cynics and demagogues. The Charolais student's questions were inspired by the rhetoric that surrounded the Howard Beach Incident. The term was first applied to by New York's liberal Mayor Edward Koch, who said: "This attack rivals the kind of lynching party that existed in the Deep South." It was thereafter freely exploited by inflammatory speakers such as Alton Maddox, Esq., C. Vernon Mason, Esq., and Reverend Al Sharpton. Eventually it was used by Reverend Jesse Jackson.

When one hears how Michael Griffith was hounded through the streets by a howling mob until, in desperation, he ran into the fast lane of the Belt Parkway to be struck by a passing car, and how his body was thrown twelve feet and fell back to burst like a dropped watermelon, one is tempted to rhetorical excess. But graphic details cannot substitute for rational evaluation. The question was: Was Michael Griffith lynched?

No question can be answered without definition. Accordingly, I began by defining the term. There were a number of definitions I could have used. The dictionary I took to college in 1968 defined the verb "to lynch" as: "to put a person to death by some concerted action without authority or process of law for some offense known or imputed." What was, in 1987, the latest edition of *The New Britannica Encyclopædia* defined the gerund form, "lynching," as a case "in which a mob executes a presumed offender, often also torturing him and mutilating his body, without trial, under the pretense of administering justice."

However, during my period of obsession, I developed a definition built on that foundation of American justice, the Bill of Rights. Lynching is, in essence, a violation of the spirit of the Fifth Amendment, which states: "No person shall be . . . deprived of life, liberty, or property, without due process of law." Due process is a good faith attempt to eliminate reasonable doubt through a rigorous and critical examination of facts.

Advocates of a doctrine called States' Rights (which included Thomas Jefferson) maintained the Fifth Amendment applied only to federal action. Thus, the Fourteenth Amendment was needed to extend it to the states. Neither amendment applies to actions of private citizens. But the notion that no person should be punished before evidence has been presented and examined is a fundamental belief of the American Mind. Some denial of American belief is therefore essential to lynching.

Death is also essential to lynching. Most punishments can be reversed, at least to some degree. Persons illegally or erroneously deprived of liberty and property can be compensated. But a lynching victim is beyond meaningful compensation.

A mob is likewise essential; lynching is not a matter of individual action but of concerted group action—a conspiracy. It is a conspiracy of private citizens; a lynch mob has no legal authority. Since a conspiracy requires agreement, the homicide is premeditated. Since it's premeditated, it has none of the "exigent circumstances" justifications; lynching is murder.

Beyond their murderous premeditation, lynchers share a curious state of mind, which I call the expectation of impunity. Despite the obvious illegality of their actions, lynchers do not expect to be punished. Which is why they often do not bother to conceal their identities.

The definition of lynching, then, is: a murder committed by a conspiracy of private citizens, with malice aforethought and an expectation of impunity.

This definition does not mention race. Lynching doesn't necessarily have anything to do with race. The term appeared during the Revolutionary War, and referred to harsh treatment of colonists who remained loyal to the Crown. Its eponym was Charles Lynch, whose family also gave the name to Lynchburg, Virginia. Lynch was a magistrate, acting on written orders from the governor, Thomas Jefferson. He may have been overzealous, but he never lynched anybody, let alone anybody black.

Race wasn't a factor when the first lynchings did take place, sometime after December 15, 1791. Frederick Jackson Turner's Frontier Hypothesis is relevant here, because American lynching originated on the frontier. Turner's concept of the frontier was a line that, at any given time, marked the westward limit of European-American settlement. He called this "the meeting point between savagery and civilization." In less romantic parlance, a frontier is the interface between an area in which human culture—including laws—have some force, and an area where Nature's laws—as some would have it, the Law of the Jungle—is the only law.

For decades, Turner's Hypothesis was the basis of American history. Unfortunately, he made a critical error when he theorized that what made the American Frontier different was the empty land in front of it. What made the American Frontier unique, at least from the perspective of law enforcement, was that there was so much empty land behind it. When pioneers left Independence, Missouri, on the Oregon Trail they began a journey of two thousand miles. Even if they stopped before reaching Trail's End, they settled where there was no judge, no lawman for hundreds of miles, which is to say, within weeks.

They did not leave crime behind—the frontier, for obvious reasons, attracted criminals as well as peaceful pioneers. When a crime occurred, frontier dwellers had to act swiftly, lest the alleged perpetrator escape into the wilderness. Accordingly, they "took the law into their own hands," as the liberals say. In fact, in a democracy the power of law originates with the people; frontier dwellers simply exercised it. Turner's hypothesis suggests that, in so doing, they created something uniquely American. In fact, they were merely applying five hundred years of English Common Law.

Under Common Law, the sheriff was empowered to impress any male in the county (excepting boys under fifteen and clergymen) into a *posse comitatus* in order to pursue and apprehend a miscreant. In the absence of a sheriff, citizens were required to raise a "hue and cry" and pursue a suspect "with horn and voice" to the limits of the manor. In short, there was legal precedent for rounding up a posse or for forming a Vigilance Committee to run 'em out of the territory.

There was no legal precedent for summary execution, but the posse often got involved in a lengthy chase. Contemporary research has shown police officers often use excessive force at the end of a high-speed pursuit, the result of hormone-induced temporary insanity called "Post-Pursuit Syndrome." Today, most police forces require a ranking officer to remain aloof during a high-speed chase so as to be able to exercise rational and calm control after the suspect's apprehension. This was obviously impossible on the frontier; yet there is no reason to think the tendency to use excessive force was less strong when the pursuit depended on horses, rather than horsepower.

The lynching described in Wister's *The Virginian*, however, was not a passionate, post-pursuit act, but a deliberate one. Still, Wister invoked a ranking officer to defend it—the character Judge Henry Garth. The symbolism indicates that Wister, a Harvard-trained lawyer, believed frontier lynching, while illegal, was in keeping with the spirit of the law, and he was correct. In frontier lynching, there was probable cause to arrest the perpetrator. If a posse brought him back for trial, some members may have been jurors; a guilty verdict was probable. If a guilty verdict did result, death was a probable sentence. Given that the circuit judge might not show up for months, it could be argued that lynching balanced the Fifth Amendment right to due process against the Sixth Amendment right to a speedy trial, and achieved an outcome not out-of-keeping with the probable result of trial.

The key word is "probable." In America, we don't punish those who are probably guilty. We punish those who are guilty beyond a reasonable doubt. Frontier lynching eliminated the process that protected the innocent. Even frontier lynchers recognized that death of an innocent was not a mistake, but a tragic error. In frontier lynching, guilt mattered.

Guilt did not matter in another type of lynching, which I call Southern lynching, because of where it tended to occur. However, it has occurred in almost every region—there are only nine states in which no record of a Southern lynching can be found.

Southern lynchings may have taken place as early as 1791, but logic suggests they only emerged as a discrete phenomenon after 1868. However, in 1869, Mark Twain made reference to what may have been a Southern lynching in an essay called "Only a Nigger." There is anecdotal evidence that one Frank Timberlake may have been a victim of this type of lynching in Fleming County, Kentucky, in 1870.

Wister's *The Virginian*, set in 1885, suggests that by then, Southern lynching was distinct enough to permit comparison. Judge Garth says:

> I see no likeness in principle whatever between burning Southern Negroes in public and hanging Wyoming horse-thieves in private. . . . We do not torture our criminals when we lynch them. We do not invite spectators to enjoy their death agony. . . . We execute our criminals by the swiftest means, and in the quietest way.

This reference may be an anachronism. However, in 1889, the first year for which there are reliable data, it appears that only 46 percent of lynchings were of the frontier type. By 1902, when *The Virginian* and *Gabriel Tolliver* were published, 89 percent of American lynchings were of the Southern type.

Wister's Judge seemed to assume—as many Americans, white as well as black, in both 1885 and 1902 assumed—that the victims of Southern lynching were guilty. In fact, although there was usually an allegation of a crime, that was often merely an explanatory narrative, and often created after the fact. A researcher, Arthur F. Raper, who investigated lynchings in the 1920s and '30s, estimated that a third of the victims were innocent. That was based on a superficial examination; rigorous trials might have produced even more not-guilty verdicts.

Not that it would have mattered. In Southern lynching, even a legal verdict of not guilty was often ignored. An earlier researcher, a journalist, Ida B. Wells, the first person to compile lynching statistics, documented a case in Louisiana, in 1893, where an all-white jury found a black man not guilty of murder. A few nights later he was lynched.

Ginzberg reported a 1935 case in which the Louisiana Supreme Court set aside a black man's murder conviction. He didn't get a new trial. He got lynched.

Frontier lynchers executed people for committing felonies. So did frontier courts. So did Southern courts. Southern lynchers executed people for minor offenses that would not rate incarceration—if they occurred at all.

Rape was often used in explanatory narratives, but, especially at a time before modern forensics, the evidence was often ambiguous. Often it was the classic "she said, he said"—only he never even got a chance to say. Wells made herself unpopular by breaking what was, even to the black community, news: black men were not, generally, interfering with white women against their will, but with their consent—if at all.

Wells also documented cases in which blacks were lynched for "conjuring," proposing marriage, and "no offense." Arthur Raper analyzed a sample of one hundred lynchings that took place between 1929 and 1941 and found that 50 percent of the time even the explanatory narrative did not allege either murder or rape. Twenty-five percent of the time the alleged crime wasn't a felony. Two percent of the time the victim was accused of being insulting.

Some Southern lynching victims weren't even suspected of that much. Wells described the lynching, in Paris, Texas, in 1893, of a retarded man named Henry Smith, who allegedly had raped and killed a white female child. The evidence against Smith was questionable; Smith's stepson, William Butler, was never even associated with the crime. But Butler was later found hung, his body riddled with bullets.

Wister's Judge Garth, though wrong to assume "Southern negroes" were guilty, was right to refer to "burning," "torture," and inviting "spectators to enjoy the death agony." One observer of the Smith lynching wrote, "Kerosene was poured upon him, cottonseed hulls placed beneath him and set on fire. In less time than it takes to relate it, the tortured man was wafted beyond the grave to another fire. . . ." According to another observer, in Maysville, Kentucky, in 1899, "thousands" watched as an unnamed black man was skinned and burned at the stake. Children "kept up the fire around the blackened body by throwing grass, brush . . . anything combustible . . . until dark."

Pre- or post-mortem torture and mutilation was common. Smith was tortured for fifty minutes with hot irons "burning the feet and legs . . . rolled up and down [his] stomach, back and arms. Then the eyes were burned out and irons were thrust down his throat." Moreover, the event often proceeded with a high pageantry; before his torture and death, Smith was "placed upon a carnival float in mockery of a king upon his throne" and paraded about town.

Even when the event was less medieval, it involved public display, if not of the act, then of the body. In Columbus, Mississippi, in 1918, a black woman named Cordella Stevenson was questioned by police regarding the whereabouts of her son. She was found at dawn, dead, hanging from a tree, and naked, fifty yards from the main line of the Mobile and Ohio Railroad. In 1947, a University of Chicago-trained sociologist, Oliver Cromwell Cox, wrote that a typical lynching victim was "burned, hanged, or shot in some public place, preferably before the courthouse, and his remains dragged about the Negro section of the community."

But what Wister's Judge *really* got right was the racial aspect. In Southern lynching the victim was a Negro—although later exceptions were occasionally made for Jews, Mexicans, or union organizers.

Liberals have been heard to whine, "White people got lynched, too." It's true; they did. If you look up lynching in *The New Encyclopædia Britannica* you'll find that a quarter of the victims were white. But the *Britannica* statistics are broken down simplistically. A more complex breakdown, by race and state, reveals most lynchings of whites occurred in states that were not among the original thirteen—frontier states, in other words.

States in which lynching of whites most often occurred were Texas, Montana, Oklahoma, and Colorado. Most lynching of blacks took place in states that were part of the Confederacy. Here Georgia ranks second, with 492. Georgia was the fourth colony to ratify the Constitution— and the Bill of Rights. Another breakdown, by race and time, provided by Arthur Raper, reveals that 90 percent of the lynchings of whites took place before 1910. By 1932, he wrote, "in the typical lynching the victim is a Negro."

Raper's analysis is slightly off the mark, because he saw lynching as a singular phenomenon that had become racialized over time. In fact, he was looking at two distinct, albeit related, phenomena. A folkloric account suggests how distinct these two forms were. In September, 1887, in Fleming County, Kentucky, three men, two white and one black, were convicted of the same attempted rape. A mob stormed the jail, kidnapped the black man, Charles Colemen, and hanged him from a railroad trestle. The whites were left to serve out their sentences.

❧

Southern lynchings had none of the justifications of frontier lynchings. There was no trackless wilderness into which a miscreant could flee, nor was the sheriff a distant, unavailable authority. Raper, anticipating the concept of post-pursuit syndrome—and probably trying to fit his research to the frontier hypothesis, the then-dominant historical paradigm—argued Southern lynchings were a result of what he called "the Man Hunt Tradition—the traditional practice of Southern white men in arming themselves unofficially and hunting down an accused person," which, he said, "evolved on the frontier."

This tradition persisted, Raper said, "in localities where police power is least adequate." In fact, Southern lynchers often had to break a victim out of jail—if they let him get there in the first place. A later study, also by Raper, indicated that half the time at least one police officer could be found among the mob. Nor was lynching necessary to insure a publicly acceptable legal outcome.

In 1901, Mark Twain condemned a lynching in Missouri in these words: "they took the law into their own hands when by the terms of their statutes their victim would certainly hang if the law had been allowed to take its course, for there are but few Negroes in that region and they are without authority and without influence in overawing juries." In other words, Southern justice was so biased, lynching was unnecessary.

But if guilt was irrelevant and justice—even Southern justice—was assured, what was the purpose of Southern lynching? The answer was suggested by Wells in 1892, when she described the attitude of whites before a triple lynching in Memphis, Tennessee: " 'The Negroes are getting too independent,' they say, 'we must teach them a lesson.' "

Forty years later, in her autobiography, she told the story of that lynching, which took the life of one of her friends, a law-abiding, family man named Thomas Moss, who had "committed no crime against white women." What he had done, with Calvin McDowell and Lee Stewart, was open the "People's Grocery" which competed successfully with a white-owned grocery. The owner of that store, backed by a "posse of officers"—in plain clothes, but allegedly in hot pursuit of a criminal—broke into the back of the People's Grocery late at night. The black men defended their property with guns. Three "deputies" were wounded, none fatally. Thirty-one black men were jailed. For two nights an armed black militia stood guard at the jail. Then a judge, in violation of the Second Amendment, ordered them to disarm. That night Moss, McDowell, and Lee were lynched.

"This is what opened my eyes to what lynching really was," Wells wrote in 1931. "An excuse to get rid of Negroes who were acquiring wealth and property and thus keep the race terrorized and 'keep the nigger down.'"

By then, that statement was supported by dozens of cases. One of the most heinous took place in Springfield, Missouri, on Easter weekend, 1906, which had a prosperous black community, comprising ten percent of the population and a significant percentage of the voting rolls. Horace Duncan, Will Allen, and Fred Coker, all charged with rape, were taken from jail by a mob of seven thousand, hung from a replica of the Statue of Liberty in a downtown square, and burned. Eighty percent of the blacks left town—leaving their property behind.

In 1947, Cox, generalizing from this and other incidents, delineated what he called the *lynching cycle*. It began with "a growing belief among whites in the community that Negroes are getting out of hand—in wealth, in racial independence, in attitudes of self-assertion . . . or in reliance on the law." Next came a "continual critical discussion about Negroes among whites" which produced an "attitude of racial antagonism and tension." Next came "the rumored or actual occurrence of some outrage committed by a Negro upon some white." Cox said "the ideal act" was rape, but "if the tension is very high, whites will purposely seek out an incident." Next came the lynching, and a "scramble . . . for toes, fingers, bits of clothing, and the like, which are kept as souvenirs." Cox went on to describe four more phases of the cycle, and specifically mentioned "the sense of penal immunity which pervades the mob"—what I've called the expectation of impunity.

That expectation was justified. Whether the deed was done in the dark of night or in broad daylight, the doers were almost never sanctioned. In 1944, European researcher Gunnar Myrdal, in his study of race, *An American Dilemma,* claimed other types of anti-Negro violence were more common and had worse effects, while lynching was merely "a small-town custom" which "occurs most commonly in poor districts" and was perpetrated by the lower classes; according to Myrdal, middle- and upper-class whites were only "occasionally" part of the mob. Myrdal, however, had to admit that middle- and upper-class whites did "generally . . . condone the deed, and nearly always find it advisable to let the incident pass without assisting in bringing the guilty before the court"; and, also, that lynchers who were brought before the court were seldom found guilty because "the judge, the jurors, and the witnesses are either in sympathy . . . [or] do not want to press the case." He insisted Southern lynching was "a local community affair . . . state authorities usually do not side with the lynchers," but admitted that when lynchers were convicted, they were usually pardoned. Perhaps he didn't realize pardons are issued by a governor, or that a governor is a state authority.

American researchers had long known that, in fact, Southern lynchers derived their expectation of impunity from the explicit statements and actions of the highest state authorities. Ida Wells had described how, in South Carolina, in 1893, a black man named John Peterson, suspected of rape, sought sanctuary in the governor's mansion. Unfortunately the governor was "Pitchfork" Ben Tillman, who, during one campaign, had promised to help lynch any black who assaulted a white woman. He kept that promise by turning Peterson over to the mob. The raped woman said Peterson was not her assailant. His alibi proved true. They lynched him anyway. Then they elected Tillman to the U.S. Senate—four times. He died in office.

Arthur Raper, after describing the lynching of a black man named Dan Jenkins in Union, South Carolina, in 1930, added that, two weeks later, Senator Cole Blease, also a former Governor, came to Union and declared: "Whenever the Constitution comes between me and the virtue of the white women of South Carolina, I say, to hell with the Constitution."

If Myrdal knew about this statement, he missed its implications—and also those of his own writings. He wrote that, after a lynching, "In the locality where it has happened and in a wide region surrounding it, the relations between the two groups deteriorate. The Negroes are ter-ror-stricken and sullen." Cox, a black man who had lived in the South and who understood the Mind of the South, described the post-lynch-ing phase more perceptively: "Negroes become exceedingly circumspect in their dealing with whites, for they are now thoroughly frightened." In other words, the goal of Southern lynching was terrorism. Its strangest details—killing of innocents, bloody rituals, public display—were designed to do to post-Civil War blacks what, in 1835, a North Carolina woman said she did to her slaves: "Make them stand in fear."

❧

In 1987, on the basis of this analysis, I assured that black male student at Charolais State that the Howard Beach Incident had not been a Southern lynching. In 1990, I gave the same assurance to a black female student at another college, regarding another incident which also involved a car, a gang of white youths, and four black youths, one of whom failed to thrive. In 1997 and 1998, I assured myself that the incidents in Independence, Virginia, and Jasper, Texas, were not South-ern lynchings. But by then Southern lynching seemed beside the point. In March 1991 I had seen a videotape of twenty-seven Los Angeles police officers beating a black man named Rodney King, and had the nauseating feeling that what I was watching was not the same-ol', same-ol' police brutality, but a lynching in progress.

My gut reaction was not merely a matter of emotional horror, for despite the indistinctness of the images, it seemed clear that the officers were acting in concert to violate or condone the violation of King's rights. While it was not clear that they were trying to beat Rodney King to death, it appeared that they did not care if they did. But in my head, I knew it was not a lynching. King wasn't killed. And the officers were officers, with authority to pursue, arrest, and subdue. They may have abused that power, but they were empowered.

Still, though my head said this was not even an attempted lynch-ing, in my gut, I knew it was. Subsequent revelations tended to confirm

my gut. The initial pursuer turned out to be a white female Highway
Patrol officer. King was innocent of the alleged infraction—speeding;
hardly an heinous crime in Southern California—that gave probable
cause for the traffic stop. The LAPD did have policies to ensure that a
cool-headed commander would be present during the arrest phase of a
high speed chase, but in this case that officer was a leader in the beating. While the officers could hardly have anticipated videotape, they
were aware that they were under observation from nearby residences;
the beating was a display for community residents.

Transcripts of police radio communications showed that, over time,
the LAPD had code words to refer to beatings of black men. Transcripts of police radio communications about the King incident indicated officers involved had used those code words freely, suggesting
that they had little interest in concealing their behavior from their fellow officers—that they had, in other words, an expectation of
impunity. That expectation proved true. In internal investigations, officers involved were cleared of serious wrongdoing. Criminal charges
were filed, but the trial was moved from Los Angeles to a suburban
community known to be racially similar and emotionally sympathetic
to the officers. The jury acquitted them.

This additional data made me suspect my mind and gut were both
right: what I—and millions—had seen on that videotape was an
attempted lynching, but of a new type altogether.

In 1987, at Charolais State, I based my answer to the second question—"Can it happen here?"—on one of Arthur Raper's conclusions.
Raper reasoned that local reporters and newspapers were either sympathetic to the lynchers or dependent on their good will, and so failed to
publish the facts. He felt lynching could be decreased if "immediate factual newspaper reports . . . by trained newspapermen" were available.
He recommended the creation of a cadre of "expert reporters who could
be sent wherever a mob threatened."

No such cadre was formed, but technological and commercial
developments achieved the same result. In 1987, unlike 1937, most
journalists saw investigation as the highest expression of their profes-
sion. They also tended to have closer ties to national interests than to
local ones. Small-town newspapers and radio stations tended to be

owned by national corporations. Even locally-owned outlets were eager for news—and footage—that could be distributed nationally. None was likely to overlook the journalistic and commercial opportunity of a lynching.

Surely, there were locales in America where the conditions of Cox's lynching cycle existed, but it was unlikely locals believed they could hang a black man in the courthouse square, let alone subject him to the protracted rituals of Southern lynching, and get away with it. Surely, there were politicians with attitudes akin to those of Pitchfork Ben Tillman, but they did not dare say what Tillman said—at least, not in public. Accordingly, I assured the student that a Southern lynching could not take place in America in 1987. However, I added a casual caveat: that one institution in America had the power to control media access while kidnapping, isolating, mutilating, and murdering a person, and also had the ability to alter evidence and testimony to promulgate a justifying narrative—law enforcement itself.

After the Rodney King incident I began to take that caveat more seriously, listening to the excuses of the LAPD. The problem, said Chief Daryl Gates, was that officers were no longer permitted to use the "choke hold"—which had killed several minority suspects, because, he had earlier said, minority vascular systems were not "normal." In other words, the cops had to beat King half to death because they were no longer allowed to choke him to death.

I was reminded of Arthur Raper, who in the 1930s linked lynching to the tendency of police organizations to be secretive and of police officers to say nothing about the actions of brother officers; in 1991, this was known as the "blue wall of silence." I realized also that, as newsgathering became more sophisticated, so had "media relations"; by 1987, police had become adept at concealing or putting "spin" on events and promulgating explanatory narratives.

Not that I believed the LAPD—or any police force—would be able to carry out a traditional Southern lynching. But lynching, like any social phenomenon, can change over time. Historical evidence suggested that Southern lynching evolved out of frontier lynching; there was no reason another form of lynching could not evolve out of the Southern form. I recalled Arthur Raper's finding that at half of Southern lynchings there was at least one cop in the mob, and when I reexamined historical accounts, I could perceive ontogenetic structures of an emergent lynching form.

In Clarksville, Tennessee, in 1878, the lynching of a black man named William Anderson was preceded by one police-related incident, in which a black man was shot while resisting arrest, and succeeded by another, in which another black man was killed, also while resisting arrest. In Paris, Texas, in 1893, one of the men who "thrust hot irons into the quivering flesh of Henry Smith" was a deputy sheriff who had been "forced to use his club" on Smith in the past. One of the details that prompted Mayor Koch to intemperately and erroneously term the Howard Beach Incident a lynching was that, when police found Cedric Sandiford battered and bleeding profusely from a head wound, they had him assume the position, frisked, and partially stripped him—in New York, in December, and at night—and then, without offering him medical attention, questioned him for three hours about another homicide, in full view of Griffith's mangled corpse.

Fearfully, I speculated on possible characteristics of this new form of lynching. It would be a conspiracy, not of private citizens, but of law enforcers. It would occur in locales where whites in general, but particularly whites in law enforcement, held "a growing belief . . . that Negroes are getting out of hand" and prompted a "continual critical discussion about Negroes," where relations between the black community and police are characterized by "antagonism and tension," and where excessive police force was common. It would involve the death of a probably innocent suspect. It would have an explanatory narrative, perhaps supported by planted evidence. It would involve not blatant torture and mutilation, but accidental infliction of pain and inadvertent mutilation—a brutal beating or a hail of bullets—in the course of arrest or incarceration. The display would be provided by a hungry, and perhaps approving, media.

The expectation of impunity would derive, initially, from the culture of police organizations. The few officers involved would expect their brothers to shield them by carefully wording written reports and oral testimony, and perhaps even by misplacing, destroying, or planting evidence. So hampered, even vigorous internal investigation would result in exoneration. Internal investigation would provide protection from external prosecution; since subjects of such investigations can be required to testify, no evidence developed from their testimony—not even information developed from it—could be used in court. Even then, a carefully selected jury, more frightened of criminal incursion or racial aggression than of police excesses, might find reasonable doubt.

And the motive? While Myrdal insisted other types of violence against Negroes were more common and had more intimidating effects than lynching, Cox pointed out that these mundane intimidations drew their intimidating power from the possibility of a lynching. As he put it, "the threat of lynching is continually impending, and this threat is a coercive force available to white people as such." From a Machiavellian perspective, lynching would be an effective law enforcement strategy.

Further research uncovered a prototype police lynching: the killing of Black Panther Fred Hampton in Chicago in 1969—the year historians at Tuskegee Institute stopped compiling lynching records. At 5 A.M. on December 4, Black Panther Party members, including Hampton and his pregnant fiancée, were asleep in an apartment on Chicago's West Side. Fourteen hand-picked Chicago police officers, armed with a search warrant and automatic weapons, forced entry, supposedly to search for illegal firearms. They fired more than eighty rounds during a nine-minute attack. Spokesmen subsequently claimed the Panthers resisted; evidence and testimony later revealed that only one round had been fired from a Black Panther gun. Hampton never even got out of bed.

Correspondences between this incident and Southern lynching are striking. The attack was by Chicago police, making Fourteenth Amendment rights an issue. The FBI supplied the intelligence—including a floor plan—that was used to both obtain the warrant and carry out the attack. (Afterward, the informer received a $300 bonus for "uniquely valuable services.") Fifth Amendment rights were therefore also at issue. Moreover, as the alleged crime was the possession of firearms, not by an individual, but by an organization that was arguably a well-trained militia, Second Amendment rights were at issue as well. Hampton, who was very dead, was also very innocent of the weapons charges—and the FBI knew the weapons had been obtained legally. The excessive force used had an effect suggestive of mutilation; one observer reported that the apartment's walls looked "like Swiss cheese." What the bodies looked like can be imagined.

And was imagined by the local black community. Surviving Black Panthers regained possession of the apartment shortly after the attack and conducted walk-through tours so the public could see the colandered walls and the blood-soaked mattresses. How the Panthers gained control of the crime scene is a mystery. Some sanguine commentators assume police failed to seal the crime scene out of confusion or incompetence—in any case, unintentionally. It is possible, however, that law enforcement officials intentionally allowed access to achieve terroristic effect and may have suggested the idea to the Panthers through the FBI informant.

The officers involved had the greatest expectation of impunity of any lynchers in history, for the assault was supported by the highest levels of federal law enforcement. The FBI supplied not only the intelligence, but moral support through its Counter Intelligence Program, COINTELPRO, ordered by J. Edgar Hoover himself. In August 1967, Hoover wrote in an internal memo: "The purpose of this counterintelligence effort is to expose, disrupt, misdirect, discredit, or otherwise neutralize the activities of black nationalists—their leadership, spokesmen, membership, and supporters." In March 1968, in a follow-up memo, Hoover directed agents to "prevent the rise of a 'messiah' who would unify, and electrify, the militant black nationalist movement." Fred Hampton, young and charismatic, surely fit that description.

Despite my analysis of the Fred Hampton incident, I could not really believe a new form of lynching was emergent . . . until June 1994, and the beginning of the O. J. Simpson case. Then I found myself thinking almost compulsively of lynching. Not because I thought Simpson was innocent—there seemed to be, as prosecutors claimed, a "mountain of evidence" against him. But there also seemed to be, as defense attorneys later claimed, a "rush to judgment." Due process ends with a fair and public trial, but it begins with a diligent and unbiased investigation, which, in this case, seemed somewhat absent.

What was palpably present was the White Woman Theme, invoked every time some bubble-headed, bleached-blonde anchorperson referred to Shakespeare's *Othello*. And then there was the melodrama of the famous Slow-Speed Chase. When I saw the LAPD spokesman, flanked by the District Attorney, announce that Simpson was a fugitive, armed and considered dangerous, I heard an echo of the wild, wild west: Simpson was wanted, dead or alive. Knowing about the LAPD (for example, officers in some elite units received unofficial commemorative plaques for a "good shoot." In one unit, the plaque depicts a heart playing card—a red one if the victim lives, a black one if he dies), I was sure Simpson would be taken dead. I believe the tension of the Slow-Speed Chase—which for a time preempted the NBA basketball finals—turned on the possibility of a bloody end.

Or rather, probability. For this was the LAPD, which had beaten an unarmed, apprehended, and innocent Rodney King. Simpson was armed, fleeing, and had a mountain of evidence against him. Surely there was a picnic atmosphere among those hundreds who lined the streets and overpasses, and those millions who had settled down, with beer and pizza, to watch the Knicks play the Rockets. Surely some of us were thinking, with whatever complex emotions, that this time it would be seen not in a grainy, videotaped, black and white, but in clear, living—or dying—color. No picture postcards would have been needed; this was prime time CBS.

I believe that, had it not been for that huge television audience—and the cell phone that allowed the public to hear his suicidal, rather than homicidal intent—O. J. Simpson would never have had his day—or year—in court. That "mountain of evidence"—much of which was never presented at trial—would never have been tested, and most Americans, myself included, would have rationalized it as the informal execution of a guilty man for a crime which, under California law, deserved the death penalty. In fact, it would have been the violation of one of America's most basic principles—and the killing of a man whom a jury would, in time, acquit.

Is a new form of lynching emerging in America? The answer, I believe, is no. The answer, I believe, is that such a form of lynching has emerged.

When I began speculating ten years ago, I felt that the accounts of officer-involved killings, though troublingly frequent, lacked sufficient context and common elements to constitute a discrete phenomenon. Since then, a coherent pattern has been realized and ritualized. The characteristics include an explanatory narrative based on a routine traffic stop for a minor infraction, and the presence, not of a white woman, but of that contemporary symbol of power and success, an expensive automobile.

I am not suggesting every routine traffic stop is an attempted lynching, nor that every fatal officer-involved shooting is an actual lynching. Officers who fire their guns in the line of duty are usually justified; there are, as police jargon puts it, "good shoots." Even "bad shoots" can result from poor training, fear, sheer stupidity, or purely individual prejudice.

But a compilation of some "bad shoots" forms a troubling text— one that cannot be dismissed as a series of isolated incidents, although internal investigators, "hanging" judges, or juries who fear the encroachment of blacks more than the excesses of police have done just that.

October 12, 1995. Near Pittsburgh, Pennsylvania. A thirty-one-year-old black man named Jonny Gammage was asphyxiated while being restrained—face down—by five suburban police officers after allegedly resisting arrest following a high-speed chase. The chase began when one police officer observed Gammage "tapping his brakes." This suspicious action was made while Gammage was driving an expensive automobile owned by his cousin, Ray Seals, a defensive lineman for the Pittsburgh Steelers.

Three of the five officers were tried on charges of involuntary manslaughter. One was speedily acquitted outright. The other two were retried twice over the next several years, with neither jury reaching a verdict. In June 1998, a few months after the term "racial profiling" joined the colloquial "DWB" (Driving While Black) as part of the American lexicon, the wrongful death suit of the Gammage family was settled for a reported $1.5 million—but no admission of liability. One month later a local judge dismissed all charges against the accused officers, ruling that a third trial would violate their rights. In early 1999, the United States Department of Justice declined to file any charges.

April 23, 1998. The New Jersey Turnpike. Four men, three black and one Hispanic, were stopped by two white state troopers. Troopers alleged that, as they approached the vehicle, a van, the black driver, Keyshon Moore, tried to run them down. They fired eleven times, wounding not Moore, but the passengers, Danny Reyes, Rayshawn Brown, and Leroy Grant. The wounded men were handcuffed, strip-searched in view of passing motorists, and forced to lie in a ditch before being given medical attention.

Although no deaths resulted, this case marked a turning point in public awareness of racial profiling. New Jersey State Police had long denied that they "profiled" motorists, stopping those who appeared to be in racial groups linked statistically with certain crimes. Even before the Turnpike shooting, however, the U.S. Justice Department had been secretly investigating. A quick-and-dirty review revealed that, during a two-month period in 1997, 75 percent of motorists arrested on the Turnpike were members of minority groups. In April 1999, a report commissioned by New Jersey Attorney General Peter Verniero concluded that complaints about profiling on the Turnpike were "real, not imagined," and admitted the practice was fostered by ambiguous rules and a "culture" that encouraged substituting race for probable cause. A report later published in the *New York Times* revealed that, in 1996, State Police commanders emphatically declined to discourage racial profiling.

Less than a month after the *Times* ran its story, a New Jersey judge dismissed charges against the officers, saying, "Members of society engaged in law enforcement deserve no less protection from the criminal justice system than that which is afforded to other citizens." This decision was overruled on appeal, and charges reinstated.

February 4, 1999. Bronx, New York. Amadou Diallo, black, twenty-two, was observed entering the vestibule of his Bronx apartment house by four white officers of the New York Police Department's Street Crime Unit who were looking for a rapist. When Diallo pulled out his wallet—perhaps to show identification, perhaps to appease what he thought were muggers—police fired forty-one times, striking Diallo nineteen times and killing him.

The four officers were indicted for second-degree murder. A state appeals court granted the defense a change of venue to Albany, New York. In February 2000, all four officers were acquitted of all charges.

June 12, 2000. St. Louis, Missouri. Two unarmed black men, Earl Murray and Ronald Beasley, were killed when white undercover police officers fired into Murray's car in the parking lot of a fast food restaurant. Murray had, allegedly, arranged to sell drugs to undercover police earlier in the evening and had stopped in the parking lot to complete the sale. Police acknowledged that Beasley, who relatives said had simply asked Murray for a ride, was not under suspicion.

This incident was a culmination of a long buildup of racial tension in St. Louis, involving at least two police killings of black males. Local black activists were especially angered because prosecutors, while promising a "thorough investigation," refused to release copies of surveillance tapes of the incident.

I do not want to believe the conclusions to which the data have led me. Like the boy who begged Shoeless Joe Jackson, I want to beg myself, "Say it ain't so." But even if it isn't so, I must admit that I, myself, am very much afraid.

Whenever I see those red and blue lights flashing in my rearview mirror, or note a squad car parked on a street down which I must walk, I feel a tightening in the gut, and a nauseating sense that, at that very moment, my life may be spinning out of my control. Was I speeding? Does it matter? Was Rodney King really doing 115 miles an hour—in a *Toyota?* Am I unarmed and homeward bound with my door key in my hand? So was Amadou Diallo.

I am afraid, moreover, of my own thoughts and speculation. In 1968, in a book called *Black Rage,* two black psychiatrists, William Grier and Price Cobbs, theorized that there existed a disturbance in the psyche of all black Americans. They wrote:

> We submit that it is necessary for a black man in America to develop a profound distrust of his white fellow citizens and of the nation. He must be on guard to protect himself against physical hurt. He must cushion himself against cheating, slander, humiliation, and outright mistreatment by the official representatives of society. . . . For his own survival, then, he must develop a cultural paranoia, in which every white man is a potential enemy unless proved otherwise and every social system is set against him unless he personally finds out differently.

I don't know if Grier and Cobbs were right. I do know I don't want to look at my fellow Americans, or my society, that way. But, increasingly, I do.

When I hear that police officers have shot down some poor nigger for walking while black, I try to believe the police chief when he says—

as they always say—that it was perpetrated by "a few bad apples." When I saw the headline "Aides Erroneously Stopped By Police" and read all about how "two [black] White House aides were traumatized, embarrassed, and humiliated when gun-wielding police stopped them in a Washington suburb," I tried to be gratified that, this time, the cops picked on the wrong black Americans.

I believe in fact that there was no mistake; that the police knew exactly who they were stopping and why: not for driving while black, but for being prosperous, well-educated, and well-connected, while black. I believe, as my grandmother taught me, one bad apple can sour the barrel. And I believe that the barrel of American justice is soured by one bad apple—or a few, or many. I believe many white Americans work to maintain its vinegary condition—to preserve, through threat of lynching, the social status quo. I believe that many more white Americans do not mind this. I believe there exists, not some vast conspiracy, but an unspoken understanding that it is best if black Americans be periodically reminded of the ephemerality of their citizenship, of their expectations, of their very existence.

Call it cultural paranoia, or perhaps plain paranoia, but I do believe the foul spirit of that North Carolina slaveholder lives and moves and has its being in the hearts of my countrymen. I believe that many white Americans want black Americans to be made to stand in fear.

David Bradley *is best known for his bestselling historical novel about race,* The Chaneysville Incident *(Harper, 1981), which won the PEN/Faulkner Award, the American Academy and Institute of Arts and Letters Award for Literature, and the* New York Times Book Review's *"Editors' Choice" citation.*

Bradley is currently completing a nonfiction book about race in America, The Bondage Hypothesis: Meditations on Race, History and America, *and hopes that it will be published by 2003.*

© Brian Kleinecke

Passing

Theresa M. Towner

At work:

"I understand that you have an intellectual expertise in African American literature, but what do you say to the charge of cultural appropriation?"

"What are you teaching next semester? . . . Oh."

"My mom's about as light as you, and she gets &#*! all the time."

At home:

"Theresa, not EVERYTHING boils down to race, y' know."

"What are you teaching next semester? Oh."

"What I don't understand is what black people want, anyway. I mean they've got equal rights and now it just seems like they want special rights. And white people who think they should have them are suffering from what I call 'white guilt.'"

Around town:

"What people who aren't from the South don't understand is that 'nigra' is the Southern pronunciation of 'Negro' and doesn't mean the same thing as 'nigger.'"

"And what do you teach? . . . Oh . . ."

"She had her hair colored about the same as yours. It's real fine, like yours. Is this manicure set all you needed today, hon?"

And then there was the time a friend who heard the answer to the recurring question above simply picked up my hand and rubbed his thumb back and forth along the back of it, in response to my own question—"Why not? It's good stuff"—as though the color of my skin were answer enough.

What do you think he would have done if the pale had come off?

In a discussion of his film *Bamboozled*, Spike Lee said that "In the new millennium, you don't have to wear blackface to be part of a minstrel show or to be a minstrel act" (*Dallas Morning News*, 11/8/2000). That comment gives ironic voice to a thought I've had ever since I became interested in African American literature and culture: What business have I got here, anyway? By what right do I comment on Alice Walker's plot developments, James Baldwin's political essays, the Invisible Man's attitude toward women? Is it the racial version of the *droit de seigneur*, the right of the lord of the manor to take what he wants? As an identifiable woman, can I even claim *droit de seigneur*?! At what point do I just get to think what I think, write what I write, be wrong when I am wrong, regardless of my color or sex or age or zip code?

Mine was exactly the question that people of color have screamed, in life and in art, in voices illiterate and literate, in languages long forgotten as well as the ones forced upon them by the institutions peculiar to American history: What large force keeps my individual and unique self bound?

In my case, though, the answer to that question waited for me every minute in the nearest mirror, and to say that this realization was disconcerting is to so radically understate the case as to risk out-and-out lying. What kept me from belonging to a literature and culture that I deeply admired was precisely the historical reality that created both me and what I admired: white American enslavement of kidnapped Africans.

I had just performed what we call in the academy an act of racial interrogation. I had examined the position of a person—myself—in the larger context of racial concerns in America; but in the act of doing so, I discovered that like all human objects of study, I didn't much like being treated like an object, even when I was the one doing the treating. Even worse, I found myself in an ethical conundrum. Knowing what I knew, what should I do? It wasn't good enough to tell myself and others that, for instance, even though I am not a sixteenth-century Englishman, I still teach *Hamlet* with reasonable success; why shouldn't I teach *God's Trombones*? It wasn't good enough to point out that Houston Baker first trained as a scholar of British Victorian literature and then go on to lay my own claim to writing about *Song of Solomon*. It definitely wasn't good enough to adopt the so-called "enlightened" white attitude toward all racial matters and pretend to ignore my difference from these writers and thinkers. Black folks never ignore race; they can't afford not to know where The Man is, and pretending that I was not The Man or His Woman would not only be patronizing and stupid but would also cheat me out of everything I had figured out so far, even if what I had learned left me rather stuck.

The man who currently serves as my dean once told me about what he called "generative questions." These, he said, are the questions that make you ask all the other questions—the first questions, if you will, or primary interests. His own generative question was "What is heroism?" Upon listening to him talk about Odysseus as we drove down a long suburban street in America, I blurted out that my generative question would have to be "What is an honorable life?" That question—unarticulated—had prompted my ongoing examination of race in William Faulkner's later novels; asked flat-out of students about literature, that question had evaluated characters, plots, and themes by the hundreds over every century I knew; said and unsaid, attempts to answer that question in the midst of my ethical conundrum were what kept me teaching African American literature. Trying to live up to the literature I loved, I kept going back to the questioning faces in the classroom; kept wiping the sweat from my palms; kept worrying.

I still worry. I always will, because to me the day I stop worrying is the day I will have arrogated myself into the realm of the inhuman.

Here, at the moment of the millennium, I teach in whiteface.

Theresa M. Towner is the author of Faulkner on the Color Line: The Later Novels *(University Press of Mississippi, 2000) and of essays on Faulkner, African American literature, and theory. She is Assistant Professor of Literary Studies and Associate Dean of the School of Arts and Humanities at the University of Texas at Dallas.*

© Amber Novak

Black and White

Robert Jensen

I AM AN academic and a journalist, trained to step back from myself, to analyze, to be detached and "objective." Luckily, I have overcome most of that training, which is why I can begin this essay with personal stories of the anger and fear of a white boy confronting race.

The anger is not the typical white anger, the anger at "minorities" who "won't help themselves" or "won't stop complaining." And the fear is not the typical white fear of "radical" minorities who might take things from me or hurt me. The anger is directed at white people and at that part of me that is white in the same way. And the fear is a fear of myself, of seeing honestly the parts of me that are still white in that way.

Now, two stories.

I. The Anger

I once attended a symposium on journalistic ethics where the keynote speaker, a well-known journalist, talked about journalists' special role in society as guardians of democracy. Because of this, he said, journalists are sometimes allowed to do certain things that other citizens are not, such as intrude into people's private lives. This is much like doctors who are allowed to cut into people or soldiers who are allowed to kill, he explained.

Then he offered another analogy: it's like police who "have the right to beat people." I sat in the audience, momentarily stunned. I nudged a friend next to me. Had he actually said that police have a right to beat people? Yes, she said, I had heard it right.

I looked around at an almost completely white and generally middle-class audience in the auditorium of the private college where the symposium was being held. No one seemed too upset by what he had said.

The speaker went on to say a lot of other reactionary things. Later, during the question period, I went to the microphone, intending to focus on another stupid point he had made.

"But before I get to my question," I said, "I want to say that it seems to me that anyone who can say that police have a right to beat people is presumptively excluded from discussion about ethics of any kind."

The audience squirmed, unsure of how to react. The speaker winced but never responded to my challenge.

Later, during the reception, I talked to a colleague who was unclear what point I was trying to make. Surely the speaker just misspoke, he said; what the speaker meant to say was that in certain situations, police have the legal right to use force, sometimes even deadly force.

Yes, I understood that, I replied. But my point was that he used the phrase "the right to beat people." The language reflects his relationship to power. No one who comes from a class of people subject to being beaten by police would ever think of using such a phrase. Only people who don't have to worry about being beaten would make the "mistake." Beyond that, I argued, it's not implausible that the speaker and lots of other folks like him are glad they live in a world in which police sometimes beat people; it keeps the "dangerous classes" in line. "Try to imagine if he were black, even a black person with a professional career and a middle-class life," I said. "Think of how different interactions with police are for black people. Do you think he would have said that?"

My colleague shrugged and said I was overreacting to an admittedly careless, but harmless, choice of words on the speaker's part. The colleague turned, never really understanding what I thought was a simple point, and headed off to talk to someone less contentious.

I was left standing there, full of anger, wanting to scream, and feeling incredibly alone.

I looked around and realized that all around me were people just like me—white, middle-class, educated academics or professional journalists. And I hated them. I don't just mean that I was frustrated with them. At that moment, I hated them. Not just the speaker, but all of the nice middle-class white folks in the room who were too polite to say anything, to hold the speaker accountable. I even hated the three or four white people who had come up to me after the talk and thanked me for speaking up. I bit my tongue and didn't ask them the obvious question: Why didn't you speak up too, instead of leaving my comments to hang in the air, to wither and die without support?

I hate middle-class white people. And I am a middle-class white person, which means that in some sense I hate the part of myself that can't escape the identity. I don't like that feeling.

II. The Fear

Part of why I hate part of myself is simple: I can feel the lingering traces of racism in my own body. Every time I start feeling a bit too self-righteous about race, I try to pull myself out of my head, where it is easy to keep things neat and clean, and back into my body, where the world is much messier.

So, what facts about race are in my body?

It's easy to test. Put my white body next to a black body. What do I feel? What reactions kick in, immediately, before I have a chance to think? What facts about race can I feel in my body in that moment? How honest can I be about that?

The fact is, I feel something different—a certain kind of fear—next to a black body than I feel next to another white body. The difference matters, still, after years of actively trying to overcome that learned reaction. Though the intensity of the feeling of difference has lessened considerably over the years, I still feel different next to a black body. That doesn't mean I am a racist. It means that I can't deal honestly with race and racism until I can deal with that feeling, until I can talk about it without shame and guilt, without apologetics.

Here's my second story, about the fear.

I was on a panel with several other professors at the University of Texas discussing race and politics in the O. J. Simpson case. Next to me was Ted Gordon, an African American anthropology professor. I was talking about media; he was talking about the culture's treatment of the sexuality of black men.

As we talked, I paid attention to what was happening in me as I sat next to Ted. I felt uneasy. I had no reason to be uncomfortable around him, but I wasn't completely comfortable. During the question-and-answer period—I don't know what the question was that sparked my comment—I turned toward Ted and said something like, "It's important to talk about what really goes on between black and white people in this country. For instance, why am I sitting here next to Ted feeling afraid of him? I know I have no reason to be afraid, but I am. Why is that?"

People in the audience didn't know what to make of it, nor really did I. There wasn't a clear context for the observation, nor any obvious path for dialogue to take from it. So the comment hung in the air, never addressed but very much hanging in my mind.

Looking back, it seems clear that my reaction wasn't a crude physical fear of him, not some remnant of being taught that black men are dangerous and more prone to violence (though I have had such reactions to black men on the street in certain circumstances). Instead, I think it was perhaps a more basic fear that haunts white people—the fear of being seen, and seen through, by people of color, especially when we are talking about race.

In that particular moment, for a white-boy academic on an O. J. panel, the fear likely was in large part the fear of being exposed as a fraud or some kind of closet racist. Even if I thought I knew what I was talking about and was being appropriately antiracist in my analysis, I was afraid that some lingering trace of racism would show through, and that Ted would identify it for all in the room to see.

After I publicly recognized the fear, I think I let go of some, but not all, of it. I have overcome some of my deeply embedded instincts, though I still struggle with that visceral reaction, of my white body next to a black body.

The deeper fear now is that I will never fully understand where that discomfort comes from, a fear that I won't find a way to overcome it.

III. Disclaimer, Definitions, Direction

The disclaimer: I do not write this out of a sense of guilt. This essay is not an expression of white liberal angst. I do not feel guilty about being white.

Guilt is an appropriate moral, political, and emotional response when one has wronged another, when one has something to feel guilty about. There have been plenty of times in my life when I have felt guilty about racist or sexist things I have said or done, even when they were done unconsciously. But that is guilt felt as a result of specific acts, not guilt for the color of my skin.

I think many white people stay stuck in that sense of guilt about being white for two reasons. First, if one keeps the focus on that abstract guilt, one rarely gets to the appropriate guilt for racist actions; it's a convenient way to avoid accountability. Second, such guilt is a way for white people to avoid taking action. If one feels guilty, it is easy to feel paralyzed, which makes it easy not to act. A white person can say, "Look how bad I feel about racism and white privilege. I feel so bad it immobilizes me." From that position, just talking honestly about race and racism becomes too overwhelming, and people often use their own psychological pain to escape political responsibility.

Having white skin is something about which I feel neither guilty nor proud. I did not choose my skin color, hence I can't be responsible for it. But I am responsible for how I choose to deal with being white and the privilege that brings to me. I am, to borrow George Lipsitz's term, responsible for whether I make a "possessive investment in whiteness" or consciously take on an antiracist identity and work to dismantle white supremacy.

Framed that way, it is not enough for white people to denounce overt discrimination, renounce the overt forms of racism in their own lives, and call it a day. To be antiracist demands that we go beyond that kind of individualistic framework, in which racism is seen only as the obviously racist acts of specific people. In his book *The Possessive Investment in Whiteness,* Lipsitz argues convincingly that white people must begin to see the way in which a history of both overt and legal, and covert and social, discrimination has resulted in institutionalized racism in housing, employment, education, and social life. The task is not merely to stop telling racist jokes, but to transform the institutions of the society that, without intervention, replicate the inequities.

So when I ask white people—including myself—to think about our own complicity in racism, I don't mean to suggest all whites are KKK members or sympathizers. When I talk about the racism that lingers in me, I mean not only the attitudes and behaviors that the culture in which I was raised taught me, but also the tendency to want to ignore the ramifications of race that are all around me. That's why I so often talk not about racism but white privilege—the advantages that come to white people who live in a white-supremacist culture. To be antiracist is to acknowledge that privilege and take one's place in the political struggle against it.

By "white supremacist," I mean a society whose founding is based in an ideology of the inherent superiority of white Europeans over non-whites, an ideology used to justify the original sins of the genocide of indigenous people and African slavery. That ideology also justified legal and extralegal exploitation of every non-white immigrant group, and is used to this day to rationalize the racialized disparities in the distribution of wealth and well-being in this society.

White people often challenge me on these points. It is unfair, they claim, to call the United States a white-supremacist society when the legal structures of discrimination have been dismantled. My response is simple. If there is so much racial justice around, why is Shannon County, South Dakota, home of the Pine Ridge Indian reservation, consistently the poorest county in the United States? Why do African Americans on average live seven years less than white Americans and experience more than double the infant mortality rate? Why are unjustified stops of Hispanics by Immigration and Naturalization Services border agents so routine that a Mexican American student would tell me that when he and his friends drive in that area they allow extra travel time to accommodate the harassment?

Perhaps more important than the statistics is the testimony of non-white people—available in print and in conversation to anyone who cares to hear—about living day to day in the midst of that white-supremacist ideology. The ultimate white privilege is to ignore both the statistics and the stories, to hold onto a belief in the fiction of a level playing field, a fair and equitable economy, a color-blind world.

To better understand why white supremacy persists, I want to go back to my stories, to the roots of the fear and anger.

IV. Roots of Fear

It's not too difficult to figure out where my lingering fear about race comes from: go back to my childhood in an almost all-white upper Midwest in the 1960s and '70s. The only black people I saw were on television, mostly in sporting events. In my family, we were Minnesota Viking fans. The running backs for the Vikings at that time were both slow, plodding white guys, real Midwestern types. Then one year, the Vikings got a fast guy, a flashier guy, a guy who didn't plod. A black guy. He was good, but he was different. He wasn't as trustworthy as the white guys. He fumbled more often, or at least it seemed that way. He was good, but we had to be careful. He was a n——.

"Look at that n—— run," my father said to the TV set, and to us.

The fear in me comes because I grew up in a world, in the United States, where blackness is associated with difference, and the difference can't be trusted. Even when the difference is greater skill and expertise, the difference can't be trusted because it is within a framework of lesser-ness, of presumed black inferiority. There has to be a downside to the superior performance, because we all know blacks are lesser. Even when they are better, they are lesser in other ways.

This is never explained in detail. It doesn't have to be. It simply is. $1 + 1 = 2$, and black = degraded + degenerate.

In short, I was raised to be a white American.

I went on to be a good liberal teenager and college kid, in reaction to my reactionary upbringing. I supported the most liberal candidates.

I criticized U.S. foreign policy. I had some vague sense that corporate capitalism doesn't deliver freedom and justice. I assumed I was antiracist and antisexist.

Then I got out of college, and three male college friends and I started hanging out regularly, doing that male bonding thing. In private, we told jokes and laughed. Two of them told openly racist jokes, and all of us indulged in an all-too-common misogyny around sexual issues. I was uneasy about the racist jokes, but I said little if anything. (I barely even recognized the misogyny, which is a story unto itself not to be told here.) I controlled my reaction, laughing enough to not be seen as a drag on the fun but not so much that I would feel overly racist.

I was raised to be a racist. I rebelled, ever so slightly. But I couldn't break with the training completely. I was stuck, and I knew it. But because I had no serious friendships with non-whites at that point, because I still lived in an almost all-white world, nothing propelled me to change. There were no structures of accountability in my life.

V. Struggling to Get Beyond Fear

Five years later, I returned to graduate school. I started studying feminism and gravitated toward the most radical analysis. I started to see how patriarchy works, how structures of domination and subordination are naturalized and rendered invisible. The ways in which sexism and misogyny were woven into my life started to come into focus.

By this time, the Women's Movement had started to address race and racism more clearly and coherently. Ignoring race in social analysis and personal reflection became impossible for me, not just because it was being talked about, but because seeing one axis of oppression makes it difficult to ignore others. I started to see how white supremacy works, which was different than patriarchy in some ways, but with the same pattern: domination and subordination, naturalized.

Working out how that works out in the world is complicated, but the basic insight is simple. So simple, but so easy to ignore in an almost all-white world.

My world then shifted from graduate school in Minnesota to a faculty job in Texas. The University of Texas struggles with race and diversity issues, but the place is not as almost-all-white as my previous worlds. But it is also a fairly segregated place, no longer by law but in reality. The interstate highway that splits the city—into a mostly middle-class and wealthy white part of town and a mostly low-income black and brown part of town—is such an imposing reminder of white supremacy that it is difficult not to think about race.

My life is about as segregated as the average white professor in town. During the day I am around many folks of different races and ethnicities, both U.S. and international. But I go home at night to the white part of town, and my closest circle of friends is almost exclusively white. For the first six years here, I still had virtually no structures of accountability.

That changed in some fashion when I began working closely on political projects, and then became close friends, with three non-white people. Two are American-born of (Asian) Indian parents, and the other is Turkish. We gravitated toward each other because of a shared political analysis and concerns. As I spent more and more time with them, things I knew intellectually about race became more real. One key realization was about just how often and to what degree dark skin or a foreign accent resulted in radically different treatment. It also became clear that I was unaware of all but the most obvious manifestations of that.

While those friendships have had an important effect on me in other ways (more on that below), they also highlighted that when it comes to the black/white divide, my life is still almost as segregated as the city in which I live.

VI. Roots of the Anger

We live in a morally lazy society, and that makes me angry.

I do not mean morally lazy in the same sense that traditionalists and fundamentalists condemn contemporary America. The problem is not a decline in family values (whatever those may be), but the ease with which people who could intervene on the side of justice—primarily the white middle class—not only don't, but refuse to acknowledge the scope of the problems and their own connection to them.

How does one move an affluent and protected class of people to work for fundamental change in regard to an issue such as race? And how does one make people see the connection between the racism that lives at home with the brutal racism, both economic and military, in U.S. policy abroad?

Some of the great thinkers about race, especially W. E. B. DuBois, saw this connection. As a socialist and an anti-imperialist, as well as a critic of race relations in the United States, DuBois could see clearly the country's seamless history of oppression.

I invoke DuBois not just because of the keenness of his insights or eloquence of his writing, but for quite strategic purposes. The connections I want to make between our economic system and the actions of the U.S. government in world affairs are often dismissed these days with arrogant talk of the inevitability of markets, the naturalness of capitalism, and the grand victory of the West in the Cold War. If he were alive, DuBois would surely scoff at such self-indulgent triumphalism.

As he put it in *The Souls of White Folks,* written after World War I as the United States was claiming to be the world's exemplar:

> It is curious to see America, the United States, looking on herself, first, as a sort of natural peacemaker, then as a moral protagonist in this terrible time. No nation is less fitted for this role. For two or more centuries America has marched proudly in the van of human hatred. . . . Instead of standing as a great example of the success of democracy and the possibility of human brotherhood America has taken her place as an awful example of its pitfalls and failures, so far as black and brown and yellow peoples are concerned.

Nothing that has happened since DuBois wrote this passage would change his fundamental analysis. The United States continues to pursue an economic and military policy abroad that offers as its underlying assumption a simple, but quite bizarre assertion: the primary beneficiary of the resources, both human and natural, of developing countries—that is, the countries of the "black and brown and yellow peoples" of the world—should not be those people but corporations and wealthy investors in the United States. Such logic leads to things such as support for terror states in Central America, the direct invasion and devastation of Vietnam, and the imposition of brutal economic sanctions against Iraq throughout the 1990s and into a new century.

Should it be a surprise that a country founded on genocide and slavery moved on to consolidate its power and wealth through the subjugation or destruction of non-white peoples elsewhere? DuBois certainly would not be surprised. Nor should we be.

If we care about justice—racial justice—we should be, individually and collectively, moved to oppose both the government that carries out these policies and the economic structures in which they are rooted. Yet, for the most part, the class that could have the most effect politically— the white middle class, the class to which I belong—remains passively complicit in, or actively supportive of, these policies.

So, perhaps I am not yet fully comfortable next to a black body. But I also am no longer comfortable next to most white bodies, not because of my race training, but because of the alienation that comes from recognizing the truth of DuBois's analysis. When I first started doing antiwar and anticapitalist political work, I did not see this particular relationship between race and class. I was able to do that work, yet continue to live a fairly "normal" life as a white middle-class man.

Those days are now mostly gone, and "normal" is largely closed off to me.

VII. Struggling to Get Beyond the Anger

Why do people choose not to act, indeed, even not to know about injustice? How am I to deal with the anger at that inaction and my alienation?

One of the non-white friends I mentioned above is not optimistic about those questions. He is blunt in his analysis: "The problem with most Americans is that they have no soul." He uses the term soul in a political, not a theological sense. He means that people so comfortable materially can easily lose sight of anything other than the maintenance of that level of comfort. Without even thinking about it, they can trade their souls for affluence.

I am more upbeat than he is, not necessarily because I analyze the situation differently, but because I have no choice. To believe in the possibility that the American white middle class can change is, in essence, to assert a belief in myself, and in the possibility that I will not drown in this anger. That especially matters to me because the anger never stays in me as anger; it almost always turns to a deep sadness. I can live with the anger; I can manage it and find ways to vent it in the company of allies and friends. But the sadness is less controllable; it simply sits in me. Putting that sadness into words so it can be vented is more difficult, sometimes impossible.

So, I have no choice but to try to get beyond the anger, lest I be consumed by it and trapped forever in the sadness. That means I have to find ways to talk with people from whom I might otherwise want to separate myself. In short, I have come to realize that my political work as an American middle-class white man is primarily with the white middle class.

But that work is always more than simply providing information or analysis. More important is breaking through the willed ignorance, the purposeful not-knowing about the racialized consequences of our social, political, and economic structures and policies—the not-knowing that makes possible the comfortable lives we lead. The task is to give people who otherwise need not care about justice a reason to care.

That requires humility and hope. I have to reign in my instinct to feel self-righteous, and I have to understand that in every human interaction there is the potential for connection and transcendence. I have to talk in a fashion quite out of sync both with the surface triumphalism of the post–Cold War era proclaimed especially by politicians and pundits, and the deeper cynicism that many ordinary people feel.

There is much more to say about the on-the-ground political strategies, but this is not an essay about strategy. So I will end this section with a reminder to my brothers and sisters of the white middle class that one of the greatest gifts that people with unearned privilege can receive is the gift of being made uncomfortable, for that uncomfortableness is often the first step to reconnecting to our own souls that we have lost.

VIII. Beyond Black and White?

I will end with a story about what makes me uncomfortable.

It is commonplace to assert that discussion of race in the United States has moved beyond a simple black/white paradigm. Latino and

Asian American issues have taken a more clear place in the conversation, although the genocide against, and ongoing colonization of, native peoples continues to be largely ignored as part of the race question.

But something always nags at me, even as we expand the discussion beyond black/white and continue to push forward the analysis. In pushing forward, what are we leaving behind?

It is a difficult fact for most white people to acknowledge that most of us have internalized a hierarchy of racial discrimination. There is great individual variation, of course, but it is not uncommon for white people to find it much easier to deal with Asians, Asian Americans, and Latinos than with black people. In this, I am not uncommon.

After publishing essays on white privilege, I was invited to several college campuses to speak. At one, I was at a lunch with students and the African American administrator who had organized my visit. When people took up the "beyond black and white" discussion, the administrator drifted out of the conversation. Later I asked her if she had been upset by what was said.

Not upset, she said, just tired of the way in which white people are so quick to use that dodge. The most serious racial problems on that campus were all about black and white, she said, about the inability of university officials to take seriously the racism that the small number of black students on campus endure. My conversations later that day with black students made it clear how true her assessment was.

The fact is, she said, that many white people can find a way to change the way they react to Asian Americans or Latinos. (Sociologist Andrew Hacker says white people see members of these groups as "whites in training," available to be mobilized into the category of white when the relative decline in the European American population threatens whites' majority status.) But, she said, even progressive white people don't seem to be able to do it quite so easily with African Americans.

I squirmed when she said that, because she had named the struggle that goes on inside me. I squirmed, but I was grateful for having been made uncomfortable. I was at the college to be the invited speaker, the person to whom others looked for answers about race. That is an inherently dangerous position for a white person to be in, a situation in which it can be difficult to hold onto humility. I was glad I had raised the question with her and glad she had been honest in response. The uncomfortableness I felt never completely left me during the visit, but when she and I made the long drive early the next morning from the small college town to the metro airport, it was with a new sense of why there is reason for hope.

IX. Lord, Save Us from Well-Intentioned White People

People ask me, why do you write about white privilege? Why do you spend time trying to deconstruct a privilege that benefits you? One person, trying to be supportive, asked, "How come there are so few well-intentioned white people like you?"

I don't want to be well-intentioned, and I don't think we need more well-intentioned white people. Non-white folks have been suffering the good intentions of white folks for long enough. What we need are honest white people who can act not only out of a concern for justice, but out of the urgent need to find, and save, our own souls. I have a conception of social justice that underlies my analysis and informs my political activities, but that alone isn't enough to spur most of us to act.

I became politically involved—I started organizing, speaking, and writing—when I could no longer bear to not do those things. Part of the motivation was knowing that I would always be much less of a person than I could be as long as I absorbed the privileges and comforts of the classes to which I belong without challenging them. I became active when I could no longer look at myself in the mirror and see a whole person without acting.

James Baldwin had it right when he talked about whiteness not as an intrinsic identity but as a moral and political choice, and bluntly told white folks that deciding to be white was "opting for safety instead of life." That doesn't mean one can opt out of the privileges that come with white skin in this culture or pretend to be black. It does mean actively choosing an antiracist identity and making good on it through self-reflection and political action. For years I was well-intentioned on matters of race, and yet I did nothing to change myself or be part of a movement to eliminate white supremacy. It was only when I started scrambling for my own life, to rescue myself from the degraded and degenerate whiteness that was the default identity for someone with white skin, that I began to act in the world. I started searching for people with whom I could talk and analyze and organize and laugh.

That doesn't mean I've escaped my whiteness. Put my white body next to a black body. I still will feel my whiteness, and I will feel the blackness next to me. I will have to deal with the fear, no matter what is sparked in me by the particular black person. I will have to resist the move to associate that blackness with lesser-ness. Even when I am successful, I will know I had to work to overcome something and, if I am lucky, I will hold onto humility and hope.

Put my white body next to a white body. I still will feel the whiteness. I will have to deal with the anger, no matter what is sparked in me by the particular white person. I will have to deal with the complicated emotions that bind me to that person and make me want to distance myself at the same time. If I am lucky, I will hold onto hope and humility.

Can we move beyond black and white? In one sense, of course, we have to. But we also can't yet afford to.

Robert Jensen *joined the University of Texas faculty in 1992 after completing his Ph.D. in the School of Journalism and Mass Communication at the University of Minnesota. He teaches graduate and undergraduate courses in media law, ethics, and politics. He is coeditor with David S. Allen of* Freeing the First Amendment: Critical Perspectives on Freedom of Expression *(New York University Press, 1995); coauthor with Gail Dines and Ann Russo of* Pornography: The Production and Consumption of Inequality *(Routledge, 1998); and author of* Writing Dissent: Taking Radical Ideas from the Margin to the Mainstream *(Peter Lang Publishing, 2001). Jensen also writes opinion and analytic pieces for popular media, both alternative and mainstream. He was a founding member of the editorial collective producing* The Working Stiff Journal, *an independent monthly paper in Austin for and by working people.*

© Mary Levin

For Colored Girls Who Have Resisted Homogenization When the Rainbow Ain't Enough

JOYCELYN K. MOODY

You do not have to be me for us to fight alongside one another. I do not have to be you to recognize that our wars are *the same*. What we must do is commit ourselves to some future that can include each other . . .

—Audre Lorde[1] (emphasis added)

To act as if power does not exist is to ensure that the power status quo remains *the same*.

—Lisa Delpit[2] (emphasis added)

> The idea that one can analogically feel *like* another person feels can be overshadowed by the paradoxically narcissistic and self-negating desire to feel *with* that other person, to imagine that the experiences of two subjects entirely coincide.
>
> —Glenn Hendler[3]

ASKING ANGELA TO meet with our writing group to discuss a draft of this essay on the significance of "race" in my life, I flash back to Women of Color in Academia (WOCIA), a lecture series, then support group, she formed during 1995–96. All the members are dispersed across the country now, but those awful days were bearable only because we turned, untenured, to each other twice a month. We were black, Puertorriqueña, Indonesian, and Chicana during that year when three female colleagues—black, Latina, South Asian—were forced to trade in their tenure-track jobs for instructor positions.

I meet Shirley, another colleague, the next day for coffee and suggestions on how to tackle this essay. She and I are Chinese American and African American, respectively: two lesbians, literary critic and historian, both African Americanists, in our early forties, friends "separated" by power differentials. Though I am a couple of years older, she is my "senior" in that she has been Associate for several years now, whereas I am new to the rank; she is Chair of her department, and I'm not only newly tenured in mine, but tangential to it as well. I am Adjunct in her department, so she is my "boss." I remember when I first got my tiny office in the same wing as hers—before she moved into the Chair's office. We regularly ate lunch together, with another woman, a Jewish graduate student.

Shirley was the first of my colleagues that I came out to. I have sweet memories of our drive one wintry Sunday in 1993 to Roslyn, Washington, to tour the site of *Northern Exposure*. Out herself for years, she was stunned, especially since my lover was one of her students—a very young white woman whom she disliked for what she mistook as her predilection for dating women of color.

From the first, I have known Shirley to be a feminist for whom color counts in meaningful and appropriate ways. These days I cannot imagine my life without her. At coffee, we talk about the shorthand we use in the presence of whites, how various oppressions have taught us almost to read each other's minds, to know viscerally what the other feels. Her advice on this essay? Pithily, she urges me to say that our sameness sustains us in the academy.

Later, on a mid-afternoon shopping errand, I confess to Shirley my ongoing fear of being deserted and lonely when I am old. I plaintively ask her, "But who will love me when I am old?" "*I* will," she says, without hesitation. The firm promise of that moment thrills my needy soul.

And in that moment I realize: black folks too often think that unconditional love comes to us exclusively from "our own." I make a mental note that my contribution to this book will proclaim that someone who is neither black nor white has promised me eternal friendship and a steady(ing) presence.

Walking back to our offices that afternoon, Shirley bitterly expresses her anger that racism killed both of her parents. She loved her father for his spirit and his determination to disprove whites' stereotypes of Asian Americans. But she believes that that pursuit of an "American" identity and white endorsement led to stresses of assimilation and ultimately to illnesses that killed him. She also blames racism for her mother's recent death by emphysema: her mother had taken up smoking in the 1950s, desperately trusting that if she could look like those Hollywood starlets poised so prettily with their cigarette holders, then she could leap transformed from Boston's slums into an idealized Chinese American matronhood.

Although Shirley's present partner is white, she hates whites for what their racism has cost her. She has the same righteous revulsion I've heard in black folks' voices when they too start tallying up their personal losses to racism. I match her stride as we cross the campus together through hordes of white students changing classes.

The next week I eat dinner with the other two black women in our seventy-odd-member department. I wonder about the *tableau* we make, given that we are three completely different (kinds of) black women. Neither knows the other as well as she knows me, situated as I am between them in multifarious ways. We represent three different geographic regions, three different areas of African American literature, three different stages of life, three different points on a sexual continuum. We whoop at one woman's hilarious caricatures of her brothers-in-law—one a white Californian, the other a black Mississippian. There is so much she need not explain; these men are our relatives, too. The steps to their cultural dances we've rehearsed well. Later I ask the other woman, Colleen, for ideas for this essay: what should I write? I marvel that her urgent response is the same as Shirley's: say that our sameness sustains us in the academy.

But do I dare to say that our sameness is a contrivance as well? Would I betray my black women colleagues, were I to write of our differences rather, to observe that a slight strain undercuts our rapport and glittery repartee? Can I say that "sameness" is what most nonblack others impose on three black women professors gathered in a bar, whatever we share or don't?

Another week goes by. I attend a campus production of *The Sign in Sidney Brustein's Window,* Lorraine Hansberry's play about interracial and intercultural marriages. Appropriately, I am with a mixed-race lesbian couple, Caroline and Lendy. Over dinner Caroline, who is Eurasian, and I rant about racism in the academy. She and I have come of age together in the English Department, and our fate was sealed as we co-authored an essay in the summer our tenure clocks wound down to the witching hour. Tonight we deplore not merely the loss of feminists of color, but the stark absence of more of *us* on campus. Racism and its kinsman, tokenism, have yielded only a handful of colleagues who look like Caroline and me. We draw close around the fire of our nonwhite ethnicity and our sexuality. But in truth, outnumbered and nearly overwhelmed by the academy's exclusivity, we conclude that we have constructed a certain "sameness" of necessity. We are women who love other women, and women for whom race and class signify fiercely, women bound by literature and philology. Yet moments before the lights turn on Hansberry's tragedy, we admit to each other in the theater's dark the illusion of sameness.

Days go by before I can work up the nerve to return to this intimidating assignment to write candidly about my life as a "race(d)" woman. Meanwhile, I've had a few revelations—and a blast from the past. Just before Thanksgiving Day, a black lesbian who loved me twenty years ago, before I was ready to live queer, had found me through the Internet. She told me she is "married" now, living happily with partner and daughter in upstate New York. Her spouse is a woman of color, too, an Arabian ophthalmologist. She said her partner is often mistaken for (read exoticized as) white—unless they are traveling, in which case Customs transforms vacation into nightmare.

My old friend sent this e-mail just as I was fighting for weeks with my own partner, Randi, a light-complexioned Latina, about our different experiences of race and racism. Randi makes Thanksgiving dinner with her mother in northern California, while in Seattle I declare my home luxurious "All Black Space," hosting only black guests for the holiday meal. It's a rare treat for me; one drawback to being with Randi has been that whenever we socialize with others, even if they are all of one "race," because she and I are interracial and intercultural, the social event becomes interracial and intercultural. Making black space in Seattle in my forties requires an effort I never had to exert growing up in Mobile during the 1960s and '70s.

The morning after Thanksgiving Jean wakes me. I have slept in because Mae stayed until midnight, helping me wash dishes so we could carry on an intimate sister-girl conversation about our lives as black mothers and daughters and sisters, and as black women in the academy. Jean phones to thank me for the extraordinary evening. She also teaches, and though her college and home are on Seattle's multiethnic south side, it seems she, too, rarely inhabits an all-black space. Later in the morning, Lois, a black feminist colleague, calls about a manuscript she wants me to edit. They are the only people I talk to in an otherwise contemplative day. All day I manage to keep the world at bay, basking alone in my guests' leftover love, wholesome as cornbread.

Throughout the holiday weekend I brood about my unresolved conflict with Randi. A brilliant psychologist researching the formation of racial identity, she recently told me about a conversation with a black psychologist friend in which Randi said that she "sometimes forgets that we are not the same." On the one hand, we are indeed "the same": it is our same-sex love of women, after all, that renders us lesbian. On the other hand, even lesbians differ one from another. And though she tried persistently to assure me that she meant that our racial ideologies are virtually identical, I can only comprehend this disclosure as that for her, I am not always black, or that she is sometimes black. Both interpretations unsettle me: either means she does not understand the effect of black skin in the United States.

I am rocked, knocked completely off balance: how is this possible? Many of Randi's friends are black, and all of her women lovers have been black. I have teased her about a "fetish," but never believed it true. Now I find myself completely unable to admit this lapse of hers to any black person I know; her dirty little secret has become mine, and its stench is on me now, too. My beloved elder brother has guessed that something is wrong between Randi and me, but I cannot bring myself to tell even him. I know too well what I would be saying to any black person—man or woman, queer or het—if s/he told me that her non-black lover had said this! I hate myself for judging Randi, but nothing calms my tremors of vulnerability. DuBois's veil has dropped between us, and I wrap myself protectively within it. All weekend I wonder what it would take for me to get over this insult, and worry what kind of black person am I for *wanting* to get over it. I spend a lot of time thinking about wanting, about desire.

Days later I will perceive that what Randi has said is what I have been advised to write here by women in WOCIA, in Women Studies, and in my home department: she has said that our sameness sustains her.

And later still I will confront my own lapse. We have loved each other for over three years now. Our romance has been based, I would insist, on mutual respect, tender affection, and endless "processing." I thought I knew her deepest, most complex thoughts on race. Yet for all of our discussions on the subject of Race American Style—intellectual and teasing, reflective and signifyin'—we have managed never to have a single conversation about our different subject positions, as it were, about what bell hooks calls "eating the other."

In the meantime, however, when Randi and I talk over Thanksgiving weekend, I bitchily emphasize that she would not have fit into the heady, intimate, holiday dinner conversation because she is not black. I know that had she been with us, we would not have had the same conversation. Does this mean that Shirley and Angela are wrong, that non-black women—lesbian or straight—and I are not "the same," after all? It certainly means that the "sameness" invoked by my black colleague is not the same "sameness" that Shirley means, that Randi means.

Since the onset of this fight with Randi, I have begun to think acutely about the difference that blackness makes in multiethnic, multicultural women's solidarity—to say nothing of its impact on interracial lesbian liaisons. I want to avoid ranking oppressions or claiming some oppressions graver than others. Something stops me. My scholarly studies and my international travels have supplemented my life experiences: I *know* that ain't no body like a black body, that black bodies are subject like no others to unspeakable tortures. And no, I do not mean an expansive "black" body—as in, say, the postcolonial black body of India, nor "black" as a category that contains all nonwhite groups, as in "colored." I mean of African descent. Period.

But my hesitation is not just about torment; it is about skin color privilege, about the color-caste system Americans live by. The second epigraph I cited at the beginning of this essay puts the matter succinctly; to put Lisa Delpit's words another way, when light-skinned people of color discount the power acceded them for their appearance, they discount the degree to which they must struggle alongside us darker folks for full human rights. Folks so privileged must be assiduous: they must actively resist the racial allowances—a.k.a. "passing," whether they will it or no—that whites grant them. For me, Randi's very (or *mere*) appearance nullifies any likelihood that, were it even desirable for me, she and I could ever be "the same." Moreover, I am only a "shade" darker than my Chinese American friend Shirley, and yet I doubt anyone in the United States would ever mistake her for black and treat her "accordingly." Which is not to say that, like both Randi and me, she hasn't got her own set of racialized problems. After all, white racism killed her parents with *the same* deftness and indifference it picks off black folk every day.

Pondering Thanksgiving, I must acknowledge that Randi would have fit into our after-dinner conversation after all: She is the daughter of a woman who struggled after Randi's philandering father left to keep their three children, but in the end despaired, and relinquished them to their father. Around my table, late into Thanksgiving night, we three women had captivated each other with stories of "non-mothering mothers," Mae's designation of her compelling scholarship.[4] Because Randi's mother believed herself unable to rear her adolescent children alone, Randi, no less than my black guests and I, fits within the contours of Mae's research. Too many colored girls across the rainbow, Randi's mother included, share this grievous sameness—in myriad forms.

Talking over coffee with Shirley, I proposed to write this essay on the false black-white binary, one that excludes some of the most important women in my life: Shirley, Caroline, Angela, Saraswati, and other colleagues, and, of course, Randi. Inasmuch as my personal life pirouettes around my professional work in a racist, sexist, homophobic academy, I have learned to find and to treasure allies in various, sometimes unpredicted places. Still, fondly recalling a series of recent evenings spent alone with black women, I know that my survival depends not simply on colored women's space but in large measure on exclusively *black* women's space. I need both. In the end, I find that I am stunningly narcissistic. I have thought so before; indeed, I *feel* it every time I look into my son's lovely black face and find the traces of my own.

But neither is narcissism enough; blackness alone does not sustain me. When Shirley and Colleen urged me to "say that our sameness sustains us," they invoked a multifarious amalgamation of qualities we share—chiefly gender, and/or ethnicity, and/or sexual orientation, and/or scholarly expertise, and, in both cases, nonwhiteness. Right before school started, though, I felt alien, not akin, to a black, heterosexual colleague who teaches multiculturalism across campus. We were gabbing on the phone when suddenly she railed against Asians and Asian Americans. Midway through an innocuous anecdote, she denounced them as "chameleons," "untrustworthy" because "they can pass—and they do!"

Even in the moment, I knew my silence betrayed every Asian woman I profess to love. Is it enough to say that shock and horror rendered me mute? Shame indisputably did. Bound by blackness to this "sister," I put on her shame like a hair shirt. The incident verified the capacity blackness holds for perfidy and irrepressibility, and it frightened me. Has blackness stifled an empathy for subjugated others in her that it has not in me? Why has it not in me? Is it a queer identity that has sustained in me a largesse and empathy for others that my straight colleague lacks? Was it my own blackness that made me treacherous in that phone call? Will it again—perhaps when I least suspect it?

Thinking about race for this essay, I mourn my faithlessness in that moment; I grieve racialized blindness everywhere. I think how black men's sexism parallels whites' racism. I think of Anna Deveare Smith and her performance, in *Twilight,* of the Korean woman shop-owner-

cum-shooter of a long-legged black girl. I think of my Midwestern relatives who assume that the Latinas who bus tables in urban cafeterias
are undocumented workers, who complain that "those foreigners"—
from anywhere—cannot speak English. Where does such myopia come
from in a subjugated people? And where do our damaging double standards and restrictive myths originate?

In the week after Thanksgiving for my graduate seminar on African
American Feminist Epistemology, I get depressed reading an essay on
the sexual harassment of black women across the academy. Bizarrely, at
first I appreciate my good fortune in never having experienced the kinds
of injury the essay describes. Gradually, though, I begin to recall one
episode after another that I have suffered in my sixteen years in higher
education—most brazenly, unabashedly meant to harm me. I think of
the gamut of harassment that black women suffer, recognize my initial
"forgetfulness" not only as the stuff of survival, the lull of Lethe, but
as a symptom of my suffering. I have forgotten, for example, the Ku
Klux Klan youth corps leader who disrupted my class, then slammed the
door shut on the two of us when I held her after to speak about it.

Women of color, black and not, experience such incidents across the
academy; we are surely the same in this way. I remember a woman in
WOCIA sharing harassment an Asian immigrant professor suffered: on
the course evaluation form, one student wrote, "Dumb Brown Bitch"
over and over around the borders of the page. When a Latina lesbian
was appointed Chair of UW's American Ethnic Studies Department,
the student newspaper ran her photo with a marksman's crosshairs centered over it. Compared to a Midwestern lesbian friend's once having
been threatened by letters addressed to "Nigger Woman," who was then
stalked and required a police escort from her campus office, my own
encounters with intractable white boys who resent studying *David
Walker's Appeal* seem bearable. Next to hers, my pain seems petty, so I
minimize it.

What does it take to alert me to this toll on my health? For me to
figure its costs? Authors of the essay, Jacqueline Pope and Janice Joseph,
argue that black women in the academy should receive "combat pay."
A good friend who doesn't teach uses precisely this phrase to talk about
what she thinks black women professors deserve for the crap we put up
with. When we women of color get a merit raise, the administration

never notes that it's for another year of PMS: putting up with (white) men's shit.

Then there are the incidents involving white feminists. In my current seminar I am the only black woman; of the eight students, only one, a Filipina, is not white. Recently I taught Dawn Bennett-Alexander's contemplative essay on being a black lesbian in a Southern law school together with Nellie McKay's instructions for surviving white academic racism. Both texts argue for dignity as a viable tool of resistance. My students misread "dignity" as passivity, take the texts as advice from handkerchief heads—though they believe themselves enlightened, they do not know this slang phrase. In the ensuing class, I offer Nikki Giovanni's "nikki-rosa" and a poem McKay mentions, Pat Parker's "for the white person who wants to know how to be my friend." I resist the mean temptation to insert "-looking" between "white" and "person"—just to cover all the bases. The irony of my gift-poems is lost on my savvy students. All term we read black women theorizing the difference that blackness makes in feminist activism and epistemologies. During our discussions, I often feel brutalized, and feel sorry for myself that as professor I don't have the option simply to ignore them, to will myself someplace very far away from them. Part of me assesses their naïveté and PC positioning as decisive indications of what I need to teach them. Part of me simply wants to vanish. It is a benign enough feeling, but too familiar: I leave class devastated by the implications. Collectively, they have implied that they constitute a "different kind of white woman" from those who usually harass me. Thus, they are the worst kind: "disintegrating" themselves from what they'd call racist whites, while not recognizing their own racism. And yet, in contrast to many past students, they are so earnest and diligent that, in the end, it is one of the most rewarding seminars I have had taught in years. Hell yeah, I want my combat pay.

All fall, I deal with the fact that I am in an interracial romantic relationship with a woman of color, a race expert, who experiences race as the most salient fact of her life, but who homogenizes my blackness in one fell blow. Can she see that as important and vital as my relationships with nonblack women are, they insufficiently sustain me? Especially in Seattle, where one can go for days without seeing another black face, I need blackness. What did Nikki write? "Black love is Black wealth."

And Lucille, even more precisely: "a perfect picture of/ blackness blessed." I want to be *that,* to feel *that.*

Yet the pinnacle of my blessings requires Shirley's presence in my life as much as Lauren's: blackness alone also insufficiently sustains me.

Sometimes I am surprised at the primacy of race in the most central relationships in my life. Blackness and something more than blackness—perhaps *narcissism*—together with "sameness" and something more again—indisputably *family, familiarity*—are operative in a pair of conversations I have with my mother the week after Thanksgiving. I talk to her one night for almost an hour, and the next morning for another two. So much during the work week is rare, but that morning she somberly explains that she needs me as her "sounding board," and I know that no one else can help her think through an incident she'd experienced after we had hung up the night before. I wonder that one of her sisters might not have filled her need, but she called *me* to provide for her. The bond I share with her is based on blood certainly, but on blackness, too, and womanness, and motherhood, and on, and on— a series of common traits that render us "the same."

On the way home from school that evening, I meet up with a familiar black student at a campus bus stop. As it happens, this woman has my mother's name and, like Mama and me, also hails from the Deep South. Catherine has enrolled in one of my undergrad courses for next term. I am excited about this, but also wary because she and I have an intimate history: a year ago, she spent Saturday afternoons in my home, helping me maintain my fledgling dreadlocks. (I laugh as I write this. It is true: every essay by a black woman eventually gets around to the hair thang.) Twilight deepens while we wait. Catherine and I slip softly into the colloquialisms we used in my home, the lilt of our black-woman-speech turning heads at the bus stop. I speak in expressions I do not use with my seminar students, colloquialisms I cannot use with Randi.

At home, I stop on the first floor of my building to ask Mae to come up for Thanksgiving leftovers. We revisit her research topic and share more stories, continuously intrigued, as new friends, by our very different backgrounds—she is from working poor in Watts, and I am from Southern wannabes, god bless 'em. As we eat and confide, I find that I cannot get enough of black women that single day—despite hours on the phone with my mother, my intellectual work with writings by black feminist theorists all afternoon in seminar and before, my shopping for a Boston friend's birthday gift, my extraordinary e-mail correspondence with scholar Jacqueline Jones Royster, and my serendipitous hookup with Catherine at the bus stop. Never enough.

Nor is my time with Randi, Shirley, Caroline, Angela, and Saraswati ever enough. The white academy at the center of my life has seen to that.

Finally, it is December 1, one day before I actually force myself to begin crafting this essay. I tag along with Angela to a Latina luncheon, mainly to avoid eating alone and looking conspicuous in the faculty cafeteria. I apologize for invading her Latina separatist space, but she waves off my apology, pronouncing me "Latina for a Day!" She giggles, repeating it to the women who interrupt their enthusiastic greeting of her in Spanish, who switch abruptly to English as Angela introduces me. Everyone is polite, but we all know that I am cramping their style, that their issues are not precisely mine, that though invited I am eavesdropping, trespassing; if I weren't there, they'd be speaking Spanish. I eat quickly.

Later I tell Randi about the experience. She quips poignantly, "Does this mean that we are not an interracial couple any more?" I go on reflectively, thinking aloud, as if Randi were not Latina—my own momentary lapse that she and I are not "the same"? —musing that I was happy to be Latina for only an *hour*, that I felt intrusive—and I was, that it was too great a burden. I stop short. The words are out, and of course, I must clarify them. I pause, reflect, then avow: "It is too great a burden to pretend to be something I'm not."

Epiphany: the profound differences that separate me from my feminists of color colleagues hold. As Lucille Clifton corrects Chinua Achebe: "Things don't fall apart. Things hold. Lines connect in thin ways that last and last . . ." Moreover, I can count on these faithful women to hold me; the ties may be contrived and wire-thin, but we wrap them 'round ourselves to hold each other. Sameness *does* sustain us, but for each of us, integrity rests in an intricate web of identities we cultivate, that we help each other nurture, sometimes, paradoxically, by withholding, by our very absence.

Although all of the opinions expressed herein are mine, I gratefully acknowledge the editorial assistance of the following brave women: Kathryn Friedman, Angela Ginorio, Lorraine Martínez, Caroline Chung Simpson, and Shirley J. Yee. Outstanding scholarship by Tamiko Nimura generously suggested the opening quotes to me.

———

[1] Audre Lorde, "Learning from the [19]60s," *Sister Outsider* (The Crossing Press, California, 1984)

[2] Lisa Delpit, "The Silenced Dialogue: Power and Pedagogy in Educating Other People's Children," *Harvard Educational Review* 58:3 (August 1988): 290-298, at 292.

[3] Glenn Hendler, *Public Sentiments: Structures of Feeling in Nineteenth-Century America* (University of Chapel Hill Press, 2001)

[4] Mae C. Henderson, "Non-mothering Mothers: An Examination of Women's Experience Within a Social Contract." *The McNair Journal CSULB,* 3 (1999): 74-82.

Joycelyn K. Moody, Ph.D., *is Associate Professor of English at the University of Washington, where she teaches courses in nineteenth-century African American literature, women's writings, and autobiography. In 2001–02, she holds the Jane Watson Irwin Chair in Women Studies at Hamilton College. She is author of* Sentimental Confessions: Spiritual Narratives of Nineteenth-Century African American Women *(University of Georgia Press, 2000)*

Her publications include numerous essays on slave narratives, black autobiography, and teaching in virtually all white institutions. She has taught Zimbabwean students at the University of Zimbabwe (Harare) and U.S. students at the University of Cape Town.

© Bernestine Singley

Anatomy of a Fairy Princess

Patricia J. Williams

"What's a radical-left black single-mother intellectual like you doing reading *O*?" asked an unusually annoying friend of mine who knows exactly how to make me defensive.

"I subscribe," I said evenly.

"Why?" he asked and made a face. I threw popcorn at him as he beat a hasty retreat.

Why indeed, I thought, as I settled into an article about the mathematically unlimited ways to accessorize the same blouse and skirt over the course of a week. Hadn't I read this someplace before? And what has it got to do with the national crises about which I usually write—suspect profiling, the death penalty, eugenics, human rights?

The truth is that I buy *O, The Oprah Magazine*, for an accumulation of little reasons, not one of which is earthshaking, but which together allow me a comfortable moment of the mundane.

The attractiveness of the comfortably mundane—I suppose that says more about me than it does about black women in general. But our culture teeters crazily between exceptionalizing and sensationalizing us on the one hand and, on the other, rendering us ugly and invisible. This is deeply wearying. In a land generally given over to the cult of appearances, it is harder and harder for anyone—male, female, minority or not—ever to just walk through the day unselfconsciously. Add that to the ingrained hierarchies of racism, and black women end up categorized in ways that never allow us to feel casually normative.

When I was in college, living in those just-post-adolescent pressure cookers called dormitories, I marveled that most of my white friends struggled with the fear of looking like everyone else. My black friends and I, on the other hand, struggled to "fit in," tending to find the middle ground of "ordinary" something of a relief—even a luxury. This is a purely anecdotal observation, I admit, but it makes me wonder about the source of such social forces—and how they shape us. For me, the paradox of African American attempts to become mainstream is that the very rituals of proving that we are "just like" the girl next door are themselves the proof of our marginality.

Back in college, we worried about women's magazines selling fewer copies every time they put a black model on the cover. Hopeful little sisterhoods all over the country would run out to buy the occasional copy of *Glamour* or *Elle* just because a black face had been sighted on the supermarket news rack—always in the tenacious belief that our pumping up sales would "show them" that black beauty is no less than white. Twenty-five years later, little has changed at those magazines; the sisterhoods grew tired long ago, many abandoning the quest for integration with the advent of *Essence*.

If the world were a different place, I suppose I might join those who have sneered that *O* is just another yearning-for-a-middle-class-lifestyle magazine like *Martha Stewart Living*. But however obvious the similarities may be, for me the distinguishing feature of *O* is its visualization of a mixed society as "normal." I don't mean that it's colorblind. Rather, it purposefully arranges people like bouquets of wildflowers. People with differing looks, opinions, tastes, and ages are put side by side to ruminate about random things—marriage, money, books, etc.

It's equalizing in a very quiet sense, this pictorial impression that the soap opera of life's little issues touches everyone.

Of course, I still read Foucault and *Jet* and the kinds of New York-based political journals that keep me testy and sarcastic. But *O*, for all of its aromatherapeutic take on life, is the most integrated magazine on the American market. Yes, it serves up calculated fantasy, is studiously apolitical, and is rather long on fluff, but where else can you find images of women who are black, white, Asian, large and small, mothers, wives, singles and sisters, braided, dreadlocked, and hot-combed, on a budget or with Oprah's money to spare—all just girlfriends together?

Then too, I like *O* because Oprah Winfrey graces each and every cover, positively glowing with unconventional good looks. I suppose she's just playing the print version of her role as television hostess, welcoming us into this paginated living room of hers, but in the process she has turned herself into the most consistently employed cover girl in the world. Perhaps it's good for her self-esteem—but it's also good for mine.

This musing is driven by my age, I suppose. You see, it is a kind of nice confusion to wake up, as from a dream, and find oneself in the Age of Oprah. When I was growing up in the fifties and sixties, the only black women in the national eye were Marion Anderson and Hattie McDaniel. They, in their very polarity, symbolized the rock and the hard place of African American womanhood: the martyr and the mammy, the hyperarticulated classicist and the folksy frump, the chin held high and the ample, encompassing bosom.

These were the most visible models. There were also cartoonish renderings of Jezebels and Sapphires, exotic hoodoo women in skirts of bananas, insurrectionary half-white witches whose "gift" of half-a-white brain was always undone by the curse of a really bad black attitude. Suppressed but haunting us too were the archetypes of Pansy and Prissy—the silly trollops in *Gone With the Wind*, the ones with the squeaky voices who knew nothing about birthing, and who made terrible servants, but very fine comics. White people would wink and laugh, in the parlance of that time, about certain little black girls having "grown like Topsy" when they mysteriously turned up pregnant. The babies would always be light-skinned and fatherless. "The night has no eyes," my grandmother would sigh.

We live in a great memory-gobbling global marketplace now. Our sense of racial history has expanded and contracted in marvelously complicated ways. "Growing like Topsy," insists William Safire, now means nothing to people beyond Harriet Beecher Stowe's original reference in *Uncle Tom's Cabin,* to wit, a young slave "untutored in religion." And the array of black women in the national imagination ranges from Toni Morrison to Li'l Kim, from Rosa Parks to Lani Guinier, from Erykah Badu to Carol Mosely Braun. While almost all the aforementioned have been objects of controversy, if not attack, I guess none of us ever expected any of this to come so easily.

But despite all the progress and the multiplicity of purveyed images, each battle seems not to have built on the last; rather our collective status as black women, like that of all who labor within stereotypes, remains at stake in every struggle. Each time one of us is on the line, so is the public image of the black woman. This makes for a precariousness, a fragility, a vulnerability, a political resonance to the erstwhile romantic fluffiness of Terry McMillan's term "waiting to exhale."

Indeed, *O* is perhaps the nonfiction equivalent of McMillan's books, which created a genre of black bodice rippers. I'm not a particular fan of this sort of Danielle Steele-ish literature, but I confess also to a certain gratitude that Oprah reigns as fairy princess in the dream world *O* creates. No other magazine has ever left me fantasizing about what it would mean to do yoga on the deck of my yacht in red silk lounging pajamas. But then, what other magazine has ever featured a black woman who owns a yacht?

This is not something I aspire to in a material sense: this sort of fantasy serves psychic longings, not physical needs. But the image of a less stressed, more escapist me with tropical breezes rippling over my bare shoulders, my dark eyes flashing in the moonlight, is oddly attractive, a kind of little-girl dream, like that of being the perfect bride. "Like" because Oprah herself seems to have grown past the perfect-bride phase and gone on to envisioning the perfect life. And since I, like Oprah and many of my generation, was never a bride but was nevertheless socialized to want something like that, the Oprah fantasy of happiness ever after—with personal trainer and spoiled-rotten little dogs—is a particularly satisfying substitute.

When I was growing up, fairy-tale contentment was always the property of white girls and women. In my mostly white high school, life was driven entirely by the promise of fairy tales, and there was always a singular golden girl whose looks captured that promise at everyone else's expense: for me, she was a constant reminder of what I did not look like, or what I did not have. I resented her because she was so, well, golden, although I do not mean to imply that I didn't have an amicable enough relationship with her. It's just that she had boyfriends and I didn't.

The Golden Girl—I'll call her GG for short, but she could have been Muffy or Melinda or Babette or Martha Stewart—was the blondest girl in my whole school, and that had a currency with no relation to how nice she was. She was destined for bliss in Connecticut and everyone knew it. No one cared whether she was nice or not; she was just so perfect. I always tried to be very, very nice to everyone, not just blondes, but no one ever looked at me the way they did at GG because apparently being seen as nice always seemed to depend on being seen to begin with.

I was pretty invisible in high school, or at least I felt it. Didn't we all? (Another of the great integrating sentiments upon which Oprah capitalizes.) Maybe GG did too, but somehow I doubt it. In fact, I suspect she might have felt too visible, or at least she gave off the kind of vulnerability that made you bet some prince would come along and protect her from the rest of us by sticking her behind high palace walls, or at least in a nice gated community. Last I heard, she was on her third prince, third palace. Some people have all the luck.

So here I am, at that glorious intersection called middle age, still with this ghostly sense that being nice is not enough. My ghosts are small and petty, I suppose, for which I maintain a consistent stance of gratitude, and for which I hope the entire category of good people who just happen to be blonde will pardon me. Some of my best friends are blonde.

But what is this haunting adolescent anxiety of which Oprah makes me aware and then soothes?

The only way I can explain it is by way of contrast. I remember running out to buy the October 1998 issue of *Vogue,* just after the debut of the movie *Beloved*. Oprah was on the cover, and all of us determined, middle-aged, middle-class black women made the pilgrimage to the newsstand to show our support. There she was, wasp-waisted no less, reclining on a hammock, looking positively sultry in a little black nothing of an evening gown. So, I thought, here I am, almost thirty years out of high school, and when I see Oprah Winfrey gracing the cover of *Vogue*—a black woman literally *in* vogue—I cannot help thinking: what a very good thing. This thought was immediately followed by another, as I remarked upon the cotillion-style evening gowns that she and *Beloved* co-stars Thandie Newton and Kimberly Elise were wearing: what an unsettling thing!

The cover of *Vogue* is so complicated as a cultural symbol. It's the province of Helmut Lang's spiky, emaciated teenagers in white lipstick, cashmere underwear, and shoes designed for those who have little occasion to ride the subway. In that space, Oprah appeared so . . . unusual. She was thin, all right—that was what you saw first and foremost. But she was also too substantial in a way that had nothing to do with weight. It wasn't even a visual thing; perhaps part of it was that her television persona allowed me to feel as though I *know* her.

Oprah, after all, has made her career on the friendly revelation, the girlfriendy tell-all. Like a sweet kitten that rolls over and shows its belly as a sign of concession, she loads a wagonful of the equivalent of her lost belly fat and rolls it across the stage. Who could fail to find that endearing, if in a weird kind of way?

But I also feel as though I know Oprah because she likes potato salad made the Southern way, my grandmother's way. Or because she runs marathons and sweats as much as I surely would were I ever to run a marathon, which I most assuredly will not. Then there was that pedicurist on her show talking about corn removal. That chat with Jada Pinkett Smith about depilatory practices. The weepy confessions about the sorts of biological shortcomings generally covered by that handy blanket of a word, *funk*.

So when I looked at the cover of *Vogue*, I could only marvel at how completely embodied Oprah was—how completely enfleshed, indeed, all black women tend to be seen, at least on some imagistic level. We are known by our aches, pains, and appetites. We have ashy legs, big butts, and "bad" hair that does not flow or swing. Flat, as though in ungrateful opposition to Barbie, feet. Hard-to-be-a-ballerina-looking-like-you-do. We little girls of a certain era grew up in freshly pressed sausage curls and fluffy tutus, looking like hope, feeling like failure. The front maintained in a world that did not love, desire, or romanticize you. You could not trust, and so you maintained an edited self, a well-groomed self, a commercial, compressed, and well-oiled self—prepared for presentation, straining to provide only certain parts of yourself in a world that invents you, projects upon you, mixes you up, makes cyborgs with your parts. Your best bet is to rationalize it as artful rather than as keeping secrets, as choice rather than deference, comportment rather than disguise.

All said, we've had to claw our way through so many stereotypes that "getting real" has become our meta-stereotype, our very own archetype.

Perhaps part of Oprah's great genius is the ability to take a cultural history of being owned and turn it around. She has taken a personal history of being known too intimately, too violently—a history of invasion and rape—and instead of letting her molesters own, as secrets kept, her deepest scars, she's made a business of their revelation and remediation. She's not only mastered the fine art of self-exposure, she's made it a mirror—a great big social mirror, reflecting the biggest audience share this sort of stuff will ever have.

Again, I think of how completely embodied Oprah appeared in *Vogue*. I look at past copies of *Vogue* and think how completely disembodied everyone else who's ever been on the cover has been—a long procession of icons to the illusory, the airbrushed, and the unattainable. It wasn't as though Oprah didn't have all the right moves for *Vogue*; she reclined like an odalisque, so fey, so vulnerable, so . . . unlike herself somehow. I think of the literal meaning of "odalisque"—not a pose in a painting, but "female slave or concubine"—and a certain discomfort befalls me.

What happens when the very substantial Oprah Winfrey enters the space of this particular kind of romantic mirage? What happens indeed when any living breathing person, white or black, blonde or Jhericurled, becomes the malleable, reclining odalisque? Will she actually be able to expand the symbolic territory of anxious anorexics? Will the general "desirability" of African American women be maximized by Oprah in *Vogue,* or will we be drawn into the neurotically self-conscious world of the anemically seductive GG? (Oh, did I mention that

GG was completely body-obsessed? She was acutely aware of how much her place in the world depended upon the approving gaze of others.)

I guess I wonder if—in these interesting times when Bill Clinton could spark debates about whether he was our first black president—the *Vogue*-ish Oprah could vamp her way into becoming our nation's premiere icon of white womanhood.

I don't mean to imply that Oprah was "acting white" in the way some people use that term when they want to describe a black person who is hoping no one will notice that he or she is black. Rather, my interest is focused on the iconic nature of whiteness and womanhood. I'm always trying to place her—and myself—in a culture where white womanhood has always embodied the essence of femininity and black womanhood has too long been seen as its opposite. While white women have fought for sexual liberation and recognition of their strength in the workplace, black women have sought liberation from stereotypes of being strong, overly sexualized workhorses. While many white women have struggled to liberate themselves from femininity as constraining destiny, most black women have never stopped hunting for the perfect adornment, that little bit of fabulous frippery that will render the wearer "pretty."

So it was that Oprah, by appearing on the cover of *Vogue,* represented an odd intersection of these two incongruent cultures within the Women's Movement. Who was Oprah in that moment? The collective projection of best girlfriend? That rock-solid confidante of us all . . . primping like a coltish debutante and dressed like a Southern belle, complete with gardenias in her hair and diamonds at her throat? There she was resting on one elbow, knocking back champagne while all the rest of us were still stuck at home in that same old terry bathrobe, eating Mallomars, longing for the days when she was on a diet too, because then you could both languish in the camaraderie of mutual self-loathing turned safely outward and aimed at the silky person of GG.

I am, of course, not condoning this small-minded behavior. I make the observation not only because I own a terry bathrobe and several boxes of Mallomars, but also because my life has been characterized by this kind of nagging doubt—by a sense of limit and not belonging, by a sense of being under surveillance and measured and always being inadequate. I am always caught up in the question of self-presentation.

I am always listening to myself, I am always watching myself through other's eyes. This was the precise anxiety that seeing Oprah, airbrushed in *Vogue*, stimulated in me.

Oprah in *O*, in contrast, comes closer to negotiating a resolution between the common longing to see oneself in idealized terms and the tyrannically perfectionist images modeled in most women's magazines. It's a subtle distinction, I suppose. Although Oprah Winfrey is exceptional by every measure—extraordinary wealth, extraordinary power— she nevertheless projects an image of Every Black Middle Class Woman. No, that's not quite right: She projects an image of Every Black White Yellow and Red Working Middle and Upper Class Woman for All Seasons Castes and Creeds. My point is that despite the fact that there are few human beings on the planet as well-situated as she, the most endearing part of the Oprah myth is that You Out There—Me?—Yes, You! can be all that she can be.

Oprah Winfrey's talent for what is called "crossover appeal" has the potential for forcing the culture to rethink other categories of desire, particularly romantic and associational desire. But I say "potential" because others before her, like Bill Cosby, have achieved crossover appeal on television without as deep or lasting an impact as might have been hoped. Oprah Winfrey has risen to powerful heights because she has been so savvy in shaping her role as communal friend and helpmeet.

After all, what really is there not to like about her? Cynical New Yorker that I am, I actually find some of her programs mildly annoying because she is almost too nice, too accommodating. She stands for nothing if not shared values—moderation in eating and drinking, getting lots of exercise, clean living, self-motivation. She's no threat to capitalism— every girl should have such a corporation. She stands for team spirit as well as radical individualism, down-home as well as high fashion. She loves all hues and views of humanity. She is kind to fools and Klan members, and publicly encourages reading, reading, and more reading.

I don't want to be understood as overstating Oprah's significance in a world as encumbered by the aesthetics of history as ours. In particular, I do not wish to style my thoughts about her as any kind of political analysis. But given a history in which certain bodies have been ruthlessly deromanticized as a first step in that process of dehumanization that has imagined some of us as "suspect profiles," "undesirables," and "human trash," I wonder if Oprah's romantic humanitarianism isn't such a bad thing.

The mass media have become our most important font of collective imagination. Oprah takes the stories of confused, abused, generally less-than-normative people and meticulously tracks the misfortunes and bad choices that have brought them to their lot. Then, like some kindly force of Anti-Fate, she unravels the mess, shakes it out, sets *les miserables* on the path toward "Happy Ending," and gives them a friendly shove.

It's an art, this treading of thin lines through emotional dilemmas that perhaps risk exploding in passionate polarization but that also harbor opportunities for personal reflection and deep empathy. It is magic, the ability to control and broadcast information, a test of whether that seductive power will be used for narcissism or good will.

Again, Oprah is hardly the revolution. But as a tiny turning point in a culture that has not easily opened doors to those who don't conform, she beats Martha Stewart any day.

Patricia J. Williams, *a 2000 MacArthur Award winner and 1997 BBC Reith Lecturer, is one of the most astute commentators on the racial divide in America. She received her undergraduate degree from Wellesley College and her law degree from Harvard Law School; she is now a Columbia Law School professor, a popular columnist for* The Nation, *and a frequent contributor to the* Village Voice, Ms., *and numerous national law reviews. She is the author of three books:* The Alchemy of Race and Rights: Diary of a Mad Law Professor *(Harvard University Press, 1991),* The Rooster's Egg *(Harvard University Press, 1995), and* Seeing a Color-Blind Future: The Paradox of Race *(Noonday Press, 1993).*

© Donn Young

A Rambling Response to
the Play Marie Christine

KALAMU YA SALAAM

The following essay was commissioned by the Lincoln Center to appear in their theatre program guide for Marie Christine: A New Musical, *words and music by Michael John LaChiusa, starring Audra McDonald and Anthony Crivello, at Lincoln Center, NYC, December 1999–January 2000. The essay did not appear.*

I

Here is my initial reaction:

It is difficult, if not impossible, for me to respond to this play, mainly because I am not interested in responding to racist fantasy. Of course, that statement raises the question: What do I mean by "racist"?

From my perspective, this is a play repeating and reinforcing the notion "it's in the blood" and the white supremacist thesis that there is a major bio/psychological species difference between black and white.

This is a play that ignores history to present fantasy. It is a play that offers decontextualized research masquerading as historical fact. It is a play glorifying the white male penis and its desire for the "color struck" mulatto female vagina.

It is a play about the "tragic mulatto," a figure who was, historically, created in the main by white male rape and extralegal liaisons. It is a play about fantasy and sublimated desire, a dangerously well-crafted artwork that is attractive in its production values but repulsive in its meaning.

It is ultimately a play about celebrating racist patriarchal power relationships, rather than human relationships.

I could go point by point through the play—the assumptions, the mixing of time periods, the ignoring of historical accuracy—but to argue at length only dignifies an object that does not deserve serious scrutiny.

Towards art for life,
Kalamu ya Salaam

&

The above response is pretty standard political rhetoric—standard in that, like all political rhetoric, what I say is absolute rather than relative, abstract rather than concrete, and, ultimately, addresses what I "think" while avoiding how I feel.

But I decided not to stop with a rigid position. I decided to enter into conversation with myself, to engage, at an emotional level, an issue which is difficult to grasp. I have decided to talk a bit about this: "As a heterosexual black man, what is my relationship to black women and to white women?" and see where that takes me.

But first, a definition. Mulatto can specifically mean the child of biracial parents (one of whom is black and one of whom is white), or mulatto can generally mean anyone of a mixed racial (again, the emphasis is on black and white) background. I use mulatto in the general sense. Mulatto also connotes a person who appears to be closer to "pure" white than to "pure" black. Moreover, in the United States, mulatto is not about whites mixing with other ethnicities, e.g. Native American or Asian. In the final analysis, when we say mulatto, we are talking about a white-determined American preoccupation with the intersection of race and sexual desire.

Once, when I was in my twenties, an elder woman said to me, "I don't know why a man would need to go outside our race to find a woman because we have any kind of woman he might want among us." We were in New Orleans, passing a bus stop.

The physical variety of skin tones, body types, hair textures, even eye colors among "black" women in the Crescent City requires a computer monitor that can display at least 256 colors to even come close to representing it. (I know somebody is about to ask, "But if she has blond hair and blue eyes, how can she be black?" Well, you see, blackness is color, culture, and consciousness; in very important ways, blackness is not simply nor solely a biological absolute but is also and more importantly a collective experience as well as a personal choice.)

My first wife was reared as what some would call a "Creole" because of her light skin and the Catholic/French-speaking heritage of her family. We had five children whose skin tones range from cinnamon to nutmeg, all of them with thick curly "naps." And they were reared to consider themselves and all of their friends, family members, and acquaintances as black regardless of the shade of skin.

Unavoidably, however, there have been bumps on that road of intraracial equality. One daughter remembers her shock when she heard her mother say she wished her children were darker. My daughter was shocked because she never thought of herself as light skinned and was taken aback that a lighter-skinned mother thought her darker-skinned daughter was "light" or at least "lighter" than the mother had wanted the daughter to be.

Later in Brazil that same daughter is told that she is a "mulatto" and she is doubly shocked.

I have fought against reducing the human spectrum to absolute biological colors and defining individuals by their biology, but, just like my daughter, I too have been affected by the race-based ideologies of this society. Only as I have grown older have I realized that much of what I thought was just my personal taste as a young man was in fact an unconscious adoption of prescribed, race-based notions that "black is beautiful" inverted, but did not deeply and thoroughly address. For beauty, like biology, tends toward diversity rather than absolutes.

Although I have had dark-skinned lovers, the truth is that the majority of my lovers have been my skin color (which is dark brown) or lighter. This fact forces me to ask: Is the female mulatto intrinsically more attractive than either the white woman or the black woman?

Based on what I have witnessed, I say, yes, "mulatto" women have proven to be more attractive to men than dark-skinned women. Moreover, judging mulattos more attractive than dark-skinned blacks is generally the rule for both black men and white men. Even a casual perusal of rap and pop videos will support this conclusion as, ironically, you will probably find more dark-skinned women in pop videos than in rap videos. This preference is a socially induced preference, the result of being reared in a racist society that unceasingly prioritizes the male consumption of both a Eurocentric definition of physical beauty and a male-dominant definition of female sexuality.

Within a racist society, the female mulatto represents the highest taboo. She is usually envisioned, to one degree or another, as having the looks of the white woman and the sexuality of the black woman. But racism also splits sexuality into the too often mutually exclusive duality of procreation and pleasure. It is easy to see how a racist dichotomy could lead to white procreation and black pleasure.

The assumption of the play is that the mulatto woman is the object of desire, but the American truth is that the mulatto woman exists because of white male attraction to black women. Not to mulatto women, not to women who look white, but to black women. Black women. Black. Women.

As to the inverse: are black women fixated on white men? I don't think so, not in America. Indeed, while a brother might be proudly defiant or defiantly proud of his "snaring" a white woman, black women who are with white men tend to pursue their lives quietly, almost apologetically. Part of the reason is that in this society women have been reared to please others, not to offend others, especially family and friends. But part of it is that both the reality and the mythology of white male rape of black women is so painful, so long-standing, and, yes, so real that a black woman who chooses to be with a white man

seems (at least at first glance—on the sociological surface) to be a traitor to her own history and to her people's history.

So while we might have the same result, i.e. an interracial union, the
dynamics are very, very different depending on the "color" of the male
and the "color" of the female in such a union. I don't believe the play
addressed any of those dynamics, even though ostensibly the psychology of the Creole is a major plot element.

While color continues to be a major psychological issue for many
black people, the subject of interracial sexual relations is tiresome and ultimately wasteful, especially when divorced from class and gender issues.

Interestingly enough, as far as the play was concerned, I, as a black
man, did not exist. The non-Creole black man literally plays no role in
this production, while the Creole male is merely a foil to be ignored or,
when he gets in the way, eliminated. For as long as I, the black male,
am not thwarting the actions of white men, and as long as I am not running around raping and killing white women (à la O. J.), I am acceptable (à la the O. J. of the glory days). There is a reason that Othello
remains relevant to this society.

Although *Marie Christine* is male-centered, this play is not about
black men and the views of black men, whether well-balanced or
deranged. Regardless of its other themes, this play is specifically about
the color fetish of white male sexual desire. One would think that by
now, this concern would have been worked through, but not so. Even
after close to five-hundred years of white-male-dominant contact, their
mulatto fetish does not seem to be diminishing.

So what's up with this need to consume women of color? (Check
the liquor, cigarette, and fashion advertisements, not to mention tan-
ning and lip enlargements.)

To be clear, I am not saying every white male wants a black woman.
I am saying that a major fetish in the arsenal of American sexual
desire/fantasy is the sexual consumption and/or domination of a black
woman. That is a norm that may be completely absent in some white
men, but to one degree or another is a part of most men's sexual fantasies. Moreover, the dominant influence of male sexuality in deter-
mining and/or shaping mores and behavior in this society is much larger
than most of us are generally willing to admit. For example, white

women are constantly dealing with questions of sexual adequacy vis-à-vis black women, hence the seldom-discussed rift between heterosexual black women and white women on gender issues, a rift acknowledged but not explored in the play.

Suffice it to point out that, unavoidably, there is a major tension around physical attractiveness whenever white women perceive themselves to be competing with black women. Although color complicates the attractiveness issue, ultimately, in this patriarchal society, women make themselves sexually attractive due to a *socially perceived* need for male protection and support, even when there is no *actual* need. In other words, the female is "encouraged" to feign a submissive posture in order to attract the desired male.

Thus, the bedroom becomes the most complicated room in the house. The social emphasis on sex is complicated by the moral emphasis on monogamy and the racial emphasis on purity. Given that this is a male-dominated society, sorting through all of this is both complicated and easy. Complicated if one chooses to avoid discussing the intricacies and intersections of color, class, and gender; easy if one acknowledges the brutal fact driving and dominating American social interactions: the white male's insistence on sexual conquest.

I'm simply saying men like to copulate. (I would say "fuck," but given mainstream tastes, the use of an euphemism is preferred, if not outright required, in public discourse. Moreover, the need for euphemisms reflects the American inability to admit sociological realities, but that's another discussion for another time. Why else would Viagra . . . need I say more?)

But let's get back to the issue at hand: racist obsession with black female flesh. I think white men want it both ways. They want to propagate the white race, hence a "white wife," and they want black sensuality, hence a black or "mulatto" concubine, kept woman, or prostitute.

On the other hand, without "white wives," the white race would, in a matter of a few generations, blend into the general colored populations of the world. From a racist position, that would amount to racial suicide. Or, to flip the script: as I ask fellow blacks whenever someone expresses a deep distaste for interracial unions, "What would you rather see, white babies or mulatto babies?"

I'm sure to most whites that's a shocking statement, but it's a factual one. White people cannot spread out all around the world, have human interaction with all the peoples of the world, and remain "pure white" unless they enforce a racist system that values white purity over racial diversity.

My position is that I support racial diversity over the essentialism of so-called purity, whether white or black. Indeed, realistically, what other position could I hold, given that the overwhelming majority of African Americans are of mixed heritage?

The natural result of human intercourse unfettered by racist ideology is diversity. Indeed, race mixing has been and will continue to be the inevitable result of multiracial societies in modern times, racially supremacist ideologies notwithstanding. Yes, even under the most racist system, if the system is also patriarchal, you can bet that there will also be race mixing, because by definition, within a patriarchal system to be a man is to be able to consume any and all women.

If American history proves nothing else, it proves that white men are going to be white men and that they will continue to be fascinated by black women. And this sexual fetish will manifest itself, consciously or subconsciously, in the artwork of this country, especially that artwork which reflects the dominant ideologies, regardless of the particular ideology, gender, or race of the artist, unless that artist consciously, honestly, and fearlessly decides to confront just what it means to write yet another play about a tragic mulatto.

II

AND WE STILL AIN'T READY!

When I was first asked about writing the essay, I asked, "Are you sure you want me to write for you?" The editor assured me that she knew my work and did indeed want my participation. True to her word, once I turned in the essay, the early stages went remarkably well. The editing process was straightforward and helpful. Everything seemed to be everything.

Then, while I was in residence at the Providence Fine Arts Center, less than two weeks before the issue was to go to press, I received a call from the editor's boss. Seems the galley copy was circulated to the cast of the play, and . . . well, here's the relevant text from the formal letter I received about the decision not to print the essay:

Dear Kalamu,

Josselyn indicated that you'd like us to write to you as a follow up to our phone conversation of two weeks ago. I'm happy to do so.

We decided not to run your article "A Rambling Response to the Play *Marie Christine*" because the artists of the play felt your preface to the article would hurt the perception of the show. As you know, we inquired whether we could run the main body of your article alone, and when you declined, we decided not to run the piece at all.

I'm sorry this worked out this way, since we all liked the body of the article very much.

Sincerely,

Anne Cattaneo
Executive Editor

She's right. It was my call to say run the whole thing or don't run it at all. Publication in New York never hurts, especially if the publication is from Lincoln Center. Moreover, offending editors is a risky proposition; as huge as New York may be, the publishing circles are really not that large. It didn't take me long to reach the decision I did, and so here we are, another failed attempt to bridge the gap.

On the one hand I fully understand that publishing the above essay in the official program would have been daft—if I were them, I certainly would not have done it. But then again, I certainly would not have been producing that play, either!

I know there are many other black writers who would have been tickled to write a non-offensive essay for Lincoln Center. My position, however, is simple: I'm not the one.

To me, the play was offensive, and to respond politely and inoffensively to such a play just is not an option. Ultimately, what liberal America wants is to be integrated and at the same time continue perpetuating their fantasies.

I don't know who called the final shots. I don't know who strongly objected to my article, but I do know I sleep well at night. I do know they are clear that there is at least one intelligent black person who finds their play offensive and is willing to tell them so in a forthright and unambiguous manner.

None of this is life-or-death serious, and in the grand scheme of my career and the careers of the cast, crew, and creators of the play, this little incident is but a minor skirmish. Nonetheless, this was, in my opinion, a battle that had to be fought.

Some of us are not glad just to be accepted into the mainstream. Some of us are not for sale and we will speak up, even if the "we" is just one writer refusing to co-sign patriarchal fantasies about mulatto sex.

In the final analysis, it is these quiet battles, the ones outside of the limelight, the ones that others may never even know happened—it is these principled engagements that will determine how far we have come and how far we have yet to go before we can honestly engage in dialogue across the racial divide without biting our tongues or censoring our thoughts.

A luta continua (the struggle continues) . . .

Kalamu ya Salaam *is a writer, artist, actor, and activist with a track record that spans more than thirty years. Among his numerous awards are the Richard Wright Award for literary criticism; the Deems Taylor/ASCAP Award for excellence in writing about music; and the Deep South Writer's Contest Award for prose.*

Salaam's published work includes numerous poetry, fiction, and personal essay collections, the most recent of which is entitled What is Life? *(Third World Press, 1994) and* 360 Degrees—A Revolution of Black Poets *(Black Words Press, 1998).*

Salaam, founder/director of Nommo Literary Society, a black writers workshop in New Orleans, Louisiana, was a 1999 Senior Fellow at the Providence Fine Arts Center. He currently edits and manages a very popular online discussion group devoted to African American arts and culture around the world.

© Jennifer C. Johnson/J3 Productions

Black, White, and Seeing Red All Over

SHAWN E. RHEA

I.

It is spring 1995 in New York City. I descend the steps of my brownstone apartment in Fort Green, Brooklyn, and before I even hit the last one I am caught up in the glow. The sky is a bright, azure blue, kids are playing in the park across the street, people are actually smiling at one another, and I can feel the warmth of the sun hitting my shoulders. It is the kind of day that renews my love affair with New York. It is the kind of day when I like to walk the streets of my neighborhood—an area that has been dubbed the Black Arts Mecca.

I have an affinity for black men, particularly artistic, culturally aware brothas—poets, musicians, and artists who sport dreadlocks or untamed afros and wear baggy, casual clothes that may even be splattered with paint. For the past decade this neighborhood has been the place to find them in abundance. It is not unusual to step into a cafe and see table after table of black couples huddled together, looking as if they're sharing a wicked secret, or walking down the street hand in hand as if they hold the strength of creation between their palms. But recently the neighborhood has become more multicultural. There are signs of gentrification everywhere, from the new massive Pathmark grocery store to the rising rents to the white homeowners and tenants who are becoming regular faces at local haunts. And as I turn the corner I am confronted with another surefire sign of urban gentrification: I see an interracial couple coming in my direction, walking hand in hand.

The brotha is dreadlocked, brown, and beautiful. The woman is attractive, shapely, and sporting a gelee head wrap. I have seen black men with white women in my neighborhood so often recently that I no longer have to have that embarrassing internal conversation with myself: the one that says I am being racist, petty, and insecure when I become upset over a brotha's choice to be with a white woman; the one that I would never repeat out loud because my parents didn't raise me to have such feelings. I am consciously struggling to be more accepting of each person's right to choose whom they love. I am trying to not take personally any one brotha's decision to sleep with, date, or marry a white woman, so I keep walking, and I force myself not to throw any glances that may be interpreted as disrespectful. I do not want to pass judgment on this couple, these individuals whom I have never met. But then, as we pass each other, the woman's eyes meet mine, and in hers I believe I see a look of defiance, boastfulness almost. The brotha shifts his head so that he can avoid our making eye contact. Suddenly I am angry. There are no words, no internal dialogue that can quell my feeling of betrayal—my feeling that, like the Trojan Horse, an enemy has been welcomed into our homeland, and it is only a matter of time before it gleefully and irreparably destroys the very bonds of our nation.

II.

I do not want to be diagnosed with Angry Black Woman Syndrome, so I constantly check and question myself. I wonder what is truly at the root of my feelings. Is it my own fear of ending up alone, without a mate who truly appreciates and understands me? Is my own sense of worth and beauty threatened by the thought that black men who date white women have opted for a physicality that is impossible for me to realize, and, in doing so, have rejected me at my core? Do I simply need something, someone to blame for the fact that I haven't been in a serious relationship for some years now? I toss these questions around, vacillate between answering "yes" and "no" to each, check to see which response feels more like the truth and gets me closer to understanding. But the only thing I find is more questions.

Now I ask, why are my ill feelings specific to black men with white women? I am not faced with the same uneasiness when I see brothas with Latinas, Asian, or East Indian women. Then again, the history between our people is different. My ancestors were stolen, raped, beaten, killed, and permanently enslaved by their forefathers and foremothers—a legacy that, no matter how much we want to disregard it, is still reaping a stunted harvest. But I'm determined not to be a slave to this history, so I tell myself that this hostility toward black men dating white women is irrational, unfounded.

The truth is, every important man in my life, from my father to my oldest brother to both of my deceased grandfathers, has devoted his life to building a strong, enduring, supportive relationship with the black woman who is or was his wife. I remind myself that most of the brothas whom I've known to date white women at one time or another have ultimately ended up building their lives with sistas. I develop a list of affirmations that I employ whenever I feel myself falling prey to the ugly, hurtful, unexplained belief that black women have been abandoned by the very men who should protect and cherish us. My invocations go something like this:

- I will not let someone else's choice define how I feel about myself.
- I will judge people based on their actions, not their appearances.
- White women are not my enemy: oppression, racism, sexism, and classism are.
- Happiness does not always come in a convenient package.
- There are good brothas, kind brothas, culturally aware brothas, loving brothas in abundance, all around me everyday, who cherish and value black women, and could never imagine their lives without us by their sides.

III.

I am at home one evening right before the Labor Day weekend when a friend phones. He is upset over a recent breakup with his girlfriend. This man and I dated at one point, but have long since become platonic. He is thirty-two and the sista who has broken his heart is several years younger. In fact, she is only twenty-four, relatively new to the city, a struggling model/waitress, and a bit of a wild child who enjoys, among other things, multiple sex partners and large quantities of liquor and cocaine. I have felt almost from the very beginning that their relationship was doomed. He is looking for love, she for sponsorship. Whenever he calls me complaining about something that she has done, I ask him why he is attracted to her.

"She's a little crazy, and I've always liked women who are slightly touched," he tells me time and again.

"Yeah, but she sounds certifiable," I always respond.

When we speak, he is livid, railing over her most recent behavior. His pain becomes an indictment of black women. "You see," he says, "sistas just don't know when they got a good brotha. Y'all are too hard to please; that's why I'ma have to open up my options. I'm through dating black women." His tone is joking, but I feel, on some level, he actually believes what he has just said.

"Crazy is crazy," I snap, no longer sympathetic to my friend's pain. I feel that he has unjustly turned it on me. "If you date crazy women that's how they'll treat you. It doesn't matter what color they are. I have a ton of single girlfriends who are attractive, smart, successful, loving, and sane, so that's utter bullshit."

"Yeah, well why are they by themselves? Probably because they're high maintenance."

"Do you call wanting respect and commitment high maintenance?"

We begin arguing and end the call by hanging up on one another. Later that weekend I break down in tears telling a girlfriend how hurt I was by his comment and our ensuing fight. He and I don't speak again until November, when he calls to wish me Happy Birthday. I muster up the nerve to ask him about the argument and whether he has truly sworn off black women. He tells me no, says he had only meant what he said as a joke, but that I had blown it totally out of proportion and taken it way too personally.

He wants to know why I was so offended, but I am only able to discern bits and pieces of a rational reason, and I know that any attempt to explain it would only cause another argument. So I simply say, "It didn't feel like a joke at the time, but maybe I did misread you."

IV.

My cousin Jamie is like a sister, closer in many ways than most sisters. She is also my best friend, and she knows every secret about me that I would ever draw breath to repeat. Our bond was sealed as babies, when she came to live with my parents and me shortly after I was born. Her parents were drug addicts and were unable to take care of her. She was only with us for a year, but my mother says that after her parents came and took her away I cried for weeks asking when she would be coming home. As children we were inseparable.

Jamie's father was an amazing singer, who even recorded a hit record in the fifties. Her mother, I am told, was very attractive as a young woman; she is also white. Jamie received her father's face and beautiful singing voice, but she got her straight, light brown hair, fair skin, and hazel-green eyes from her mother. When we were little, people never believed Jamie and I were related. "Are y'all jus' play cousins?" or "How come y'all don't look nothin' alike?" were the questions that newly acquainted friends and even their parents felt compelled to ask us. But Jamie and I were family, and we were determined to honor that bond, so we became fiercely protective of our kinship. "No! We're real cousins," both of us would vehemently declare to whoever dared question our shared bloodline.

We became even more protective of that bond as teenagers. Jamie was easygoing and popular; I was sharp-tongued and took longer to warm up to people. New acquaintances, men in particular, always gravitated more readily toward Jamie, and that was painful for me. She is one of the most endearing people I have ever known, and this was clearly part of what drew them to her. But there was another reason, an unspoken reason that neither of us knew how to name as children or teenagers: her looks. There were people who wanted to be close to Jamie just because she had long hair, fair skin, and light eyes. And there were others who disliked her for the same reason.

We didn't realize it then, but I made it my job to be a buffer between her and those whom I felt were disingenuous, and she made it her job to defend me against folks who thought me too acerbic, bossy, and aloof. Sometimes Jamie and I disagreed about people I thought were phony, but she wasn't willing to write off. The arguments sometimes strained, but ultimately strengthened our friendship. Years later, when she moved to Los Angeles and I to New York, distance did not weaken our loyalty to one another. I remember clearly her desire to seek an ugly revenge on a Los Angeles-based brotha who broke my heart, and I recall seething when she told me about a particular brotha who would not date her because he thought her skin too light and hair too straight. Then there was the white female coworker who had wondered out loud why Jamie "admitted" to being black when no one would ever have guessed.

Experiences like those have become so commonplace for Jamie that, though they are painful, she has developed a serious ability to check folks and leave them holding their own crap. When we were younger, however, I was just beginning to understand that being close to my cousin often gave me an uncomfortable view of racial dynamics that most folks only speak of in the abstract. It would take years for me to realize that our friendship and kinship were the genesis of my internal battle against black folks' coveting of "the Other."

V.

Jamie has come to New York to celebrate New Year's. One evening during her stay we are visiting Charles [name changed], a man I've been dating. Tony, a mutual friend, is also there. The four of us are having a wonderful time listening to music and drinking wine when Charles starts teasing me about a guy who, at a club the night before, was determined to talk to me despite the fact that I was obviously with someone. The brotha planted himself in a seat at our table when Charles went to the bathroom and all but refused to get up when he came back.

I remind him that that was not the first time something like that had happened to us. "Remember that time we were at that club and that white woman came and stood in front of our table? She started dancing by herself and throwing kisses at you. She saw me sitting right there; she saw me looking at her like she was crazy and I was 'bout to kick her ass, but she just kept on going."

We all laugh and shake our heads in disbelief. But I am not content to just compare notes with Charles about whose admirer was craziest. I begin making blanket commentary about white women. "They are a trip," I continue. "Why are they so blatantly sleazy when they're going after men?"

I do not notice it at first, but Jamie has become quiet. I go on to make some other less than complimentary remarks. When my cousin can no longer bear my comments, she blurts out a command that silences me in mid sentence. "Shawn, stop dogging white women!" she snaps angrily. "You know, my mother just happens to be white."

Despite her venomous tone, I see only hurt. "Sorry," I say. Charles quickly changes the subject, and I realize that I have hurt my cousin in a way that I would not have intended even at my angriest moment. I know that my apology can never compensate for the pain that I've caused her.

At home later, I remember something that Lisa Jones, daughter of Hettie Jones and Amiri Baraka, wrote in *Bullet Proof Diva*, her book of personal and political essays on race and culture in America. Jones, whose mother is also white, has struggled for years to come to terms with her own multiethnic background. In one piece she describes her feelings about brothas who pass over sistas in favor of white women. But she also writes that she fiercely loves her own white, Jewish mother, and that if one particular black man had not lain down with one particular white woman, she would never have been born. I think long and hard on that statement, and I realize how much it rings true in the case of my own cousin and best friend—someone whom I could never imagine not having in my life.

That night I begin some serious soul searching. I am disappointed that I have let my initially protective feelings toward someone I love fester into rhetoric that pains her. Before Jamie leaves New York, I give her

my copy of Jones's book, hoping that she too will find something familiar and helpful in it.

VI.

It is July 1999, and I am preparing to move to New Orleans. The
unyielding pace and expense of New York City, coupled with a severe
case of writer's block and restlessness, are causing me to flee southward.
I am looking for a more nurturing and productive environment. Also,
I am convinced that I am never going meet a man with whom to share
my life in New York. Over the last year I have seldom dated. Then
again, my days have been so crammed with story deadlines and moving arrangements that I've rarely had time to think about men.

While packing for my move, I stop to browse through some pho-
tos and I come across one of myself with a former boyfriend on vacation in London. I keep flipping and find more of myself with other
exes—in Jamaica, in D.C., at parties, and so on. Usually these pictures
fill me with a small sense of regret and longing, but this day it dawns
on me that my fear of being perpetually single has subsided. Though I
definitely still want a partner, a husband, a man with whom to raise a
family, I no longer wonder what I will do with my life if this scenario
does not materialize. I know that I will build a content, fulfilling existence. I find peace in this awareness.

I keep looking through the pictures, and eventually come across
one of Jamie at her graduation dinner. She is obviously tipsy, her eyes
narrowed into small slits. It is a telltale trait of inebriation that we both
inherited from our fathers. I think about how often Jamie and I have
visited each other in Los Angeles and New York, and I realize that a
chapter in my life is closing. I also remember how much I hurt her the
last time she was here. But like everything else, our bond survived, and
I have grown at least a little.

Now I rarely have a visceral reaction when I see black men with
white women, and that is something for which I can thank my cousin.
I am not sure when this particular union stopped feeling so threatening to me, but now I can actually say, "People need to be with the folks

who make them happiest," and not strain under the weight of my own politically correct assertion. I can truly believe it . . . most of the time. But I also know that, even though I no longer feel like marriage is the ultimate prize and I can accept relationships beyond the color boundary, I want to be someplace where I can possibly meet a brotha with whom I can build a life.

I move to New Orleans in August and meet Franklin [name changed] my first week there. We are immediately attracted to each other. We are both writers, both new to the city, and we each have eclectic taste in music. Neither is anxious to acknowledge an interest beyond friendship, however. He is a bit cautious, I suspect, because there is someone in his life. My suspicions are confirmed when, at a party one evening, I meet his girlfriend, who is visiting from out of town. I am somewhat surprised to discover she is white, but I am relieved when I let it go at that. While I had never considered the possibility that Franklin's significant other might not be black, I feel neither angry nor territorial when I learn she is white.

Over the next few weeks Franklin and I meet for coffee, go to poetry readings, play pool, and take in movies. We talk late into the night, sharing our struggles to find our voices as writers—our concerns that we probably don't devote enough time to writing.

We talk about our personal lives and relationships. I tell him about the challenges of being a single, thirty-something woman. I reveal that I am used to living by myself, and that my family believes I'm becoming too intolerant of other people's idiosyncrasies. They hint that I might not be fit to share a home. I confess fearing that they might be right. He divulges that, having made the choice to date a white woman, there have been uneasy moments: moments when people's judgments and assumptions have intruded upon the sanctity and peace of their relationship; moments when he has felt the stress of their obvious cultural differences. But he says that he long ago learned not to let other people's expectations dictate his own choices.

Over drinks one night, it becomes obvious that neither Franklin nor I really want to remain strictly platonic. We talk about the complications of our getting involved.

"Long distance monogamy is just not very realistic," he tells me in a confessional tone.

"Yeah, I hear you, but I don't want to be the thing that you do until the real thing gets here," I admit. What I don't tell him is that more than being concerned with whether I might be entering a relationship with a man who may eventually have to choose between me and another woman, I am concerned about the fact that this other woman is white.

I ask myself if he's dating a white woman because he has issues with black women, or because he just happens to be attracted to this particular woman? I want to make sure that he is not—as my cousin so aptly describes black men who are infatuated with white women's looks— "O.J.-icized."

But the proper words for posing such a sensitive question never come to me. How can I respectfully ask someone, especially a man with whom I ultimately wish to be intimate, whether he has racial identity issues? Would asking him directly get me an honest answer? After all, few folks struggling with race identity and allegiance issues are willing to give voice to them So I bite my tongue and force my uneasy feelings back down.

I watch his actions instead, convinced that they will provide a more truthful answer to the question I can't ask. I tell myself that any successful relationship requires a leap of faith in its early stages, and that this is the point at which I must make mine if I am going to truly find out if Franklin and I have a future. He and I agree not to put any limitations on the relationship and to see where it takes us. We officially begin dating, but our romantic endeavor is short lived. One morning, several weeks into our involvement, Franklin tells me that the guilt and emotions of trying to juggle two relationships are becoming overwhelming and complicated.

"I didn't expect to develop such strong feelings for you so quickly, and I can't let myself go there because I already have someone in my life."

I am disappointed and upset. While I shoulder much of the blame for ever getting involved with a man who is already in a committed relationship, I can't help but feel betrayed. A big part of me is angry that he has chosen being with a white woman over being with me, but I never say this out loud. How can I reveal such an ugly, antiquated insecurity? Instead, I put on my best game face and confront him about everything but the one insult clawing hardest at my gut.

I remind him that we discussed the possibility that we might develop serious feelings for one another and assumed that risk. He says he didn't realize how big a risk it was and that he still wants to be friends. I say friendship is not a subject that I care to discuss now, but that I do want to know why this guilt has suddenly overcome him. Angry tears well up.

"Hurting you is something I never intended to do," he says. I realize that he has mistaken my anger for a desire to be placated.

"It's time for you to go," I say.

VII.

It is spring 2000, and I am riding down Interstate 10, enjoying the breeze blowing through my windows. It is turning the intense Louisiana sun into a stream of sensuous warm air flowing over my still winter-pale brown skin. The radio is blasting tunes from my seventies childhood, and I become particularly enraptured when the deejay spins a seldom-played track, the Stories' "Brother Louie." I croon along, belting out the lyrics about love across racial lines.

The song's whining guitar immediately takes me back to the summer when I was eight years old. Several girlfriends and I are swinging from monkey bars as we sing the tune. Back then I liked the track not only for Ian Lloyd's gritty vocals, but also because, even at that age, I appreciated the defiant image that it painted: two people refusing to let a societal taboo regulate their capacity to love, nurture, and claim one another. I felt hope and a powerful subversion in that image.

So what happened along the way? Why can't I find these feelings now when I come across a black man who has chosen to break the taboo? I wish that I could be that little girl again: the one who saw power in the type of relationship that I now struggle not to resent.

I can never be her again. My feelings about interracial dating, specifically black men with white women, are forever colored by a racial and sexual caste system that assigns black women the role of unfeminine, difficult ball breakers, while white women are cast as easygoing, sexually accommodating, and physically desirable.

Of course, these are only stereotypes. Women, black or white, cannot be reduced to or explained by such derogatory definitions. Nor can we be held accountable for any man's physical, cultural, and emotional preferences. But these still powerful stereotypes are bandied about so often that people have embraced them as truths. For some, they provide easy excuses for complex choices, while for others, like me, they trigger feelings of rejection and low self-esteem.

This epiphany hits home: despite the self-love and acceptance gospel preached by modern-day therapists, the consistent encouragement and esteem-building dialogue of loving parents, and the support of a community of friends and extended family, at least part of my self-worth is inextricably linked to a need to be loved, desired, and cherished by black men. It is an innate want, as strong as instinct, determined to be satisfied.

I am not an animal chasing her prey over open prairies or mating with a male solely to procreate. I am a woman—a black woman—who must constantly separate the instinctual from the societal, the individual from the stereotype, the truth from the assumed. And I must find myself somewhere amid these contradictions. I must be willing to ask myself the hard question: By what am I motivated—fear or love?

Will I ever be totally free of this demon? Who knows? What I do know is this: I want to be free of it enough to love whom I love, and secure enough to accept someone else's choice if they decide not to love me.

Shawn E. Rhea *is a journalist, essayist, poet, and fiction writer. She is a contributor to* The Source *magazine, and has also penned articles for* Essence, Black Enterprise, Teen People, *BET.com, and the* New Orleans Times-Picayune. *Her short fiction has been featured in the literary publication* Anansi, *and her poetry and essay work are set for publication in the* *forthcoming anthologies* Speak The Truth To The People *(Runagate Press) and* Unheard Voices.

Rhea received her bachelor's degree from Howard University and her master's degree from Columbia University's Graduate School of Journalism. A native of Detroit, Michigan, Rhea, thirty-six, currently lives and writes in New York City.

© *Dallas Morning News*

Race Fatigue

IRA J. HADNOT

I AM TIRED of race. Bone-weary of thoughts about race. Fatigued by our society's silence about race. Too broken down in spirit to shoulder the mantle of race.

As Paul Laurence Dunbar wrote, "We wear the mask that grins and lies . . . "

More than four decades after the sixties, we are still wearing race on our sleeves.

There is the pretense of understanding and of tolerance. Yet we have a black man chained and dragged to death on the Texas road where he once played as a child.

The spines of my white colleagues stiffen with the slightest reference to race. Black Americans are either "too sensitive" or "too angry" to sustain an intelligent debate. It seems, affirmative action and O. J. Simpson aside, race still is about us and them. It will always be about black and white.

I want you to know that once it was not this way for me.

I never wore a mask—not until being perceived as a threat myself, my frustration mistaken for anger and my impatience to succeed for not being a team player.

This skin I am in first experienced blackness from the front porch of a white family in a community that was 98 percent white. I was younger, and it was elastic enough to absorb the hopes and beliefs of the VISTA and Peace Corps workers my parents invited into our home.

A VISTA program that paired inner-city kids with suburban or small-town white kids was my introduction to the color line. It was less emotionally damaging because the Foxgrovers were truly kind and compassionate people. It wasn't them or their little girl I played with who made me uncomfortable in my own skin.

It was their neighbors who lined an Appleton, Wisconsin, street that summer in 1968 to watch and point at me as I walked to the Piggly Wiggly for a soda. That sidewalk felt like a long conveyor belt. I felt as though I would never get to the end of the block and off display.

Some days, that experience comes racing back. It finds me here in Dallas, Texas, and reminds me that it's not me they see but my color. My race is recognized before I am. I will always be on display or out of context.

My husband and I were shopping in one of those huge home construction and remodeling warehouses when I saw a colleague from work. I called him by name and he looked at me blankly. I moved closer and called him by name again. When my husband and I got right up on him, he blinked and asked, "Ira? Ira? Hey, I didn't recognize you." It still baffles me that someone I have worked closely with for fifty-two weeks, someone who gets just about as much face time as my bathroom mirror, would not recognize me with a shopping cart in my hands.

I am standing at my local grocery store at the end of the cash register in the checkout line. I am waiting for my grocery receipt when an older woman tells me that she wants "paper, not plastic." I am wearing a business suit, but she hasn't seen that. I am at the station where a bagger is supposed to be. But I am not wearing a uniform.

Again, she says more emphatically, "I don't want my groceries in plastic."

"Well, I do want plastic for mine," I replied. Only then did her eyes connect first with my clothes and then rise to my face. She realized I wasn't her bagger. I was seething inside, smiling on the outside. Is this the station for persons of my race?

One evening, I was on my way to the opera and I left home without my earrings. Feeling naked, I rushed into Neiman Marcus to the jewelry counter. I stood by a carousel of pearl necklaces, bracelets, and earrings in a black velvet evening gown. I was undecided about changing all my jewelry. After a few minutes, a woman walked up and shoved some clothes into my arms.

"Would you ring these up for me?" she asked.

Incredulous, I said, "What are you talking about? I don't work here." Then she said it again.

"Would you ring these up for me?"

It didn't matter that I was dressed for *Madame Butterfly*, she simply saw a black woman and assumed that I was there to do her bidding. It is the twenty-first century and white folks still expect us to serve.

After a while, these little daily indignities take their toll.

And now I am simply tired of comporting myself to the expectations of white people. I am not going to be superwoman and I am not going to be mammy. Mine is the generation of integration and assimilation. Yet I do not want to be a social experiment any more. Mine is the generation of opportunity. Yet I have never felt so oppressed.

As my friend Ellis Cose writes in *Rage of the Privileged Class,* we've played the game, mastered the rules, and prepared for that corporate seat only to have the prize slipped right out from underneath us.

Discrimination lawsuits are on the rise. Corporate America has made many of us sick enough to seek psychological treatment; others have simply disappeared inside themselves, coming to work as holograms.

"We wear the mask that grins and lies . . ."

But I want you to know it wasn't always this way. Not with once-idealistic me.

My mother was raised in the Mississippi Delta as a sharecropper's daughter. She was an excellent student, fluent in French by the twelfth grade, and a superior orator. She spent her formative years learning how to be deferential to white people. As an adult, she had to be careful not to offend even a white child.

Her race lessons came to me in the form of "Watch what you say" and "Sometimes, you have to take low." That my mother survived with a gentle personality and a positive outlook on life truly shocks me. Yet I learned to suppress my anger and to swallow hypocrisy with a Southern belle sweetness.

My father was raised in East Texas as the child of a man who owned his land, worked for the railroads, and never wanted to be beholden to white people for anything. Grandfather ran white squatters off his land, even under threats of nightly visits from the Klan. He had a voice that could melt butter and a disposition that defied racism at every turn. My father inherited his father's defiance and passed it on to his children. I developed a resistance to being defined by anyone.

It is not easy some days to know which side should respond when race matters. The older I get, the more at odds each side is with the other. They fight for dominance. The contest can be exhausting.

I don't want to be spent on race, completely wrung out from race. I don't want to become a racial invalid, like some friends who rail themselves to sleep at night. They are caught up, 24-7, in what makes the world of white people turn.

I want peace and quiet and an end to this struggle for recognition. It would be nice to burrow inside the comfortable ethnocentric bosom of an all-black middle-class neighborhood. I am for dropping out of the pretense of race relations.

At forty-five, I am not convinced integration made me a smarter, better person, if that was the objective. The better of me seeks just to be. I know that I am run through on race and racism. I know that I am tired of veiled characterizations and of having points to prove. Concealing my passion now seems the best course. This is no place to be a confident black woman who refuses to wear the mask, grin, or lie.

I am tired of race. Bone-weary of thoughts about race. Fatigued by our society's silence about race. Too broken down in spirit to shoulder the mantle of race.

Ira J. Hadnot, *who has been an editor and reporter for the* Dallas Morning News *since 1992, can trace her family's ancestry to eighteenth-century Texas, when Julius and Ellen Hadnot had eight sons. This is no mean feat for an African American, especially one born and raised in Wisconsin. Ira, named for her father, is an uncommon blend of Yankee sensibility, feminist consciousness, sharp ear for politics, and down-home storytelling. This combination has won her numerous journalism awards throughout her career.*

III. Exodus

© Michael T. Klare

Choosing to Be Black—
The Ultimate White Privilege?

BEVERLY DANIEL TATUM

I RECENTLY HAD the opportunity to speak to a group of first-year students at a small selective liberal arts college in New England known for its liberal campus environment. It was the beginning of the new semester, and I was the opening speaker for their orientation program. The auditorium was packed full of the eager and wide-eyed faces so characteristic of the first day of school. It was a diverse group, young men and women, white and of color, sporting a range of hair and clothing styles. While waiting to be introduced, I noticed shaved heads, dreadlocks, hair dyed bright blue and red, bodies pierced in various places, and a slight buzz of excitement that suggested to me that this would be a lively discussion. And in fact it was.

My book, *"Why Are All the Black Kids Sitting Together in the Cafeteria?" and Other Conversations About Race*, had been assigned as required summer reading for all first-year students, and I could tell they were already talking to each other about it. I was eager for them to talk to me about it too, and after a few introductory remarks, I invited them to ask me questions about what I had written.

The first was about affirmative action. A young white woman said that she had read my chapter but was still confused by the concept. Wasn't it really just "reverse racism?" I responded at some length by talking about the many ways that racism still systematically provides white people with greater access to education, employment, housing, quality health care, and media representation, just to name a few examples.

On the blackboard I drew a diagram of a seesaw, one end tilted down, representing the accumulated effect of racial discrimination on people of color, and one end tilted up, representing the elevating effect of white privilege. We need action—affirmative action, I explained, in order for us to reach the ideal of the "level playing field"; in order for us to counter the insidious ways that American cultural messages and institutional policies and practices still benefit white people in educational and employment settings.

I also talked about why at a college, for example, diversity in the student body as well as in the faculty and staff was important, and how students of color need to see themselves represented in their environment just as white students almost always do. It was clear by the heads nodding in the audience that many students agreed with me, but it was certainly not unanimous.

In fact, a young white man standing in the back of the room spoke repeatedly about his belief that the emphasis on race in affirmative action was misplaced. "The issue," he said, "is class, not race." This blond-haired, blue-eyed freshman did not see himself seated on the elevated end of my seesaw. "I grew up in the inner city," he said. "I went to the same crummy schools that the black kids did. Most of my friends were black. What systematic advantage did I have?"

It was a question that I have heard before, and I invited some of his classmates to respond to his comment. They did. Without minimizing the economic struggle that this young man had experienced, classmates, both white and of color, pointed out the benefits that come simply by virtue of skin color—when dealing with the police, when shopping at the mall, when sitting in a class with white professors. One young woman, a Latina, who had attended the same high school as this young man, pointed out the benefit of the tracking system that had disproportionately advantaged the white minority in the school, and the ways whiteness conveys the benefit of the doubt in many situations. But the young man remained unconvinced.

At the conclusion of the evening's presentation, a number of students lingered to ask individual questions, and this young man was among them. When everyone else was gone, he told me more about his experience growing up in a poor family, one of few white children in his neighborhood, the first in his family to go to college. He resented racial categories, and rejected the label white.

As he spoke earnestly about his identification with the black people with whom he had grown up, I couldn't help noticing how literally white he was—his pale skin, blue eyes, and Nordic blond hair. And then he startled me by saying that as his own personal protest against racial categories, when asked to indicate his racial group membership on institutional forms, he always checked the "black" box.

Up to that point, I had been sympathetic to his perspective. The intersection of race and class is not always what the stereotypes would predict. I know that from my own experience. People often assume that because I am black I grew up poor and in an urban ghetto or that I am a first-generation college student. None of these things are true. I grew up in a small, predominantly white New England town in a solidly middle-class family, the daughter of a college professor and an elementary school teacher. Even in my earliest memories of school, I knew I was going to college: there was no question about it. Everyone I knew in my family had.

In fact, not only am I a fourth-generation college graduate, I am a fourth-generation college professor. Education has been the family business since the early days of institutions like Tuskegee Institute and Howard University. I was born in 1954, the year of the *Brown v. Topeka Board of Education* Supreme Court decision outlawing legalized school segregation, and my educational experience is unique in this regard—every school I have attended or taught in has been predominantly white. My children's experience mirrors mine. They are the sons of college-educated parents, both of whom are college professors. They have attended excellent schools, though deficient in the diversity of their student populations.

As I stood talking to this young man, I realized that he was in many ways the polar opposite of my son, also a college freshman at a prestigious New England college. While this young man grew up poor in an inner city, my son has always experienced relative suburban affluence and has had the educational benefits found in that environment. I imagine that both of these young men are excellent students—I know my son is, and I imagine that this young man had to be in order to be admitted to his college. What meaning does race-based affirmative action have in the context of these race and class reversals?

It is a question my own son has asked me. When he was in the tenth grade, he had the opportunity to participate in a summer program designed to encourage students from underrepresented groups to pursue careers in science. It was not for students of color exclusively— white students from isolated rural areas were included in the definition of underrepresented groups—but clearly the majority of the participants were of color. My son read the materials describing the program, concluded that it was designed for disadvantaged youth, and questioned its appropriateness for him. "I am not disadvantaged," he said.

"It is true that you are not economically disadvantaged," I replied, "but as a young black male, you are underrepresented, and that is a different kind of disadvantage."

Our class status provides many benefits but it does not protect my children from the relative absence of positive images of black men and women in the curriculum or in the media. It does not protect them from the assumptions others make about them solely on the basis of their skin color, reflected in women's nervous clutching of purses or the sounds of automatic door locks on cars as they pass by. It does not protect them from teachers who don't know their parents and who may make erroneous assumptions about their ability or potential as "troublemakers." It does not protect them from the real threat of a deadly encounter with police officers. It does not give them the benefit of the doubt that white skin so often conveys.

Of what value is the benefit of the doubt? Priceless? Certainly its value is frequently underestimated and perhaps more often completely unacknowledged by white people.

This point was brought home to me in a 1994 study conducted by a Mount Holyoke graduate student, Phyllis Wentworth.[1] Wentworth interviewed a group of female college students, who were both older than their peers and the first members of their families to attend college, about the pathways that led them there. All of them were white and from working-class families where women were expected to graduate from high school and get married or get a job. Several had experienced abusive relationships and other personal difficulties prior to coming to college. But I was struck repeatedly by the "good luck" stories they told: stories of apartments obtained without a deposit, good jobs offered without experience or extensive reference checks, encouragement provided by willing mentors.

While the women acknowledged their good fortune, none of them discussed their whiteness. They had not considered the possibility that being white had worked in their favor, that being white had served to give them the "benefit of the doubt" at critical junctures. This study clearly showed that even under difficult circumstances, white privilege still operated.

While I respected the young man's sincere discomfort with the "white" label society forces him to wear, I resented his unwillingness to acknowledge the racial privilege that comes with it, whether he wants it or not. Choosing the "black" box does not change that.

But what did this young man really hope to convey by choosing the black box? Was he being a "race traitor," as Noel Ignatiev would call him? Ignatiev and his coeditor John Garvey wrote in the inaugural issue of their journal *Race Traitor*, "The existence of the white race depends on the willingness of those assigned to it to place their racial interests above class, gender, or any other interests they hold. The defection of enough of its members to make it unreliable as a determinant of behavior will set off tremors that will lead to its collapse. . . . *Treason to whiteness is loyalty to humanity.*"[2] I'm not sure that my conversation partner had ever heard of Noel Ignatiev, John Garvey, or their journal, but it was clear he wanted to defect. Why?

One reason is that the label "white" did not convey to the world his economic struggle as someone who had endured a life of poverty. Calling himself black was a statement about that pain. Was it also an expression of solidarity with those whose poverty and neighborhood he had shared? I suspect it was, and in that sense his desire to be an ally is commendable. But can one really be an effective ally without acknowledging one's privilege?

His escape from his inferior high school and the poverty of his neighborhood to the private college campus where we both stood was made statistically more likely by his white skin, and, as an ally, I expected him to acknowledge that. I now wonder what he expected from me. Did he want a greater acknowledgment of my class privilege than I was willing to make?

As we stood there engaged in our dialogue, we embodied our multiple identities—he is white (however reluctantly), male, poor, young— I am black, female, middle class, middle aged. I am also heterosexual, Christian, and currently able-bodied. I don't know how this young man identified on those dimensions—but it was clear that each of us was speaking from the part of our identity where we have felt the most targeted. He wanted to emphasize class. I wanted to emphasize race. Our conflict was not surprising.

In her essay, "Age, Race, Class, and Sex: Women Redefining Difference," Audre Lorde captured the tensions between dominant and targeted identities coexisting in one individual. This self-described "forty-nine-year-old Black lesbian feminist socialist mother of two" wrote:

> Somewhere, on the edge of consciousness, there is what I call a *mythical norm*, which each one of us within our hearts knows "that is not me." In America, this norm is usually defined as white, thin, male, young, heterosexual, Christian, and financially secure. It is with this mythical norm that the trappings of power reside within society. Those of us who stand outside that power often identify one way in which we are different, and we assume that to be the primary cause of all oppression, forgetting other distortions around difference, some of which we ourselves may be practicing.[3]

It is easy to feel impatient with white people who appear not to recognize their white skin privilege. But my own impatience is tempered when I remember how much of my life I spent oblivious to the daily advantages I receive simply because I am heterosexual, or the ways in which I may take my class privilege for granted. I know I am still a work in progress, capable of distorting others' differences, but that did not change the fact that I was irritated by this young man's choice to check the black box.

Why did his decision so bother me? In the context of our conversation, it symbolized to me the essence of unacknowledged privilege. He said he was making the choice because he felt he had more in common with black people than with whites, but could the situation be reversed? Could a black person who had grown up in white neighborhoods and felt identified with white cultural norms and experiences realistically choose the "white" box? What would happen if someone did? Historically we know what has happened.

Consider the case of Susie Guillory Phipps, a Louisiana woman who checked the wrong box. In 1983 she was denied a passport because she had checked white on the passport application although her birth certificate designated her race as "colored." She was a victim of the "one-drop rule," the legal and social practice that classified anyone with known African ancestry as "black," or in this case "colored," and reserved the label "white" only for those with no known African ancestry. In this instance, the "colored" designation had been made by the midwife who delivered her, presumably based on her knowledge of the family's status in the community; but the information came as a shock to Mrs. Phipps, who had always considered herself white.

She asked the Louisiana courts to change the classification on her deceased parents' birth certificates to "white" so that she and her siblings could be legally designated as "white." They all appeared to be white, and some were blue-eyed blondes. At the time, Louisiana law indicated that anyone whose ancestry was more than one thirty-second black was categorized as black. In this case, the lawyers for the state claimed to have proof that Mrs. Phipps was three thirty-seconds black, which was more than enough African ancestry to justify her parents' classification as "colored." Consequently, she and her siblings were legally black.

The case was decided in May 1983, and in June the state legislature gave parents the right to designate the race of newborns themselves rather than relying on the doctor or midwife's assessment. In the case of previous misclassification, parents were given the right to change their child's racial designation to "white" if they could prove the child's whiteness by a "preponderance of the evidence."

But the 1983 statute did not abolish the one-drop rule. In fact, when Mrs. Phipps appealed the case, the state's Fourth Circuit of Appeals upheld the lower court's decision, concluding that the preponderance of the evidence was that her parents were indeed "colored." In 1986, when the case was appealed to the Louisiana Supreme Court and then to the U.S. Supreme Court, both courts refused to review the decision, in effect leaving the one-drop rule untouched.[4]

The case of Mrs. Phipps is not unique: a lot of so-called white people have unacknowledged African ancestry, while it is estimated that 75 to 90 percent of black Americans have white European ancestry and about 25 percent have Native American heritage. Most biologists and physical anthropologists tell us that racial categories are social constructions that have little biological meaning.

Though populations from particular geographic regions can be distinguished from each other by commonly occurring physical traits such as hair texture, skin tone, facial structure, or blood type, there is no such thing as a "pure" race. *All* human populations are "mixed" populations. Yet the categories have power because they have been imbued with social meaning. Does checking the "wrong" box change that social meaning or challenge the social inequities that have so long been associated with our systems of racial classification?

I know that for many reasons, perhaps most notably the dramatic increase in biracial children being raised in multiracial families, the use of those boxes is in flux. In reality we could all check new and unexpected boxes—but without a commitment to other strategies for social transformation, our systems of social inequity remain unchanged, and ultimately that is my concern.

I know this conversation has not ended. The young man took my e-mail address, and I fully expect to hear from him. When I do, I will introduce him to the work of David Wellman, a white sociologist who grew up in a black neighborhood in Detroit. In an autobiographical essay about identity, Wellman wrote: "Until recently, my racial identity had no name I would answer to. Whiteness was never an unmarked category for me. I've not taken my whiteness for granted, or experienced it as normal, invisible. My self-conception has been in a permanent state of war with the socially constructed version of who I'm supposed to be."[5]

Like that of my young friend, Wellman's construction of his life experience did not fit with the white label. But there is a crucial difference: Wellman has recognized the inescapability of his privilege. Describing himself as a "border person," one who has learned to juggle cultures and move between multiple communities in a pluralistic world, he acknowledges the privilege embedded even in this identity, writing: "The borders I live on are porous. My crossings are opportunities as well as options. I can choose to live on borders, or avoid them. That choice is privilege, even when experienced as pain. My colleagues of color don't choose border identities. They can't refuse them either. And they can't move between them as easily as do I. The elements of choice and privilege in my life mean I cannot be otherized in the same way as people of color."[6]

That is the point I want this young man to understand. Wellman's awareness comes from experience and thoughtful, sometimes painful, reflection. Mine does too.

Perhaps my young friend and I will never come to an agreement on this point, but it was a conversation worth having. We are all works in progress.

---

[1] P. A. Wentworth, *The Identity Development of Non-Traditionally Aged First-Generation Women College Students: An Exploratory Study* (Master's thesis, Department of Psychology and Education, Mount Holyoke College, South Hadley, MA, 1994).

[2] John Garvey and Noel Ignatiev, "Editorial: Abolish the White Race—By Any Means Necessary," *Race Traitor,* 1:1 (1993); 1–8.

[3] Audre Lorde, "Age, Race, Class, and Sex: Women Redefining Difference," in P. Rothenberg (Ed.), *Race, Class, and Gender in the United States: An Integrated Study (3rd ed.)* (New York: St. Martin's Press, 1995), p. 446.

[4] See F. J. Davis, *Who Is Black? One Nation's Definition* (University Park, PA: Pennsylvania State University Press, 1991), chapters 1 and 2.

[5] David Wellman, "Red and Black in White America," in B. Thompson and S. Tyagi (eds.), *Names We Call Home: Autobiography on Racial Identity* (New York: Routledge, 1996), p. 29.

[6] Ibid., p. 38.

Beverly Daniel Tatum's book "Why Are All the Black Kids Sitting Together in the Cafeteria?" And Other Conversations About Race *(Revised Edition, Basic Books, 1999) hit bookstores just as President Clinton's "Initiative on Race" was taking shape. Shortly after the book's release, Tatum became one of three authors to appear with Clinton at his national town meeting on race in Akron, Ohio.*

A renowned authority on the psychology of racism, Tatum uses real life examples and the latest research to illustrate how we can—and why we must—overcome the barriers that stymie conversations about race.

Appointed to the Mount Holyoke College faculty in 1989, Tatum is a dean, a professor of psychology, a clinical psychologist, and a highly sought-after consultant and trainer. She and her work were featured prominently in the New York Times *"Living Race in America" series in 2000.*

© Felicia Gustin

White Like Me: Race and Identity Through Majority Eyes

TIM WISE

"How else except by becoming a Negro could a white man hope to learn the truth. . . . The best way to find out if we had second-class citizens, and what their plight was, would be to become one of them . . ."

THOUSANDS OF HIGH school students read these words every year, having been assigned the classic from which they come: *Black Like Me* by John Howard Griffin. Teachers are especially quick to assign the book to white students, in the hopes that it may get them to think seriously about the issue of race in America. Black students, who by then pretty well understand what it means to be perceived as the racial "other," are less likely to require such an instructional. But for us whites—only 12 percent of whom, according to surveys, will have significant interactions with African Americans while growing up—this reality-based novel is often our first exposure to a real discussion of racism and its consequences.

As the reader of *Black Like Me* learns, its author took skin-darkening medication and traveled throughout the Jim Crow South in 1959 to learn first hand the viciousness of our nation's apartheid system. His descriptions of the crushing weight of racial oppression were stark, and caused a minor furor when first published nearly forty years ago.

Yet I can't help but find it interesting that America has taken so well to Griffin's words while largely ignoring the most obvious irony of his work: namely, that for whites to take seriously the words of a black man writing about his experiences, those words had to be written not by a black man at all, but rather a white man only posing as black until the drugs wore off.

Though plenty of flesh-and-blood black men—not to mention more than a few black women—could have enlightened us as to "whether we had second-class citizens, and what their plight was," it was Griffin to whom white America turned for the bad news. Though the work of Baldwin, Wright, Ellison, Hurston, Hughes, and dozens of others were available then and still are today to help whites learn "the truth," it is rare that we digest the words of such folks, no matter how eloquent. We are much more comfortable listening to one of our own describe the reality of others. It's more believable, one suspects, coming from family.

Perhaps even more important, *Black Like Me* is based on the premise that whites can only learn what racism does to its victims by reflecting on what it means to be one of them—to be black, for example, which we can never fully accomplish in any event—as opposed to what it means to be exactly what we are: white, in a system established by people like us for people like us.

I would imagine it far more meaningful for young whites to read a book entitled *White Like Me*, since it is as whites in this culture that said readers must live. Fully understanding one's own position in society is perhaps the clearest way to truly appreciate the position of others. But of course neither *Black Like Me* nor any other book on the typical student's reading list encourages whites to think about what it means to be a member of the dominant racial group, or indeed, to think of race as his or her issue at all.

This unfortunate tendency to think of race as merely a black or brown issue is at the root of much of the white condition today: one that renders us largely impotent when discussing issues of race, identity, and our place in a white supremacist system. Indeed, it is our inability to conceive of race as fundamentally about *us* that makes it impossible for most whites to even comprehend that the system is, in fact, white supremacist. We think of white supremacy as something preached by the Klan, skinheads, or neo-Nazis, rather than as the default position of American institutions since day one. And when it comes to our own complicity with the maintenance of said system—well, it is there that the discussion falls apart altogether.

Yet I wouldn't want to give the impression that I have always understood this matter: for indeed, there was a time, not all that long ago, when I most certainly did not.

It seems like only yesterday, though in fact it has been over ten years now: the third day of a hunger strike intended to persuade the trustees of Tulane University in New Orleans to divest from companies still doing business in what was then white-ruled, apartheid South Africa.

There I was, one of two representatives from the campus anti-apartheid organization, debating two defenders of continued investments in South Africa who claimed that blacks there would be harmed by a corporate exodus.

The debate itself was no real challenge: my colleague and I had little trouble convincing the audience that Tulane was financially and symbolically on the side of white racist rule. Events like this always had the effect of stroking my ego and enhancing my reputation as the school's primary "campus radical," and this was to have been no exception.

No exception, that is, until the closing minutes of the question-and-answer period, after the formal debate had ended. It was then that a young African American woman rose from the audience to speak. She began by noting that she was a freshman at Xavier University: the nation's only historically black Catholic institution of higher learning, located about a mile away. Further, she was appalled that Tulane still invested in apartheid-complicit firms, and as a New Orleanian she said she was embarrassed by that fact.

Sensing a friendly, softball kind of question on the way, I smiled, nodded, and basked in confidence about what I assumed would come next. And this, as it turns out, was a terrible mistake. For it was then that she turned to me, and asked something for which I was not the least bit prepared. After inquiring as to how long I had lived in New Orleans, and hearing my reply—four years—she asked, as if she already knew the answer (and indeed she probably did), "Tim, in the four years that you have lived in this city, *what one thing have you done to address and ultimately eliminate de facto apartheid here in New Orleans? Especially since, being white, you have benefited from that apartheid?*"

I cannot adequately describe the feeling that came over me at that moment, but it was not unlike the feeling one gets upon noticing the flashing blue lights in the rearview mirror. The lights that say, you *thought* you were going to get away with that move you just pulled, speeding through here like no one would notice, but now we've *got you*, so pull your ass over and start explaining.

And just like the motorist caught speeding on radar, I was busted. And just like the last time I actually got a ticket for speeding, I spent a few panicked seconds trying to figure out what clever answer I could offer that might allow me to escape the trouble into which I had stepped.

And just like the last lame excuse I gave to a traffic cop, my response to this young woman was so pitiful I can barely stand to repeat it. After stumbling around for a few seconds, I found myself saying something to the effect of, "Well, you know, we all pick our battles." This was an answer that, even as it escaped my lungs—before that, in fact, as the syntax formed in my brain—I knew was beyond bullshit. I had been called out, and I knew it. What's more, about three hundred other people knew it too. Until that moment, I had given no thought to what now seemed obvious: namely, that I had done exactly nothing to address the evil in my backyard—an evil that was linked to the one half a globe away in South Africa, and from which I did indeed prosper, but which I had largely ignored, despite the obvious connections.

I can't remember how the rest of the night went. I only recall leaving the debate, returning to the shantytown we had built in front of the administration building, and trying not to deal with what had just happened. But as days became weeks (and the hunger strike mercifully ended), I was faced with a reality I had never anticipated. I began to realize that despite my activism, despite my good intentions, despite how "down" I perceived myself to be with the cause of justice, I was still part of the problem. I was actively receiving the perks of whiteness, and collaborating with the system of white supremacy, whether I liked it or not. Every day in which I had attended class in this white school, set up by plantation owners for the children of plantation owners, in the midst of this black city, and remained silent about the myriad injustices taking place all around me, I had been implicated in them. And graduation would not release me, for that implication was only manifested most recently at Tulane. In actuality it was far more interwoven into the tapestry of my life than I had realized.

To take inventory of one's life is not an easy thing, and I'm sure I have forgotten ten times more than I actually can recall. Nonetheless, when I finally sat down to take stock—something I felt I had to do now that the veil had been snatched from over my eyes—I was stunned by how many things began to come back to me; how many examples of privilege flooded my consciousness; how many times I could remember collaborating with racism.

Privilege. It had been waiting for me, even before I had entered the world, to be handed down by a family that was not wealthy, to be sure, but had obtained significant advantages: parents who attended segregated schools, in the best parts of town, where only they could live; a grandfather who had graduated from an elite university in 1942, at a time when blacks could only hope to sweep the floors there; another grandfather who, upon retiring from active military duty, was able to climb the ranks of the civil service at a time when people of color—even veterans—were routinely relegated to menial positions; families that had been able to obtain property that was strictly off limits to those with dark skin.

It had been there on my third day of life, when we moved into an apartment complex in an upper-middle-class area of our hometown: a complex from which, we would learn, blacks were excluded—legally at first, and then, after the Fair Housing Act went into effect, by custom and subterfuge.

It had been there when one of my black classmates and I disrupted a reading lesson the first week of first grade, and only he was punished, though I had been the primary instigator of the morning's chaos.

It had been there in the repeated placement of me and virtually all the white students on the advanced track, and the parallel placement of most of the black kids on the remedial track: a placement that would follow us throughout our school years, no matter our promise or potential.

It had been there in middle school, when the drama club—of which I was an integral part—put on play after play with no black characters, thereby forcing blacks interested in drama either to work the lights, pull the curtains, build the sets, or more likely just receive the message that theatre was not for them: one more option foreclosed.

It had been there in the afternoons of sixth grade, when our English teacher would signal to those of us in the "honors" program, and we would quietly yet conspicuously rise and leave the previously mixed-race class. We would depart like a receding tide of pink skin, disrupting the learning of those left behind, as we made tracks for the enriched educational experience that was waiting down the hall for us, the chosen few.

It had been there throughout high school as this process of tracking and sorting continued, to my benefit, no matter how lousy my grades were; no matter that I cheated—that's right, cheated—my way through four years, *and got caught repeatedly*, but suffered no punishment as a result.

It had been there in the curriculum: literature, history, civics, economics. No matter the subject, the lesson was clear: everything wonderful, everything good, everything worth knowing about had emerged from the foreheads of those who were *white like me*. Even the discussions of racism, to the extent they existed, mostly concerned noble whites who had rushed in to save blacks, either individually or collectively: the fictional Atticus Finch in *To Kill a Mockingbird*, or Huck Finn "rescuing" Jim, or Abe Lincoln "freeing the slaves," who, one would gather from reading the approved texts, did almost nothing to liberate themselves. And, of course, there was *Black Like Me*.

Privilege had been there when I got my first job at a local grocery, extended to me because my grandmother put in a good word with the store owner: a man who would openly discuss not wishing to hire too many blacks, or to accept food stamps, because doing so might attract "those people."

It had been there when parties I attended in white neighborhoods were broken up by police because of noise complaints, and yet those same officers would overlook the flagrant underage drinking and drug use in ways they surely would not have done had we been black.

It had been there when I was caught skipping school the month before graduation—a violation that could have resulted in my suspension and jeopardized my college plans—yet was cut slack by a vice-principal who knew I was lying to him about why I wasn't in class, but who, with a wink and a nod, simply told me not to let it happen again.

It had been there when recruiters from Tulane had seen fit to travel 540 miles to pluck me out of Nashville and bring me to their school, but couldn't seem to find the time to walk two blocks from campus to Fortier High and recruit black children, whose parents were apparently good for cleaning Tulane toilets, and cooking Tulane food, and cutting Tulane grass, and collecting Tulane garbage, but not for raising Tulane graduates.

Indeed, it had been there even in my activism: the quickness with which local media and school administrators fixed on me as the "leader" of the antiapartheid movement, even though when we had started our coalition had been mostly made up of black students. And it was there when the movement—which had initially linked divestment to other issues such as enhancing affirmative action and resurrecting the Black Studies Department—became focused solely on South Africa, thereby emphasizing the issue with which whites, including myself, were probably more comfortable. (And to think I had been perplexed about why the black students drifted away from the movement!)

And it had been there in the cavalier attitudes we white activists expressed about potentially getting arrested for our protests if need be, and going on hunger strike: two things that didn't appear so romantic to black students. After all, in New Orleans going to jail if you were black was a very different experience, and you couldn't as readily count on parents to come and bail you out. And voluntary hunger was just plain stupid: the choice of someone whose privilege could be counted on to tide them over to the next meal.

And it wasn't just the privileges and advantages that I remembered, but the silences as well; the times I had sat back and said nothing despite knowing that I was surrounded by racial injustice—injustice that was operating to my benefit.

As I had been settling into my freshman dorm, acclimating to a life of privileged academia, down the road in neighboring Jefferson Parish, Sheriff Harry Lee—a Chinese American loved by whites for his aggressively antiblack attitude—had been issuing orders to his deputies to stop and search cars driven by black males who appeared "out of place." This was in 1986, before the term "racial profiling" was part of the American lexicon, and Lee was openly admitting his plans to harass black motorists. At one point, he even proposed to erect barricades between the two parishes to keep blacks out.

Yet amid the obvious turmoil and racial division that beset the community where I now lived, I had looked on most of it with morbid curiosity and little more. I had not seen the fight against even such blatant racism in my backyard as my fight, as something to which I needed to lend my voice. I had not seen the flipside of Harry Lee's call for vehicular apartheid: namely, that I would be on the winning end of that equation, able to traverse the border between Orleans and Jefferson Parishes without fear or trepidation. That I was, indeed, welcome into whichever part of the metropolitan area I felt like visiting.

And I had remained quiet during freshman orientation, when school officials went to great lengths to warn incoming freshmen about the "dangerous" parts of the city, which, of course, were all black and poor areas, though the whiter spaces might have been considered dangerous for students of color. Our school certainly didn't warn African Americans about Harry Lee, nor the New Orleans police, who, as I would come to know in my time there, were among the most brutal of any in the nation toward black citizens.

And I had remained quiet, even when I overheard another white student—the head of Tulane's Volunteer Literacy program, which operated in black elementary schools—remark in class that the kids he was working with were cute while they were young, but that in a few years they would become "niggers." That silence has haunted me ever since, as it should. As it should haunt any white person who has taken a pass or rain check on challenging even the most blatant bigotry, or responded to it with nervous laughter, hoping that the moment would pass.

While reflecting on these things, as well as others, I found myself wondering how I could have been so blind, so quiet. After all, I had always prided myself on being different from other white folks. Hadn't my mother intentionally enrolled me in a mostly black preschool? And hadn't that made me more sensitive to these issues? Hadn't I been the white kid whose friends for the first six years of school were mostly black? Wasn't I the white child who had received snide looks and comments from white teachers, appalled by my close association with African Americans, and the way I would "code switch" between "standard" and "black" English? Wasn't I the white child whose mom had helped remove a racist teacher from her position after she made a comment about black children being "monkeys" and "savages"? Wasn't I the one verbally attacked as a "nigger lover" by angry white kids when my mostly black baseball team showed up in their rural community to play a scrimmage? And hadn't that experience bound me to people of color in a way that would prevent me from ever collaborating with their oppression?

The answers, as it turns out, were both yes and no. Yes, I was all of those things. But despite that upbringing; despite the values with which I had been raised; despite the experiences that had often placed me on the nonwhite side of the color line in the eyes of many in my own community; despite all this, I had been, in myriad ways, no different or better than any other white person. My "color-blindness," if you will, had rendered me, in a strange and fascinating way, blind to the consequences of color, especially my own. I was one of those whites who could say they had black friends—and in my case even mean it—and yet was mostly oblivious to the ways in which I was being conditioned and played by the system to accept, without even noticing, the perquisites of my racial identity.

I can proudly say that my mother had that racist teacher removed so she would never poison the minds of young children again, and yet must also recognize that the classes to which I returned after her removal, by virtue of preferring those who were white like me, had the effect of teaching the same lesson as that racist educator: namely, that black and brown children were lesser; that I was better; that they were "savages." The institution could impart that lesson—and did so with unparalleled efficiency—with or without the help of Mrs. Crownover.

And make no mistake: by junior high, all of my black friends—the ones with whom I had been closest for the previous six grades—had gotten the message, even if I had not. The perennial mistreatment in the schools we shared laid the groundwork for the substantial pulling away that was to follow; a separation that would last throughout high school as old friends were reduced to formalistic and largely meaning-less gestures of recognition as we passed in the halls: a nod of the head, a monotone "what's up," but rarely more. And it wasn't my fault, nor was it theirs. It was the inevitable result of institutional inequity; it was the logical outcome of being treated so differently by the same institu-tions that we no longer shared the same experiences, no longer thought about the same things in the same way.

And it was seeing how racism actually ripped apart my close friend-ships and distorted my connections to other human beings that led me to realize that racism and white supremacy carry a cost: mostly for the victims, of course, but also for the perpetrators and collaborators. That is to say, in accepting the bargain of institutional privilege, whites set in motion a process that ultimately harms us as well. And frankly, this is something about which anyone should be outraged.

Because outrage is the only proper response to the realization that a system set up by someone else has cost you some of the dearest friends you ever had. It is the only proper response when you realize that you have occasionally waded into the pool of racism yourself, like when you do what *all white people have done* (or will eventually do) when they find themselves in a black neighborhood—that is, check to see if the car door is locked, and if it isn't, try and lock it without anyone notic-ing you. And you have done this not because you are an evil bigot, but because you have been fed a steady diet of manipulated images, and have picked up the things society threw at you, the way two pieces of Velcro fit together.

Outrage is the only proper response to the recognition that we have been cheated by those who thought they were doing us a favor by offer-ing that head start: cheated in that too many of us now find ourselves unable to engage in serious and meaningful discussions with people of color, because beneath the surface we *know* what has gone down and, more to the point, we know that *they* know it far better than we do.

Outrage is the only logical emotion in the face of a society that encourages you to cut yourself off from a sense of a common humanity and instead live a lie. Because living that lie does truly horrible things to those living it, things they often don't realize until it is too late.

In my own family I have seen this play out more clearly than I could have ever imagined. I can see what the lie of whiteness did to my Jewish great-grandfather, who came to the United States from Russia in 1910 to start a new life for his family. Little did he know that the "price of the ticket," as James Baldwin might put it, would be the sloughing off of most of the meaningful traditions that had kept that same family alive, all for the sake of assimilation and upward mobility.

To become American had meant, for him and so many other Jews, Italians, Irish, and other despised European ethnics, to become white: to give up what one was in order to become what one was not, but yet had to be in order to gain acceptance. So when my grandfather—his son—was in the final week of his life, trying desperately to conjure up some story, some seminal event handed down to him by his family, some tale of what it meant to be Jewish, Russian, an immigrant, he could think of nothing to say. For that silence is what he had been given. To get along, to move up, to succeed, one had to put away the old ways, speak differently, act differently, fit in, and make others comfortable. And that is what so many Jews, my family included, did. Surely the proper response to this assimilation, which did in fact provide Jews with so much privilege, is not guilt at having undergone it, but outrage at having been forced to take the bait.

And this thing called racism has done some other strange things to white people, or at least the notion of white supremacy has. For one, it leads us to regularly sacrifice our own well being on the altar of a truly bizarre form of racial bonding.

Like the way the elderly Jewish woman told me, without even the slightest hesitation, that she would be voting for David Duke—the lifelong neo-Nazi—for U.S. Senate, because, after all, he would "get rid of all the *schvartzes*."

Like the way whites of Italian and Irish descent made Duke a regular attraction in their parades in New Orleans and nearby Metairie, despite the fact that both groups had faced vicious ethnic oppression in this land and, in fact, were often lynched, beaten, and killed by folks with Duke's ideology, precisely because they were viewed as white "niggers." That Duke had once said Sicilians—who make up the majority of Italians in the region—were intellectually inferior to Northern Europeans was of little consequence to his supporters, so long as he was promising to get tough with blacks.

Like the way whites with barely a pot to piss in defended their much wealthier Caucasian brethren in New Orleans when a black city councilwoman insisted the elite Mardi Gras Krewes' continued racial segregation was illegal, given the city's substantial subsidizing of carnival. That these Krewes would no more invite the trailer and tin-roof crowd to join their precious clubs than they would a person of color hardly mattered, as the minions of the white working class lined the streets of parade after parade, holding signs demanding "Hands Off Mardi Gras," and inviting the councilwoman—Dorothy Mae Taylor—to take a slow boat back to the Motherland.

Like the way Southern whites from the lowest rungs of the economic ladder are the ones most likely to fly the Confederate flag from the back of their vehicles or insist on the legitimacy of the flag as a symbol of Southern heritage; this despite the fact that it represents an army of a government that thought little of the interests of such "white trash." After all, poor whites were forced to go fight and die while the wealthy could skip out of service if they owned enough slaves. And the Southern elite whipped the white working class into war frenzy over the perceived threat of eventual emancipation and the possibility of blacks becoming free labor. This despite the fact that so long as blacks could be forced to work for nothing, the wages of those same white workers were obviously being held down and their own labor undercut. They had no interest in common with the slave owners who wanted and needed secession: no interest, that is, except the common bond of skin.

For, as DuBois and others have noted, there was and is a "psychological wage" to whiteness that allows whites to overlook the very real harms that stem from our continued fealty to white supremacy, so long as we can content ourselves with the notion that we are better than someone else: that there is someone or some group below us.

This is why, time after time, white workers have turned against workers of color for ostensibly "taking our jobs" instead of joining with them to improve wages and work conditions for all. It is why whites are willing to build more and more prisons to warehouse black and brown bodies—mostly for nonviolent offenses—even if it means less money is available to educate their own children. It is why whites will vote against improving public transportation service between the cities and suburbs, so as to limit people of color's access to our communities, even though by doing so we consign ourselves to longer work commutes and much higher gas and car maintenance bills.

But perhaps most disturbing of all, to be white in the United States is to be privileged yet largely unaware of just how broad one's choices are—including the choice of turning against the system that bestows privileges in the first place. Whites have done this in the past, but this is not widely discussed either in history books or in the personal family histories handed down from generation to generation, and that's a shame, for the stories are worth telling.

Whites could, after all, choose to follow the example of Ellsberry Ambrose, a yeoman farmer from North Carolina who agitated against the Confederacy and told farmers they should oppose secession and the war because only the elite would benefit.

We could follow the lead of the small yet vocal group of whites in Georgia who opposed slavery on moral grounds and petitioned the King as early as 1738 to ban the institution.

We could follow the example of white abolitionists across the new nation, like Angelina Grimke and John Brown.

We could carry the banner of modern-day white antiracists who demonstrated that there was more than one way to live in this skin: folks like Bob Zellner, the first white field secretary of the Student Non-Violent Coordinating Committee; or Carolyn Daniels, a Georgia beautician who housed SNCC workers at great risk to her own safety; or Anne Braden, whose fight against American apartheid has spanned the better part of the last half century and is chronicled in part in her classic book *The Wall Between*; or Will Campbell, the unassuming preacher and theologian who has bravely stood against the system of white privilege and the epidemic of white denial through some of the darkest days of reactionary racist violence.

That we don't know most of these names, or those of the others I could list, is an indication of just how little our people venerate their real heroes, or for that matter understand heroism at all. More to the point, our ignorance in this matter is an indication of what little regard the dominant culture has for those who challenge the prerogatives of dominance itself.

Of course, it makes perfect sense that whites would rather not think about our unflattering history: surely most persons of European descent would rather not discuss their families' role in the slave trade, or Indian genocide, or any number of other untoward historical episodes. But more than that, I have found, at least in my own family's history—on my mother's side in particular—a marked tendency to limit even the conception of what qualifies as *flattering* history: the kind all families like to tell.

It has never ceased to amaze me how white folks will go to any lengths to show their direct lineage to some obscure King or Queen of England or some largely irrelevant Scottish Count. No matter how tenuous the connection, no matter what the royalty in question actually stood for, or how they governed, it is as if simply being related to such persons makes one better, smarter, more honorable, and worthy of respect.

In the history of my mother's father's family—the McLeans—the pattern has been amply repeated, to a point that would be laughable were it not so sad. Any association with famous people, even no more direct than one of our ancestors having sat in a room with someone who knew someone who once played cards with Davy Crockett—manages to find its way into the narrative of the family history. The McLeans are lauded for their large landholdings, their great courage in warfare (has one *ever* heard a tale of one's cowardice in wartime?), and their supposedly benevolent ownership of other human beings. And of course, in the case of these latter family members—or rather property—their stories remain untold by the "Clan McLean," being considered no more relevant than the story behind any other possession, like, say, the family footstool.

Yet also missing is the description of one of the maverick family members: a nineteenth-century abolitionist who was able to convince her parents to free their slaves because, she explained, the institution was evil. Why would such a person's story be left out? A brief bio-graphical sketch of the woman in question does indeed appear in a recently compiled family history, yet somehow this minor detail remained on the cutting room floor, so to speak. It seems that to some, remembering trivial details and romanticizing life "down on the farm" is more important than honoring a person so brave as to stand up to her family and the institution of slavery at the same time. Perhaps it is feared that by honoring such dissidents, the rest of the family is cast into a particularly dim light. Nonetheless, if such stories are never told, how are young whites to ever get the sense that they have a real choice? How are they to know that they can opt for a different kind of iden-tity? How might they come to realize that being "white" does not require one to think, feel, or behave in a certain way?

Of course, the answer is that they won't. And in the long run, that might be exactly why those stories don't get told. To tell them would be anything but functional for the extant system, those who have benefited from that system, and those who continue to do so. To valorize dissent, rebellion, and equality would be to cast aspersions on those who have conformed, remained loyal to injustice, and collaborated with the main-tenance of inequality.

Now the irony here is that even the best white person in this kind of system is in fact both of these: at times a dissident, and at other moments a collaborator; at once a rebel and yet also a loyal soldier. And unless we root out the social conditioning that forces us so often into the latter of these twin roles, we will continue to undermine our best efforts at real change and an end to white supremacy.

It is time that we faced what it means to be white, what it means for those who are not members of the club, and what we intend to do about it: what we intend to do to create a new identity that is not based on privilege and position, what we intend to do to make resistance more common and lasting than collaboration. For surely we should know by now what the cost of our continued silence will be.

Tim (Timothy Jacob) Wise, thirty-one, is a busy man as one of the nation's leading young social critics and a popular speaker on the lecture circuit. A social justice activist since age fourteen, Wise has spoken to over 75,000 peo-ple in forty-two states, and on more than 200 college and high school cam-

puses, defending affirmative action; challenging institutional racism in education, employment, and the criminal justice system; and responding to contemporary assaults on poor and working class persons of all races.

Wise is the author of Little White Lies: The Truth About Affirmative Action and Reverse Discrimination *(Loyola University, 1995). His opinion columns are syndicated by the progressive op-ed service, AlterNet. He has appeared on hundreds of radio and TV programs, and is a regular contributor to the Znet Commentary program, an online editorial distribution service for leading left and radical thinkers.*

A Tulane University graduate, Wise lives and writes in Nashville, Tennessee.

© Eleanor M. Hamilton

Traveling with White People

COLLEEN J. McELROY

ONE EVENING—I must have been about five or six—I went with my grandfather for an early evening stroll before night and total darkness. We were giving the dog some exercise—and myself, if I could keep up. I skipped along to match my grandfather, his long legs taking giant steps. It must have been spring, because I don't remember a coat or galoshes weighing me down. It was warm—that much I can recall. And the dog trotted in front of us, stopping now and then to sniff a tree or a bush, a collie like Lassie, with a long, sharp nose and blond coat. We called him Rex. The air was thick with the smell of fresh-cut grass, especially when we passed the all-white cemetery. "None of our folks in there," my grandmother would say.

When we passed the cemetery, I could smell the wet grass, watered twice a day in hot weather. So it must have been spring, what with the smell of wet grass, and the dog rustling the privet hedges bordering yards with more grass and flowers. And sometimes I could see parts of the backyards where grape arbors would bloom later in the summer, when the bees gathered. But the bees weren't there yet, not in the spring, nor the fireflies. "C'mon, let's go chase the fireflies. Ten feet around my base is *it*," we'd call in a game of hide and seek.

But that evening, I was walking with my grandfather, walking the dog for exercise. And we were way outside of the safe zone.

"Don't you let me catch you on the other side of Natural Bridge Road," my grandmother would warn. I walked with my grandfather across the wide avenue, into the forbidden zone, the deliciously dangerous streets that would mean punishment if I went there alone.

Up close, they seemed so ordinary, no different from the streets where I lived. The same brick houses set back in postage-stamp yards. The same lampposts that would let off dirty yellow light once full night filled up the sky. Here and there, a porch swing. Here and there, a backyard with a clothes line still holding the day's wash.

Curtains hugged windows, porch lights were on, everything was regular—everything but Grandpa holding onto Rex's leash like he was scared Rex would run away, Rex, who wouldn't leave the yard unless you begged him. Except when my grandfather came home—then Rex was ready to go, and so was I. If Grandpa hadn't been holding my hand, I would have been running alongside the dog.

Two blocks, three blocks, four, and we heard a voice. "Hey mister."

A white boy sat on a porch. I can't remember if he was doing anything or if he was just sitting there, that evening in spring before the weather was warm enough for fireflies. It doesn't matter now whether he was doing anything or just sitting there, but he called out to us, that white boy sitting on a porch. And my grandfather stopped and turned to the boy.

"Hey mister," the boy asked, his voice trailing across that little patch of grass he called lawn. "Is that a white dog or a nigger dog?"

And my grandfather pulled me away, on to the next block of houses with windows that shut out the light. My grandfather walked straight and tall like he knew where we were going, like he had some kind of special map to the road laid out before us. And Rex, sticking his nose into every hedgerow, turned every now and then to make sure we were still with him. And my grandfather finally said, "What kind of folks teach their children to ask a question like that?"

&

Traveling with white folks began for me the day I was born into a color-struck world, where little children laughed when they chanted, "If you black, get back. If you brown, stick around. If you white, you alright." In my neighborhood, beauty was a fair complexion and big legs. On the screen, beauty was blond hair and narrow hips. I was dark and long-limbed, like my grandfather.

I loved all the dark-haired heroines of comic strips, the Dragon Lady and Lois Lane. My favorite paper dolls were Jane Wyman replicas, with bangs cut like mine. My mother was my coconspirator. After Christmas, she sent my gifts of blonde baby dolls to the doll hospital. "Oh, look, Santa Claus left the wrong baby at our house," she would say. And off they'd go, returning in February with brown skin and dark crinkly hair, suitable for our house. I'd hold them up to the mirror and sing baby versions of the songs my grandmother sang to me. In the mirror, the baby doll had my smile—a colored doll that looked just like me.

"Look like you," my friends would say. And they'd ooh and ahh, and the girls would comb her real hair, and the boys would make her brown eyes open and close, the fringe of real lashes moving up and down.

By summer, we ignored baby dolls and got down to the real business of the day: taunting the kids on the playground in the all-white school at the end of the block. Every summer until I was ten, when my neighborhood crossed over from partially white to definitely, irrevocably black, I walked a dozen or so blocks across town to the colored school. Half a block away stood Cote Brilliante School, red-brick and glorious. For whites only. Every summer, we made it our business to loosen the hold white kids had on that playground.

We'd shake the chain link fence until it jangled in protest. A dozen black kids worked that fence until the wah-wah of one link bounced against another, the whole length vibrating enough to send the white kids scurrying home. But every day throughout the summer, they returned. And every day, we rattled the cage that kept them safe until they fled. I was always amazed that they kept coming back.

"It's the weather," my mother would say. "Soon as it gets a little bit warm, they'll be there. You just leave them be."

"Living 'round white folks is more than a notion," my grandmother would say.

～

Perhaps the whole question of color is fixed to warm weather because it is then that we reveal ourselves to each other. Without coats and hats, gloves and boots, we are more exposed to the eyes of the beholder, naked, as it were, revealing perhaps more than we intend. Nobody wants to know if Eskimos tan, or why they wear bright colors so well. Tell an Inuit: Red looks so good against your skin.

My roommate, Emilie, was from Eastern Europe, not a place known for its bright, sunny beaches. We were on a tour of South America, looking for artifacts, for folklore, for bits of the past. There were ten of us, from nearly half a dozen points on the globe, scrounging around market stalls and back alleys where our Spanish failed us. Even the Haitians were having trouble, and they swore they had cousins working in every nook and cranny we passed.

After a day of trekking, we'd retire to the hotel, grateful for the luxury of hot water on demand and the endless room service of tapas. I took my refreshment in the bar. My roommate headed for the pool. "Come join me," she'd call.

I'd flex an arm. "I don't swim and I don't need a tan."

No matter what the day brought—dust, dysentery, or simply disgust—Emilie never missed an evening at poolside.

We traveled from Columbia to Peru to Ecuador and Argentina, Emilie basking in poolside glory, her tiny swimsuit revealing an ever-increasing tan. I sipped coladas and reread my guidebook to Brazil. By the time we reached Rio, I was ready. Our hotel was directly across the street from Ipanema. From the window, I could see the surf foaming white against the white sand. A few drummers were already in place, but none of their music could match my heartbeat. I was definitely ready.

When I emerged from the bathroom, humming "The Girl from Ipanema," Emilie gasped.

"Is that all you're going to wear?" she asked. I looked down at the itsy bitsy white bikini glowing against my skin, every inch tanned, the natural way.

"I could wear a cover-up to cross the street," I said, and produced a lacy shirt that all but evaporated in the light. We strolled the length of the beach, Emilie and I. In the light of Ipanema, only strong colors held true under the sun.

"Hello beautee," someone called to me.

"I don't like this place," Emilie said, and went back to the hotel. But I was at home. Every day, I took my little white bikini for a walk among the dark skinned girls: the mulattos, pasalaquas, and mestizos. Every day, the drums called me to dance and the sun laughed.

I didn't see Emilie in another swimsuit until we reached the hotel in Venezuela. She was stretched out poolside, a waiter serving her a tall drink crowned by an umbrella. I was in the bar, cooled by an overhead fan. When Emilie waved, I raised my glass to toast her.

❧

Could it be that the United States is the only country where ethnicity is a question, but color never is? Color. It moves us, stops us, turns us around, our heads spinning in its wake like some character from *The Exorcist*.

Ivory black: sounds odd, doesn't it? Ivory is anything but black . . . it's a cool black . . . what we call a "dusty" shade. Flake white has two serious drawbacks: it turns yellow, pink, or gray in the light within a relatively short time. . . . The so-called Chinese white is usually the best.

❧

We were dreaming of leaving home: Dolores G., Gracie B., and me. The three of us in high school still, three shades of brown—from that deep brown that's all about earth and wood to fair skin with just a hint of tan like an undercoat. High yellow we called it.

Graduation and we hit the road. We were getting out of St. Louis, the three of us, three black girls in different shades of color.

Gray-eyed Dolores G. bragged about her Sugah Man. Mama called her fast. "That child's headed for trouble," she said. Come graduation, Dolores G. disappeared into that trouble.

Everyone made fun of Gracie when she sang. "Arias," she told us. But as soon as she opened her mouth and the notes rolled out in languages we didn't even know existed, everyone fell silent. Her voice was bird and wind and smoke drifting into a vast sky. Now I see Gracie braced on the pages of international opera news, still mahogany brown, polished smooth and classy, her arias. Miss Bumbry, they call her.

I had glasses always in a book, and thin legs—"Shapely," Mama said when folks called me skinny. After graduation, I headed for Germany, my first trip overseas—Europe, where Josephine Baker walked a leopard on a leash.

Far from home, we would never be the same, but we promised to keep in touch. Back then, we needed to promise.

❧

American addictions: medicine, fully stocked grocery shelves, single-family dwellings. American despair: racism in a country where only one language is honored.

"Are you one of those poor unfortunates who can only speak one language?" I fought the urge to rip his Caribbean tongue from his mouth by the root. But I spent each evening practicing French—rolling my "r"s like pearls caught in a dragon's mouth, swallowing vowels and puckering up for the music of "s" and "l" and any other sound flattened by my American ear.

❧

There were seven of us in Paris, seven African American women from a city on the most extreme point of the northwest coast of the United States. We ran the gamut of colors from mahogany brown to pale. We came with the baggage of travel experience or none at all. We walked in wide movements, commandeering sidewalks, laughter scaring birds from the trees. Seven black women invading Paris.

We passed mothers on their way to market, children on their way to school, a postman, a merchant in the doorway of his shop. We passed a couple deep in conversation. She looked casually Parisian. He looked definitely Asian. Their conversation was carried on the wind. They were no different from other couples we passed, except perhaps more strikingly handsome. And they couldn't have been more than a few feet away when one of the women turned to watch their retreating figures.

"Did you see that Chinaman speaking French?" she exclaimed, speaking English with her African-looking self.

White is . . . Black is . . . Are blacks truly black? Are whites truly white? And what do we do about red and yellow?

My goddaughter is from Malaysia. Bee Bee, whose name translates to Beautiful Beautiful, is a beautiful Chinese Malaysian, six feet tall. There goes one myth out the window: they aren't all short and rice-bowl thin. In the seventies, New York fashion snatched chopsticks and stuck them into chignons. Oh, how clever, how very Oriental. It was the "must have" of the season. One day, Bee Bee appeared in class wearing a fork in her jet black hair.

"Why a fork?" one hapless student asked.

"I eat with my chopsticks," she answered.

Dashikis, beads, braids, and dreads. Blonde dreads? Short afros dyed blonde? We think we are crossing cultural lines but we are trapped in what Baldwin called the center of the arc: the gaudiest, most valuable, and most improbable water wheel the world has ever seen. We are trapped in our assumptions, trying hard to shake them or build on them or discredit them when we cross those real and imaginary boundaries drawn by lines of color.

We carry them with us, those invisible stamps on our passports. The history that is unspeakable, that reaches into the present as surely as a pickpocket lifting the freshly minted I.D.

Ask Pam Smith, black American, who discovered that her friend Ann Neel, white American, shared a family history that fell out of the same slave chapter. "Your family owned my family," Smith told Neel. They have been trying to find a common language ever since. Shake that family tree too hard and all colors fall down. The white side of a family living on one side of the tracks. The blacks on the other side. Ask the Hemmings and the Jeffersons.

꙳

"I don't need to talk about this cultural stuff," a student announces. "I'm just white." The ultimate cultural prophylactic, I think. Nothing gets past it.

In an effort to show his sincerity, a white colleague says to me, "I've studied blacks all my life."

I smile. "Really?" I say. "And I've been black all my life."

When my German professor asked me, "What are you?" I had no words that were adequate. I resorted to *colored*. I tried *Negro*. How did I know the world needed to define me by place of birth, by religion, by class and caste and preferences for food? Wasn't it enough to be American, colored or not?

꙳

In the mid-1960s I moved to Bellingham, Washington, with my children. Only two years had passed since the Sundown Law was removed from the city ordinance books. We lived on a farm, two miles from the Indian Reservation. Mornings, the fog rolled in like lace, and in the distance, Lummi Island was a pale violet shape on the horizon. Except for the Native Americans, the countryside was lily white. And except for a few students at the college, the town was nearly white. I was one of four black professors, the only one living outside of town.

The weekend after we moved in, the neighbor's child appeared in the yard. My children saw him before they heard him.

"Hey Negro," the boy called out. "Hey Negro, can you come out and play?"

꙳

"I thought you were from India," they said in Vietnam—until they heard my accent.

"Are you from Fiji?" they asked in Australia.

The Nubians yelled, "Sweet sister," as I walked through the market in towns near the Aswan Dam. More than once, I have been recognized for what I am not: my features, my profile, and yes, my color, reminding someone of someone back home.

Italy. I walked through an arcade, elaborate wrought iron and leaded glass roof curving like a Tiffany lampshade. The place reeked of money, everything elegantly expensive. I strolled past windows with pyramids of Italian leather, butter-soft I imagined, windows of delicate lace, windows of perfume. It was all so tempting. A woman stood beside me, a desert woman by the look of her clothing. Ethiopian, I guessed, with Naples so close to the jumping-off place for North Africa. Side by side, we looked at the window display, smiling at each other. For a second, no words were necessary. We were both bedazzled by the finery. Then she gestured, a delicate turn of her wrist, and said something I couldn't understand. Amharic, perhaps? I told her, "I don't understand." I said it in Italian, French, English. It was the English that drew a sneer. Or perhaps I merely imagined a sneer—me, the poor unfortunate who truly is at home only in one language.

"I just don't like Italy. The men won't leave you alone."

"Me too," I told my blonde companion. "Don't you just love it?"

I had a dancer's legs. Gracie had a diva's voice. And Dolores never had to open a door in her life as long as there was a gentleman around. We got our wish. We got out of St. Louis.

Now I am asked: Where would you live if you could live anywhere else in the world? Always I take a long pause before answering. Where would I live without the American version of racism? But racism is the snake that sheds one skin only to take on another. In other ports of call, I've stumbled upon discarded skins, like those sea snake skins I saw on the beach in Fiji, discarded like dried foreskins as the snakes head back to the safe waters of the Coral Sea. Where could I go on this planet without tripping on that old snake's hide?

I sat in the Bamboo Bar at the Metropole Hotel in Hanoi. The place reeked of Graham Greene and colonial flavor. I had seen other black faces on the streets of the city, but for the moment, I was the only one in the hotel bar. A woman had been staring at me for the better part of an hour. We were both drinking something cool and tall. She was with a friend, but she paid more attention to me sitting directly in her line of vision. She could have been British, German, Australian.

I tried smiling. She frowned. We sat in winter light while gracious women in silk *ao dais* served us. One waitress recognized me from earlier in the week. I was hard to miss, the only black woman lounging in the afternoon, reading my lecture notes as I waited for my next appointment to arrive. She refreshed my drink, chatted for a minute, then moved on. The woman sitting across from me watched all this. Finally, she got up.

"You American?" she asked. Her tone was an accusation, her accent New York. "What are *you* doing here?"

"Keeping an eye on you," I smiled.

If color rules, then we are all as flat as paper dolls.

The wonderful thing about traveling is that you go places where color is not a fence, but a window. Sometimes you share the view through the same window as your fellow travelers. Sometimes you're offered a different view through a different window.

Where would I live if I could live anywhere? In somebody's luxury hotel. With room service and freshly made beds and towels you don't have to wash. With doors that are kept locked for you and bathwater that always runs hot. With no one at the desk who will question your reservations and no other guests who will stare in half-veiled disbelief as you ride the elevator to the penthouse floor. And when some white person tells me that this is decadent, I remind them that my great-grandmothers and their mothers earned every bit of this luxury working in the fields, cleaning houses, tending children, and dying young to rest in nameless graves. This luxury is the heritage they've left me, I say, and I take it without guilt.

Where would I live? In a place where I am what I am, walking on ground that other black women have broken for me.

Colleen J. McElroy *received her B.A. in Kansas City and moved on to study in the speech and hearing program at the University of Pittsburgh. Back in Kansas City, McElroy completed graduate work in neurological and language learning patterns and earned a Ph.D. in ethnolinguistic patterns of dialect differences and oral traditions from the University of Washington.*

McElroy joined the University of Washington faculty as a professor of English and eventually became the first black woman to be promoted to full professorship at the university.

Her Queen of the Ebony Isles *was selected for the Wesleyan University Press Poetry Series and received the American Book Award in 1985. Since then, McElroy has published two short-story collections,* Jesus and Fat Tuesday *(Creative Arts Book Co., 1987) and* Driving Under the Cardboard Pines *(Creative Arts Book Co., 1990); two poetry collections,* What Madness Brought Me Here—New and Selected Poems 1968–88 *(Wesleyan University Press, 1990) and* Travelling Music *(Story Line Press, 1998); a travel memoir,* A Long Way From St. Louie *(Coffeehouse Press, 1997); and has written for stage and television.*

McElroy continues to travel extensively in Europe, South America, Japan, Majorca, Madagasgar, Asia, Africa, and Southeast Asia. Her most recently published book is Over the Lip of the World: Among the Storytellers of Madagascar *(University of Washington Press, 2001), which was selected as a finalist in the PEN research-based creative nonfiction category for 2001.*

© Chris Burns

Race: A Discussion in Ten Parts, Plus a Few Moments of Unsubstantiated Theory and One Inarguable Fact

Kiini Ibura Salaam

I.

RACE IS BULLSHIT. A meaningless line drawn in sand by men bent on world domination and oppression. It was introduced as a fixed notion, an unchangeable, undeniable fact of world order. Yet from the moment of race's conception, the amazing diversity of body types, cultures, and traditions on the African continent alone complicated race's claim on classification. In New Orleans, the city of my birth and upbringing, the color line was never an obvious fact. There were those of us whose skin tone made us undeniably black, but then there were others who walked the color line and could decide on which side they wanted to live. What is this thing called race that counts only sometimes, yet is taken as gospel by every American alive? What is race to a New Orleanian with white skin, gray eyes, and Creole parents?

A phenomenon created in the "new world," Creole was first used to differentiate Europeans born in Caribbean colonies from native Europeans. Tainted by "animalistic" African energies, these Caribbean-born whites were somehow "altered." They were still classified as white, but by virtue of their uncivilized birthplaces, they were marked: white soiled by black.

It wasn't long before "new world" Europeans (almost exclusively male) began the process of miscegenation. The enslaved Africans who cultivated the land were forced to bear children from the seed of their enslavers. These offspring, along with other enslaved Africans, widened the definition of *creole* by melding European traditions with African customs. Creole became the language born of the mixture of European and African tongues.

In New Orleans, Creole came to define a specific community whose African ancestors bore mixed-race children. These mixed-race children intermarried, creating a group that appears both black and white. As Aline St. Julien, my grandmother, notes in her book *Colored Creole: Color Conflict and Confusion in New Orleans*, "Creole ranged in color from white to dark brown with a lot of yellow and 'teasing tans' in between." To be admired in the Creole world, one had to pass the "brown paper bag test." The lightest Creoles had the honor of choosing whether they wanted to be a *passe-blanc*, one who passed for white.

My grandmother remembers growing up Creole as a wonderful cultural experience punctuated by confusing identity crises. In her words, "I have been struggling toward [knowing my identity] ever since elementary school. When I finally got my mother to answer that inevitable question that most parents of our class dreaded and evaded for as long as possible, I was told that I was a Creole. My mother really believes that we are not Negroes."

One of the strongest elements of the Creole social code was the open admonition for younger Creoles to "keep . . . in [their] class." This indoctrination insured a cultural purity, making the Creoles of contemporary New Orleans a powerful cultural force.

With black, white, and Creole as my background of racial diversity, I have mistaken whites for blacks. In New Orleans, white skin doesn't mean white heart and blue eyes doesn't mean you're not black. People who most Americans would identify as white are clearly Creole to New Orleanian eyes. Stand a white person, a black person, and a white-looking Creole person next to each other. The black person might say, "Look at my skin, I'm black. My skin is what separates me from those two." How does the Creole separate himself or herself from the white person?

It is in the context of this Creole conundrum that I reject race as the ultimate definer of humanity. From all appearances, the Creole and the white person are of the same race. The distinction between their identities is housed in their cultures. All things being equal, race quickly becomes a meaningless marker. The element that stands fast in the midst of race chaos is culture. How does my Japanese, East Indian, and African American roommate identify herself? Certainly not by her race: her race doesn't exist. She identifies herself by her culture. How does my Pacific Islander, European American, and African American friend identify herself? Not by race: her race doesn't exist. Race is bullshit; it is culture that counts.

II.

I entered the race conversation at a young age. The adults in my community organized an independent black school called Ahidiana Work/Study Center. We were African identified and black centered. I wasn't exposed to white people until the age of seven. By seven, my identity as an African in America was well developed. Through chants and songs, we learned lessons about our environment, our history, and ourselves. One of our most important songs—"Blackness"—argues that there are three components to being black: color, culture, and consciousness. As the song goes:

> Color is for our race
> From the brightest bright to the darkest face
> We are all black bred and born
> America is where we live, but Africa is our home
>
> Culture is the way we do the things we do
> We sing our songs and work juju
> But we can do more than just sing and dance

We are the builders of civilization
The original woman and man

Consciousness is self-awareness and self-control
Identifying with each other, some call it soul
Disciplining ourselves to do whatever it takes
To defend, and develop, and make our people great

Years later, I still believe in the theory of the song, but with a different configuration. Blackness (or race) is no longer my umbrella, culture is. My blackness isn't a "thing" that walks down the road before me. It is neither a barrier to overcome, nor an exalted position to live up to; it simply is. Blackness is a part of me, but you can't figure out who I am without adding in my gender, my birthplace, the economic bracket I was born into.

Color (or race) paints an incomplete picture. Rather than defining me, race is an element of me. It is a building block of my culture. Race grants every human being a set of predefined mores to work with or against. It is not a stopping place, but a starting place, a reference.

Whatever my consciousness is engaged with will come through in my behavior. My behavior—or my actions, as defined by the song—is my culture. "Culture is the way we do the things we do." Culture is a human being's ultimate expression of himself or herself. How we do the things we do *is* who we are. Race isn't the ultimate definer; culture (affected by consciousness) is the thing.

III.

Even when we say we're talking about race, we're really talking about culture and consciousness. Racial fidelity is a huge concept for people of color in America. Among blacks and other racial minorities, there is talk of "sellouts." When people take actions that do not align with the communal perception of how someone of their race should behave, they are criticized for not "acting black" or not being "true to the race." But if someone is born black (or Chinese, or Dominican), how can they ever not be what they already are? When we criticize people for selling out, we are taking issue with their actions, not their race. What are actions?

Actions are behavior. What is behavior? Behavior is culture. Race does not cause action, yet we expect people to exhibit specific actions based on the facts of their birth. In *I Stand in the Center of the Good: Interviews with Contemporary Native American Artists*, artist and curator Rick Hill explains that Indians "grow up and have to make . . . choices, like, yes, I'm going to be an Indian; yes, I will attend ceremonies; yes, I will marry an Indian; yes, I will live on the reservation; or say no to all those things." But if you are born Indian, how can you choose to be Indian? We use the same language for two different conversations. The race conversation is complete at birth. Yet we continue to use race language to define culture. By Rick Hill's definition, what makes an Indian an Indian is not simply the incident of birth, but the Indian's actions, the Indian's cultural choices. A "true" Indian, Hill argues, is one whose awareness (or consciousness) of his/her culture dictates his/her lifestyle. If indeed thoughts and actions make an Indian an Indian, then which is more important, race or consciousness and culture?

IV.

In America, race speaks volumes and skin color causes tension. Hettie Jones, a white woman who married a black man and had two black children, was often uncomfortable around other whites because she knew the racial assumptions that were her birthright. Her white skin marked her racist, and other whites related to her as if she were "one of them." In her book, *How I Became Hettie Jones*, she says, "What's missing is critical: the way I now felt in whites-only groups. Without [my husband] or the children, I felt misrepresented, minus a crucial dimension, and seeing race prejudice everywhere, shocking and painful. Other whites in black families speak of this; [a friend] who . . . is herself the mother of two black children . . . calls it feeling disguised in your own skin."

Racial assumptions have the power to do this: disguise us in our own skins. Hettie Jones's new reality was dictated by her culture: the man she married, the children she had, the circles she moved in. Aligned with her new culture, she developed a new consciousness, a new awareness of the world around her. Yet her race kept her locked in a space she no longer related to. Race falsely defines us; culture and consciousness are truer identifiers.

My mother (whose face bears a striking resemblance to the black-and-white cover photo of Hettie Jones) was a bedrock in the black activist community of New Orleans. Despite the attempts of the white nuns at her Catholic primary school to convince her of her Creole "otherness," she identified black (consciousness), married black, and lived black (culture). As her black child, I never saw my mother as other. I never thought her skin uncommonly light; she was the same as my brown-skinned uncles; she was black and she was my mother. I didn't question what it might have meant for her to struggle for black pride inside a near-white body until one day when my sister, my mother, and I were at a friend's house. A woman of my mother's complexion and hair type came in. She and my mother immediately fell into a conversation about children and life. Fifteen minutes later, a dark-skinned girl came into the house.

"Who's this?" my mother asked. "My daughter," said the woman. "Oh, I wish my children would have come out that dark," my mother said. My sister and I looked at each other in surprise. My mother, who taught us black awareness and black pride, didn't think we were dark enough?

For the first time I considered a black life in my mother's skin. I wondered what type of mistrust and prejudice she must have combated in the very community she dedicated her life to improving. Were there feelings of inadequacy battling underneath her skin? Did her Creole heritage cause tension in the pro-black community she called home?

V.

I grew up thinking I was dark skinned. At family reunions, my siblings and I always represented the darkest end of the skin-color spectrum. My mother's side of the family—peopled with thin-haired, light-eyed, white-skinned folk—was a contrast to my melanin-flushed skin tone. In the Creole world, I was quite literally black. It wasn't until I left New Orleans that I learned the truth about my skin color. Asserting my blacker-than-thou African ego, I took to calling my college boyfriend yellow. Whenever I wanted to change a conversation, I'd drop a reference to his skin color. "I've never dated anyone so high yellow," I'd tease. One day, in the middle of winter, without the color boost the

New Orleans sun gifted me with year round, I found my hand resting next to his. My mouth flew open in shock. I was no darker than him; I just browned up better in the sunshine.

We like to believe that race gives us our identity. Yet it is our culture that defines race; it is our consciousness that decides what race means. If ever I thought race was a fixed concept, that notion was destroyed during my stay in the Dominican Republic, where people are categorized strictly by skin color, and where a white person and a black person can share the same blood.

When my host family looked at a family portrait I had pulled out of my bag, they said, "Oh, your mother's white." I was horrified. In the United States, if you have black blood in your family and if you live in a black world (culture), then you, too, are black, no matter what color your skin is. Not so in the Dominican Republic. Race is mutable, manipulated by differences in skin color and hair texture.

When I first arrived in the Dominican Republic, my light skin and short Afro inspired them to call me "india" (Indian) and "morena" (brown-skinned). One semester later, after my sun-darkened skin was accented with a mass of newly-forming locks, I suddenly became "negra" (black) and "prieta" (darky). Same person, different race.

In Salvador, Brazil, I was laughed at for calling myself black. "You aren't black," the man scoffed in Brazilian Portuguese. "You're a mulatto." Acknowledging my lack of racial purity was momentarily painful. In the United States, we behave as if we were shot directly from African genes with no European interference. But the truth is black Americans are of mixed race (and it isn't only Native American blood in the mix).

Black Americans, Dominicans, and Brazilians all think they have real, legitimate definitions of black and blackness. Each of these cultures invests in racial classifications with a seriousness that is bewildering. After walking between varying racial identifications, I know that race is no bastion of truth. It is rather a delusion we use to keep history and reality at bay.

VI.

The biggest truth that race keeps at bay is that all of us are human. We look at different body types and customs and draw caricatures based on

ignorance. We drown each other in dehumanizing race-based stereotypes that leave us bound in narrow categories from which not even
the most dynamic of us can escape.

In her collection *To a Young Artist in Contemplation*, Samoan author
Sia Figiel talks of meeting a gorgeous European at an art opening in
Germany. She thought herself sophisticated and cosmopolitan; his interest in her made her feel sexy and powerful. Later in bed, he cursed her
for being too quiet. He railed stereotypes at her about women from the
South Pacific; she was supposed to be wild in bed. "Something must be
wrong with you," he said, and he threw her out.

Sia explains that sex in Samoa is, by necessity, a silent affair. Lovers
who made too much noise would be sure to wake a cousin, a sibling,
or a parent, for there was no space for privacy. But because of her race,
she was not allowed to be quiet in bed. Imagine!

We are often trapped between fulfilling stereotypes and defying
them. The dictates and assumptions of race too often deny our humanity. Like Hettie Jones's black husband who refused to eat watermelon in
public, few of us feel the freedom to simply live. True freedom can only
be reached outside of the realm of racial dictates and stereotypes.
Native American artist/curator Rick Hill asks, "Why should we pretend that we don't drink or that money doesn't matter to us? These are
the realities of our lives. . . . If we're going to live our lives by the stereotypes non-Indians have of us, we should all commit suicide."

When I leave the United States, I am no longer simply black: I
become an American. Ironically, I only learned to call myself an American outside of the United States. Surrounded by a foreign culture, I discovered that despite my foreignness within white-is-right America, my
attitudes, assumptions, and preferences are unquestionably American.
And, surprisingly, the rest of the world relates to me as an American.
Within that construct, I befriend white people I may have merely nodded to in my hometown.

Surrounded by foreign eyes, we work harder to find safety in com-
munion with each other. In an environment where our "Americanness"
is stereotyped beyond our recognition, we can cease to be opposing
racial forces. Homesickness transforms us, causing us to recognize our
commonalties (when they exist) in a way we never do on home soil.

VII.

Arthur Grimble, a nineteenth-century European traveler, wrote:

> It began to dawn on me that beyond the teeming romance that lies
> in difference between men—the diversity of their homes, the multi-
> tude of their ways of life, the dividing strangeness of their face and
> tongues, the thousand fold mysteries of their origins—there lies the
> still profounder romance of their kinship with each other, a kinship
> which springs from the immutable constancy of man's need to share
> laughter and friendship, poetry and love in common. A man may
> travel a long road, and suffer much loneliness, before he makes that
> discovery. Some, groping along in the dark byways, never have the
> good fortune to stumble upon it.

I stumbled upon this truth in the cramped narrow courtyard of a
Cuban *solar*. Overhead were clotheslines heavy with drying fabric.
Stacked beneath the dripping clothes were metal cages full of clucking
hens. Lining the courtyard were a number of small, dark apartments. I
passed one month in one of those apartments as the guest of a black
Cuban friend. I spent my days playing with the children and joking
with the adults of the *solar*.

One day as I was leaning down to kiss the withered cheek of an old
lady, I paused. For the first time, I noticed she was white. I stood up
and looked around me. It was as if my eyes were recording the truth for
the first time in days. Everyone—the children, the women, the men, the
teenagers, everyone—was white. My host was the only black person in
the entire *solar*. It is baffling how a race-conscious American such as
myself could have missed such an obvious fact.

When I lay down in bed that night, I puzzled over what could be
different about these white people that their whiteness wasn't the first
thing I noticed. Then it hit me; it was the lack of cultural differences.
These white Cubans didn't behave any differently from the black ones.
They ate beans and rice, danced salsa, smoked constantly, laughed
loudly, and screamed at their children with the same intonations. During that month, race wasn't a factor in my relationships with my neighbors because their Cuban nationality defined who they were (which is

not to say there's no racism in Cuba, but that's a different essay). In the *solar*, life wasn't about race; it was all about culture.

VIII.

Education is touted as an ideal method for eradicating racism. Once we learn about other races, the concept goes, we won't harbor so much ignorance, anger, and hate.

Hettie Jones describes her experience of marrying a black man and mothering black children as "broadening." In immersing herself in new realities, she learned so much about herself, white people, black people, antagonism, prejudice, and racism. Her intimacy with black culture expanded her consciousness. Black people have historically held the claim that they know white people all too well. "We have to know everything about you [white people]," we say, "and you don't know anything about us."

Ideally, we want white people to know more about us, and in doing so eradicate racism and embrace black people's humanity. At the same time, we are zealously protective of our culture. Lies, bogus contracts, gentrification, misappropriation, commercialization, and other offenses make us mistrustful of white people's interest in us and our cultures. We have long grown accustomed to handling our business in the shadow of white neglect. This invisibility has caused countless injustices, from misrepresentation to discrimination. Yet when I heard a white newscaster say "dreadlocks" on national television, I cringed. I felt she had no right to know anything about my culture, and whatever she knew, she shouldn't talk about it. Echoing the thoughts of many black people, I grumbled, "Why don't they leave our stuff alone?"

These are the complex contradictions we face. We are comfortable in our segregation and painfully aware that integration does not necessarily mean improvement for black lives. I want all people to unify, but not over my body, not at the cost of my peace, not with the sacrifice of my culture. I won't integrate myself until I can feel at home in the "outside" world. I can't feel at home in the "outside" world until it is no longer "outside."

I'm with Rick Hill when he says, "I think we have to come to the reality that we're not part of that scene. [I]t comes back to what are you willing to pay to become part of the club. It's like golf clubs with no blacks or Jews. Is it a victory to be the first minority in a racist club? Who the hell wants to play golf with those guys? What are the options for Indians? Tokenism? Affirmative action? A desk job? Or entrust the significance of art to people who don't know the art or can't relate to it?" We now know that integration at the price of giving up identity or accepting inferior treatment does not forward human progress.

IX.

Often, any attempt to assert that we are all members of one diverse human clan is considered suspect. Antihumanists argue that humanism is employed as a cloak to ignore historical injustice and suppress cultural differences. As a result, many of us push race to the forefront of our lives. For too many of us, race has become a badge of suffering, rather than an element of identity.

A Fijian friend tells tales of her graduate school classmates "positioning" themselves before participating in class discussions. "As a Chicana lesbian from working-class parents, I believe . . ." Each student looked for tags to deny their privilege and magnify the oppression they suffered. Oblivious to the obvious contradiction of ignoring their privilege while participating in a Ph.D. program, these students read and discussed the history of cultural and racial inequalities and argued about their right to claim themselves among the oppressed. "My parents make less money than any of these kids' parents," my friend confided, "but I seem to be the only one who knows I'm middle class."

In *Full Circles, Overlapping Lives*, Mary Catherine Bateson states, "It is true that social scientists can predict much of what each of us is likely to think or do from a set of descriptors—age, gender, class, ethnicity, and background—but there is a core that is distinctive and individual for every person."

I am fascinated by the infinite cultural combinations that can be expressed by each person's "distinctive and individual core." At the core of each human being is unimaginable diversity and similarity. When we are really comfortable in our skins, we are unafraid of the difference around us.

Why should race cause blind allegiances to constructed identities? Rather than celebrate each graduate student's "distinctive and individual core," my friend's colleagues routinely used race as grounds for prejudice and hate. In one women's studies course, the Chicana women sat on one side of the room and the black women sat on the other side.

"Where did you sit?" I asked my friend. "Right in the middle," she laughed. She was incredulous when, halfway through the semester, the class broke down under the weight of antagonism. A harmless class discussion plummeted into a bitter argument characterized by accusations of man stealing and spinelessness. The degree these highly educated women were studying to attain? Cultural studies. Race has a knack for getting in the way.

X.

On the backs of men and women who had race shoved down their throats their whole lives, I stand embracing race, while simultaneously setting it down to the side. My sights are set on the horizon, to the future where people are valued for their humanity regardless of fabricated inferiorities and imagined superiorities. Somehow race has been accepted as a humongous moat that can't be bridged. We behave as if the differences between races are debilitating and race discrimination is a done deal. While grumbling about race, we live in partnerships and homes held together by two forces with radically different perspectives.

Even knowing that many people have failed to make the union of male and female work, we are optimistic about our abilities to balance the yin and the yang and create a future together. If men and women can manage to get along, live together, and raise families, certainly all the races of the world can unify.

"Yeah, but what about racism?" I can hear a little voice crying out. What about it? Sexism is just as powerful. Men and women have different physical appearances, different thought patterns, and different modes of behavior. If men and women can be partners despite sexual harassment, domestic violence, rape, denigration, murder, gender oppression, and disrespect, certainly members of different races can come together despite negative forces. The question comes down to a commitment. What are we really committed to? Race is a convenient excuse to be fragmented, but is it a valid one?

As Mary Catherine Bateson notes, "variation . . . is ignored by the crude oversimplification of the color line." Embedded in our constructs of race is the myth of homogenousness. When I say I was born into a black family, grew up in a black city, attended a black college, and sleep in a black neighborhood, the mind immediately starts constructing its own visual image of what my black life must be like. It appears as if I'm talking about one culture: black culture. Yet each of those elements—my black family, black city, black college, and black neighborhood—consists of radically different cultures.

The family I was born into was vegetarian, intellectual, and agnostic. Every element of my home culture was at odds with the dominant culture around me, with the black city in which I lived. My city was hedonistic, Southern international, and violent; completely different from the affluent, Christian, middle-class culture of most of the students at my black college.

Currently I am immersed in Caribbean culture. The rhythms, food, and languages in my neighborhood are distinct from anything I grew up with. When I call all of these elements of my life black without providing further details, I invest in the lie of race as culture. Within race there are many different cultures, each a world unto itself.

The lie is that we gather together because we have more in common. We believe we take comfort in people of our own race because they are more like us and can understand us better. But the true comfort in gathering in communities with people who are like us is the freedom to be an individual.

Bateson breaks it down best when she says that in the mainstream community, there is the "expectation that [blacks] will be interchangeable" with other blacks. Whereas in all black settings there is no "implied obligation to represent the group." Amazingly, it is only in similar groups that human beings are allowed to become individuals. In Bateson's words: "There is a more subtle dynamic than similarity when groups withdraw from the majority and hang out together, and this is the pleasure of differing among themselves." Bateson's clear communication of this paradox has given me a profound understanding of my own life choices.

My attitude toward white communities is not one of anger or even mistrust; the word that best expresses my feelings is disinterest. I'm just not impressed. Yet I'd be lying if I said I was impressed with many black communities. No, it is not that my community is inherently better, it is rather that my community is mine. In my community, I am not a minority, I am not an "other"; I am simply an individual, a human being with unique identity, perspective, and interests.

A few moments of unsubstantiated theory and one inarguable truth

Curriculum theorist Tayari kwa Salaam constructs conversations that dissect life's complex contradictions. Life, she argues, is not "either/or," it is "both/and." Both of these things are true: race is bullshit and racism is real. While I argue inclusion and humanism, I am a realist. I am aware of the harsh realities of racism: economic, political, social. Black and urban schools really are more neglected than predominantly white and private schools. Black people are routinely paid less and harassed more in places of business. Black people are sentenced to prison more frequently for the same crimes white people are acquitted of. And then there was slavery, colonialism, and Jim Crow. But is racism personal? I don't believe so.

Sure, white people fear people of color. They parrot racist crap and reinforce both mindless and intentional racial inequities daily. But do they eat, drink, and sleep hatred toward black people and people of color? No. It is more accurate to say they don't care. They remain intentionally unaware of racism (both institutional and their own) so they can avoid dealing with it. Remaining willfully ignorant of the realities of racism, they discriminate against people of color because it is convenient and because racism cements their own race privilege.

In a capitalist society, in a "me-have-power, me-oppress-you" world, someone has to be at the bottom. Rather than researching people's opinions and choosing to oppress a group based on something tangible (attitude, mental aptitude, moral fortitude), the people in power have chosen the dark ones, then pegged stereotypes (amoral attitudes, low mental aptitude, and corrupt ethics) on us. In the white world, people of color stand out. In homogenous societies, where everyone looks the same, a different arbitrary marker for oppression is required. Religion or tribal identity becomes the basis for oppression.

Race is a bullshit distraction—a maze from which few of us emerge with our clarity and sanity intact. In America, racism is vilified as the evil of all evils. But I cannot look the ethnic warfare of Rwanda and

Serbia in the eye and claim one "ism" more heinous than the other. I can't read about genital mutilation and child prostitution and proclaim racism the face of all that is criminal.

There is too much horror in the world to ignore this reality: humans are cannibals. When hungry, we feed on each "other." When insecure, we drink an "other's" blood. When angry, we dig our claws into someone "lesser" than us: be it a person of color (racism), a poor person (classism), a woman (sexism), or a child (ageism). Racism is something human beings do to each other. It should be dealt with as a human flaw. It should be eradicated in the name of humanity.

For people of color in the United States, insane inequity and debilitating oppression exist. "Whites Only" exists. Racial profiling and police brutality exist. Educational inequalities exist. But none of these hurts can alter the fact that race is a flawed and inconsistent concept. The proliferation of race-based social ills cannot force truth to be false.

Dismantling race is key to dismantling racism. Not by force, but by transformation of thought and deed. Until racism is eradicated, we will march and scream and lobby and hate. And greed will rear its head and power will rip our rights to shreds. But when the tide turns, there will be nothing racists, race haters, and oppressors can do or say to obscure one inarguable truth: there is but one humanity.

Self-described as a feminist and a humanist, **Kiini Ibura Salaam***, twenty-eight, a writer, painter, and world traveler, joins her father in this anthology. Since age seventeen, she has written short stories, essays, and poetry that celebrate and question the mysteries, victories, and challenges of life.*

Since 1993, Salaam has enjoyed extended stays in the Dominican Republic, Brazil, Fiji, England, Jamaica, and Trinidad. Passionately committed to self-development, Kiini Ibura promotes travel as an ultimate tool for personal growth and expansion.

Salaam's work has appeared in anthologies and magazines nationwide, including When Butterflies Kiss *(Silver Lion Press, 2001),* Dark Matter *(Aspect, 2000),* Dark Eros *(St. Martin's Press, 1997),* African American Review, Essence, *and* Ms. *magazines. College students and radio listeners nationwide have been her audience. She maintains the KIS.list, a weekly e-report featuring reflections on writing, social issues, and travel.*

© Meika Neblett

A Funky Fresh Talented Tenth

TOURÉ

I ALWAYS LOVED the first day of the year at Milton. Prep school people arrived fresh from Nantucket, a little sand still in their loafers, clutching new books and strolling to classes in ivy-covered buildings that stood over us as they stood over students a hundred years before. I loved being educated alongside extraordinary people, even though some were extraordinary only because they had extraordinary problems. I loved late Saturday afternoons, after all the games and matches and meets were over and sweat-drenched warriors ambled toward those open-stall showers and across the campus you could sense the embers of competition cooling. I loved finals, the pressure so audible the campus hummed like an electric current and for a week your mind was on its toes. I loved graduation and the boys marching in blue blazers and the girls floating in white dresses. On my graduation day the rain held off until the ceremony was nearly over. When it came time for everyone to sing, then-Headmaster Pieh, shielding his face from the drizzle with his hand, announced they would conclude the ceremony without the planned singing. With benign defiance we launched right into it. And as the drizzle landed on us and our parents and our grandparents, we sang. I walked off that day confident I knew how to dance through life the Milton way, a style that serves me even now. Some of the time.

Two years before that drizzly last day, on the next to last day of sophomore year, I had a short talk with a senior we all called Keisha Mac. She was a woman with the grace of a ballet dancer and the seriousness of Angela Davis. And, being a senior, she was, I was certain, unspeakably wise. On the third floor of the library, by the windows where you could see girls with their long hair pulled back, giggling in the sun as it tickled their bare pink feet, I asked her, "Would you send your kids to Milton?" She looked off a moment, then said, "No." A little earthquake tremor rumbled through my mind. "Milton teaches you to be white," she said. "That's just fine if you are, but for us? Coming here as a black child—and as old as we think we are, we're still children—is like learning to put your head in the lion's mouth so deep that you forget how to live outside it."

After twelve years as a black fly in the Milton buttermilk I flew to Atlanta for college. I breezed in the classroom—after Milton it was easy—and struggled with my black classmates. I pledged a white fraternity. That's when The Whisper started.

The Whisper clung quietly to my shadow through sophomore year when I began actively courting black friends and became a Black Studies major, and through junior year, when I moved into the Black House. One night there, after a party, a stupid argument turned hot. And someone, finally, stated The Whisper. "Shut up, Touré," it went. "You ain't black."

It was a searing epiphany. Years later I understood the flimsiness of that so-called spear, the ease with which almost anyone at almost anytime could be stabbed with a you-ain't-black for any number of offenses—where you live, who you love, what you think, how you walk. But still, that day there was some truth in it. There's some truth in it now. I can't simply blame Milton. It's just that I hadn't realized until it was too late that I had to unlearn some dance steps.

My truth is this: I love Milton and I hate Milton. Love and hate the way I love and hate America and my ex-girlfriend, who both blessed me and burned me, shaped me in ways I appreciate and abhor. There is nothing Milton could do to improve life for its black students—no amount of orientation or black history classes or campus-wide sensitivity, though those are good steps. It's up to Milton's black students to learn to approach Milton with equal doses of love and contempt.

Well, actually, there is something Milton could do for us. Imagine this: the admissions department institutes a Manila Folder test, demanding that all but a few students be darker than a manila folder. Overnight the student body turns bronze and beige, sable and khaki, café au lait, mocha, cocoa, sandalwood, caramel—all the colors of the ebony rainbow. After completing the summer reading, *Manchild in the Promised Land,* tanned students stroll in for a spirited first day of classes, the hallways filled with a joyous din as people swap new hairstyles, handshakes, and slang words picked up on vacations in Johannesburg, Nairobi, and Kingston. At the bell they sprint off to Chemistry, or Harlem Renaissance Poetry, or Algebra, or The History of Africa Pre-Christ, or European History From 1196 to 1945 (The Predatory Era). As the year moves on, the fourth class presents their play, August Wilson's *The Piano Lesson,* and college counselors organize trips to Morehouse, Spelman, Howard, and Hampton.

Every Sunday a Baptist preacher, backed by a forty-woman choir and a small band, delivers an exuberant sermon that rips the roof off the chapel. In class, and in-between, students and teachers discuss, sometimes with words, sometimes with glances, how to dance through life the new Milton way, moving as a black intelligenstia grounded in black culture, fly enough to stay late at the party, soaking in our mores and rituals, then waking up to slay 'em on Wall Street. A funky fresh talented tenth as ign'ant as Coltrane on a G4 and so black no one could ever put The Whisper on them. At commencement, Toni Morrison dares us to vanquish the dusty and vacuous school motto "Dare to Be True." It must've worked wonders, she says, in the days before *Catcher in the Rye* was written, but who's been able to say it with a straight face since Kent State? She suggests "Dare to Have Soul," or "Dare to Love," or, maybe, "Dare to Be Black," which is really a challenge to be yourself in a post-Milton world that will demand otherwise at nearly every turn.

Imagine that. Close your eyes and see my Milton. Maybe you'll begin to know how I felt at yours.

Touré *is a contributing editor at* Rolling Stone. *His work has been featured in* The New Yorker, *the* New York Times Magazine, Callaloo, Playboy, *the* Village Voice, The Best American Essays of 1999 *(Mariner Books, 1999), and* The Best American Sports Writing 2001 *(Houghton Mifflin, 2001). His short story collection,* The Portable Promised Land, *will be published by Little, Brown and Company in June 2002. He lives in Fort Greene, Brooklyn.*

© Lisa Dodson

On Acting *White: Mother-Daughter Talk*

LISA DODSON AND ODESSA DORIAN COLE

Lisa

Early in my life, race talk was a part of how I was taught to understand the world. I had white parents and grandparents who considered race-based hate to be an American brand of fascism, and it was their deepest fear about humanity. Authority by tyranny, politically sanctioned genocide, vanquished human rights—those were the nightmares of history. They were not kept secret from the children in my family; these were lessons about people's ways. *You had better know them.*

Our family whispered about terror and butcheries of the 1940s in the background of table talk in the late 1950s, not as Jewish survivors but as gentiles who had no right to look away. It was a child's prologue to an eventual human rights commitment of one kind or another, which in my family was akin to claiming your citizenship.

In time, civil rights and peace campaigns in the American 1960s were discussed around the family kitchen table. When I said that I was going to walk with the people seeking political and human rights, they nodded, not knowing what that might mean any better than I did at thirteen. But it seemed downright crazy to deny what you could plainly see in your own society, and *that* they certainly understood. Yet, later, it seemed that you could be called crazy—or at least extreme—to talk about color, to weave color into white conversation . . . but that came later.

I remember that the talk at my family table was of the virtue of a color-blind society. But I found that people who are boiling with pain and catching at wild dreams of justice do not seek neutrality. At a young age, I was introduced to angry, hopeful people who spoke about slavery, genocide, and the human spirit. Being there, a white child in the late 1960s with such passion all around, I had the frightening thought that there was a reckoning with *being white,* not as a fine political ideal, but with pain and intimacy.

I dreaded this revelation, and had no idea who could help me untangle the knots, because I understood it was not supposed to be about white people—everyone else, but not white people. I made a pockmarked way through my youth and early twenties, racking up countless fumbles, advances, and retreats, trying to make out how white people face up to forbidden color. If you are white in America, you have the option of retreating from dealing directly with racism, and it is one I have taken often.

Odessa

I started growing up white in an "inner-city" Boston community, one that the parents of my future suburban friends told me they would never let their children even visit. Coming from Dorchester, with a name that was "too black" for a white girl, could get quite confusing at times. When people asked me which one of my parents was black, I did not think I was being judged or discriminated against. In fact, I did not see racism as a real problem.

At my elementary school in the depths of Chinatown, I did not see black, white, or Asian; I saw friends, teachers—people. My mother and I spoke of race, but slave trading and hate crimes seemed far away. I cannot recall my mother informing me, at six, about slaves being sold. I suppose I thought it was part of the past, something one learned about in history class, and that I currently lived in a color-blind world.

Lisa

In my twenties, while squeezing my first baby into an unsettled life, it was time to figure more of this out. My daughter was white, though her name, we discovered, raises race questions. (*"Did your mama try to make you black?"* was an arrow shot as recently as this year by a black man who did not seem to like her much.) Her wild curls and face-off gaze left at least one uneasy white schoolteacher with lingering doubts.

Race talk slowly became part of our mother-daughter talk, talk about watching out for urban traffic, for "strangers" *and* "familiars" who might ask you to get in their car, for people who did not think a girl could or should play that hard or speak up that brazenly. Talk, too, about how in America there was a slave trade. Yes, that means buying and selling people. "Not the children, too, mommy?" Odessa asked, jolted, in the full-of-self way of a child's revelation. "Yes, the children, too, were for sale if their owners wanted to sell them." And the most desperate hope of all—"But couldn't their mommies run away and hide them?" She named the worst nightmare for any mother. "They did try sometimes but, no, mostly they couldn't hide them and they had no place to go." She asked for some hope here: "How could they do that? It's so mean." So, so mean. "Some white people were against it and they got together with black people and, finally, they changed the law and it stopped."

I had good girlfriends—white friends—who told me this was a little too rough for a five-year-old child to hear. And the plain truth was, her face did change in that moment, with a glimpse of horror from contemplating another child's pain, her screens not so thick and cunning yet.

OK, it was a blow. So when do we start? When do we give lessons about how people can be, about how some white people were? Nightmares were not kept secret from the children in my family. But speaking of gender and peace was often comfortable in mostly white talk, while speaking of real race history and, worse still, race today in the United States is morbid in the extreme.

I don't know if Odessa thinks I peeled back the layers too soon, but every black mother I know has spoken to their babies of the meaning of slavery in this American history. The story begins with white people, doesn't it? So when do *we* start?

Odessa

We would talk about sexism, and that helped me understand oppression first hand. I was a tough girl, strong and quick. I could beat any boy my age in a race, yet I could not fathom why I was last to be picked for the largely boy sports teams. In the fifth grade, when I publicly confronted a male teacher for rebuking the girls when they "talked rough" but ignoring the boys, my mother and I talked over the incident. It is one thing to see the truth, but another to publicly condemn a person who has power over you. (Young and inexperienced, I told my teacher that he was a sexist and had unequal standards, with the entire fifth grade present.) My mother told me, "Don't doubt what you see, but choose your moment."

I believe that sexism—preferential treatment, bias based on something as natural as your sex—brought me closer to understanding social justice. People *could* do such things, they could treat you in ways that have nothing to do with who you are, and categorize you at first glance.

One of the very first moments that pain was pressed upon my little heart was the Rodney King beating. I watched the horrifying footage—a defenseless man being beaten and destroyed by hate. It was a haunting realization for me. My stepfather was angry that I had seen such a sight, hating it himself, and furious that it had intruded into my nine-year-old mind. But my mother let me watch; we watched together.

I recognized the police, who were supposed to protect me, and whom I was told to call if I was in danger. These men were (I was sure) killing a man because of the color of his skin. I yelled to my mother, "The mean sexists!" for it was the only "ist" I understood.

I thought of my friends at school in Chinatown, and how they would feel if it had been their fathers being beaten. And worse still, what if it had been my white father? It was someone's white father who had inflicted the beating. I felt ashamed, sad, and even responsible. The following day I was relieved to return to my overwhelmingly white classroom and lose myself in the ignorant bliss of a group of people who did not even discuss the beating.

Lisa

Moving from the city to a middle-class town was a great relief, but much of that came from a fine man who willingly picked up half of the family load. Suburbia, for all my uneasiness and feeling like a foreigner, was so much easier to handle day to day, especially with children. And, of course, the schools were going to be so splendid for this daughter and the one I would have a year later. But race was on no one's mind.

Speaking of race and poverty were always part of what we were, and are: they lie beneath everyday issues, like the crime bill, the loss of rent control, the impending welfare reform in my new neighborhood. As I talked, I snagged a quick look passed between others. As I talked, I realized they saw in me a strange white woman. *What does that have to do with here, with us?* the look said.

My neighbors are proud of a yearly Walk for Hunger, diversity days in the schools, and how our community "shares the dream." They should be proud, because mostly white schools did not always promote these ideas; some still don't. But I have been gently chastised: there is a time and place, a given day, a month, even, appropriate for such talk. If you keep harping about race and inequality as vital teeming forces that reside in every part of our society, well, that makes people feel uneasy. But is it not always there in how we make our world, how we invest, educate, feed, care for, share, and grow into the people we become?

Odessa

In the third grade, I moved to an elementary school in suburbia where, to my shock, there was a classroom full of white children. This was nothing like my previous school where Asian and black students outnumbered the whites. In my new class I could count the number of non-white classmates on half of a hand. The only two black girls sat together at the back of the class. I asked my new friend with the perfect pearl earrings—dressed up for her first day of school—why they seemed so excluded and quiet. She explained to me that those girls were "Boston Kids."

The wheels turned quickly in my head: I was a Boston Kid too, yet everyone was eager to meet me and seemed to be willing to let me in where I longed to be accepted. I had been given a clue that I should conceal where I came from and, the truth is, I did for nine years. I realized that there was no reason to speak of our single-mother years, or needing some "assistance." I think I unconsciously began to "act white," act *their* class (however these new people in wealthy America acted). I released those old ways that made me fit into a black, Asian, and Latino city neighborhood. I shudder about that now. No child wants to be an outcast as a preteen.

My self-segregation continued and became more dramatic when I entered a high school that had color-coded lockers for the different graduation classes, but which in fact had become dividing lines between different races. Looking down the hallway of my high school, one could clearly see a kind of segregation. My community prided itself in having a diverse high school, yet I could never understand how we could speak of diversity with such daily division. But I was not about to be ostracized for saying what was plainly there for all to see.

Lisa

There is a quiet code white people are taught when they are young enough for true imprinting. As best I can make out, the code counsels that race in America is perilous ground. If you go there, you walk into a minefield. But when you are white, you can choose not to enter, or so the covenant teaches. This doesn't mean you can ignore racism altogether. (OK, certainly some people do, but forget them.) *Most* white people are taught that race is a major issue, one that tests the meaning of American democracy. I truly believe most white people agree on that. But we have been taught careful, covert lessons on how you race-relate. Here is one I have dug out: *Do not be spontaneous.* Know your script well. Know when race matters should come to the table, like when a black person is present and wondering about the attitudes of the white people around her, or when discussing police profiling, South Africa, or affirmative action. But also know when race and inequality talk should be kept outside, outdoors. In an all- or mostly-white gathering, discussing race is spoiling the party. I learned that term from Beth Richie, an African American college professor and writer whom I met briefly some eighteen years ago. Beth described "spoiling the party": having to fracture the façade of unity to say that she saw things differently from her white friends or white neighbors. Saying something like, "No, it is not like that for me because I am not living in America as a white person."

I know now there is a white version of spoiling the party: referring to the presence of race in the everyday, where white people have grown comfortable assuming that it does not exist. I have not come to this revelation alone. My African American and Latina girlfriends allow themselves some smug smiles and kind chuckles over some of my reported "revelations."

I have a friend, Judith, who has told me, "Leave off. Damn, girl, you will get marked as a nut." I have a friend, Barbara, who has said, "Keep on it just as far as you can go, but don't let it make you crazy." Blanca once told me to do it peacefully, creatively, not so contentiously. And Yarice, young and bold, has said, "More, don't let up, it is good."

Lucy is one white friend who willingly faces wild, hidden, white truths. She knows that race is an overwhelming story about who we are, and she also knows it can be very dangerous ground to tread, and costs *anyone* who speaks up.

Odessa

At the age of nineteen I decided I was done with expensive clothes and cars I could never afford. I was tired of going to the parties where only "cool" people were invited, ambiguously meaning privileged and largely white classmates. Before my sophomore year of college I left to join City Year Boston, a national community service organization for young adults. I needed a change. I needed another learning experience. I longed for some other connection with people. City Year became an outlet to recapture a culture that I had not realized I desperately missed.

During my first few months on the job, I had never felt so white. My first day in the after-school center, where I would work for the year, was a revelation.

When I was a child and a white "minority" in a city school, it was not that race rejection did not exist, but rather that I was not old enough to feel and comprehend it. As one of two white staff in a free, after-school program in an all-black community, I felt more than out of place. I came home to talk to my mother and told her, "Ma, I did not know that I could *feel white*, that I could be constantly feeling my color." She had been working in places where she was the only white person, too, and we talked about what it felt like, how private it was, almost like a secret for white people.

When reconnecting with my friends from high school, I heard a question about my craving to work in a multicultural setting. "You just want to be a hippie like your mom," was one criticism leveled at me when I began to stray off the middle-class teenage path to becoming a doctor, lawyer, or any other job that ensured me privilege.

"No, I just want equal rights," I said.

Lisa

I had no idea that Odessa would choose City Year, or choose to be near home as she sorted out what all nineteen-year-olds have to sort out. I did not know we would talk about being white, about why we moved to this suburb, about how her sister would get to know the world. But these surprises have been a source of quiet joy.

Odessa

Attempting to connect with the children at my center, children who had never been in close contact with white people, was a six-month challenge. The children readily questioned my motives, asking me, "Why a rich white girl like you want to work with us?"

I realized that these children were carrying the same degree of ignorance about the white population as my white friends were carrying about black people. But I showed up, week after week, and through my dedication and love for my work, the children slowly responded to me.

Just as my white friends had stereotyped the "Boston Kids," the children at the center made assumptions about me, a "suburban kid." I felt the pain of being generalized, something people of color feel every day. The children at the center would regularly ask me for money, assuming that the color of my skin was an indication of the thickness of my wallet. And it was a test, too, I think.

The children would line up to receive help with their homework, and it seemed to me that some of the black staff sat back. A fellow staff member later told me that everyone assumed I was the appropriate person to help with the homework, that I had the "book" intelligence.

I also realized everyone distrusted me—everyone. They assumed I had an ulterior motive. It seemed that people had worked there in order to "clear their consciences." I didn't feel that way; I did not come with a guilty conscience.

I was, however, naïve when I first entered the building, imagining a warm welcome and expecting to bond immediately. I found that I had to earn trust, and it was harder with some than others, and sometimes it did not happen. But I went there to find something that I could not find in books and college lectures. I wanted to understand the people that make up my country.

Some days were hard. Some of the children in the program were ready with their racism against white people. A few were not even aware that racism against white people exists. And so my effort to return to the idea of a color-blind world was futile. I had reentered a diverse world containing different classes, ethnicities, races, and religions, but not as an equal. I was forced to prove myself to every person I met and this was extremely tiring. I guess it was an exhaustion that people of color who deal in white America know well. I came to the realization that people are simply scared of the unfamiliar. And that children can be taught that unfamiliar people are the villains.

One moment during my year touched me deeply. It happened as I separated two girls in a fight. After snatching a pen away, a young, well-behaved girl told the girl from whom she had taken the pen to "stop acting so damn white." Because I called her out for this and took her out of the classroom, she did not speak to me for the remainder of the day. The next afternoon, however, when I greeted her as she entered the building, she walked directly up to me.

"I'm sorry," she said. "I didn't mean what I said. I really like you. You're my favorite staff."

I was so glad to learn that just as I had gone home to talk about what had happened, apparently, so had she.

"I was not talking about you," she continued. "You're different."

Odessa Dorian Cole is nineteen and is working on social justice in America.

Lisa Dodson is a sociologist and author of Don't Call Us Out of Name: The Untold Lives of Women and Girls in Poor America (Beacon Press, 1999). She teaches in the Women Studies and Sociology departments at Harvard University and is currently conducting a three-city study—called "Across the Boundaries"—about low-wage jobs and family life in post-welfare America. She lives in Newton, Massachusetts.

© Susan Rae Lakin

Country Music[1]

SUSAN STRAIGHT

SOME PEOPLE WERE incredulous, some amused, and some slightly unhappy when I let my three daughters listen to country music. I mean, they chose it, they changed the radio stations and sang the songs in the car and danced in the kitchen to "Prop Me Up Against the Jukebox if I Die" and "All My Exes Live in Texas." But there were people who thought I shouldn't encourage them by allowing it, by listening as they recited all the lyrics to the songs in the country top forty and chose their favorite heartthrobs: Bryan White, with teenybopper looks, and Alan Jackson, with blond curls to his shoulders.

Because, since this country classifies people according to their racial makeup, my daughters are black. Their father is African, Native (Creek and Cherokee), and Irish American. But I'm the one always in the car and the kitchen with them, the one who laughed when they sang along with Alan about waitresses and the Chattahoochee. As far as looks go, I'm as white as people come. It was my genetic heritage that, accidentally, caused the country music idolatry.

My mother is from Switzerland, and two years ago I took my entire family, husband and children, mother and father, to her country of birth for a long vacation. We met scores of relatives, which thrilled my daughters. They swam with cousins who were Swiss and Italian, they met village friends, and they communicated however children do. In evenings and on rainy days, however, stuck in our rented cabin in the high mountains, there was only one English-language TV station: Country Music Television.

It was hilarious to watch. We don't even have cable in America, and my kids hadn't been exposed to the imaginative power of videos. They were enthralled as love song after love song played, with cowboy-hatted girls dancing and kissing cowboy-hatted men whose faithfulness and/or apologetic natures were displayed with heartbreaking grins. My daughters are quick, good with words, and sentimental—like me. They fell hard, in love with the neatly encapsulated video stories, with the rhyming lyrics (perfect for elementary-school-level memorization), and with the stars. All of whom were white. Patriotic, down-home handsome, white-bread white.

My mother, who emigrated to America at eighteen and actually loved Patsy Cline and Loretta Lynn back then, was bored with what she saw as vapid lyrics and tepid vocal skills. She couldn't believe my daughters' fervor lasted all vacation and continued when we returned to California, where they made me buy *Country Music Weekly* and play Alan Jackson cassettes in the car.

My husband wasn't thrilled, either. We're in our thirties, not hardcore rap fans but funk and R&B devotees since we met in high school. While I laughed at the girls' devotion and thought it was good that they were learning to read, even if it was song lyrics about drinking and crying, and to sing, even if it was about broken hearts and dying, he was the one who took them to his father's house, since there they could watch Country Music Television on cable. Surrounded by black relatives and friends, they sang along with their country-blond favorites, not noticing the occasional frowns of people wondering if maybe our kids had started to think they were white.

White is an interesting concept to children—at least to mine. For several years, my daughters considered it merely a descriptive shade. In preschool and kindergarten, where they have classmates of all colors, they referred to children's hair and skin color merely to identify them. Race was not a complex combination of language and history and class, not a varying collection of tastes in music, food, and dress. But as they are growing older, I sense that this is what race seems to them. A construct. What a person uses to construct him- or herself, on the scaffolding of skin color.

When I examine whiteness this way, often it comes down to something as comic as definitive.

In high school, when I was already dating my future husband, I watched the chameleon-like transformations of one girl I'll call Layla. I remember her face as a blank palette: pale skin, brown hair, brown eyes, wide mouth. Her freshman year, she was a loca. Pendleton shirt buttoned to the throat, creased khakis, plucked brows, purple lips, and a necklace of hickeys. She listened to oldies, sprinkled Spanish in her sentences. Then, suddenly, she was black. Pierced her nose, wore cornrows, hung out with only the baddest crowd, listened to Cameo and ConFunkShun, and spoke with an accent between Alabama and California. But the following year, she apparently decided she wanted to be homecoming queen. I remember the surprise of all of us in the bleachers when she appeared in the parade of formal gown-wearing hopefuls, her hair upswept, her makeup tasteful, her dress pastel, her escort a blond guy from another high school, the wealthy one.

Not only did she lose, she got her butt kicked a few times after school. I heard the way people talked about her. Pulling a Layla became a definition for posing, and posing makes the inescapable fact of someone else's race seem like a joke.

During all those instructive years, I had the same boyfriend—my future husband, who was black, hung out with a black crowd, played basketball, and dated me. I was shy and solitary. I absorbed some characteristics from him, and he took some of mine. On our first date, since we were broke, we played tennis, my lonely sport. On our subsequent ones, I watched him play basketball. Eventually, many of my friends influenced my choices of music and the way I talked. But unlike Layla, I was in love with a person, not an idea. Not a borrowed culture.

Loving someone's culture, absorbing it through love, can be a good thing. I learned a lot about cooking from my husband's mother, which I added to the years of cooking I'd done with mine. So by the time I got married, I could make Swiss soul food like raui roesti, a potato dish, and Hoppin' John, a traditional black New Year's dish of rice and black-eyed peas. I think many people consider food an essential component of race. When my husband's aunts heard we were getting married, they called us over for a very serious discussion. "Can you cook *right?*" they demanded. They were worried that I'd starve the man, serve him white toast and potatoes. (Many black friends have told me their opinions of "white cooking," which they say means only salt and pepper, and those in limited use.)

My daughters have grown up eating everything. They eat "white" food sometimes, meaning boiled potatoes and hamburger stroganoff, and "black" food, meaning barbecued ribs and sweet potatoes and greens. But since a recent trip to Oaxaca, we've eaten a lot of Mexican food. We drink Oaxacan hot chocolate, eat quesadillas and refried beans.

My daughters do not like black-eyed peas. Neither does their father. He hates watermelon and won't touch fried fish. What does this say? I laugh when he and other people say about someone black that "he's not a true brother." We have had many discussions about what is true and, even more popular now, "real." Keep it real, people say.

My older daughters have called themselves black a few times now. They are eight and six. (The two-year-old says, "I still a baby.") This year, they have referred to me a few times as white. School does this— a combination of the playground and history class. I felt very white one evening at our small round table over dinner. After we discussed Thanksgiving, the older two girls said, "Everybody at the table has Indian and African in their blood. Except you, Mommy."

They all looked at me for a minute. I don't remember what I had cooked. I said, "Yup. I'm Swiss and cowboy. Gone cowboy."

"Grampa's from Canada," the oldest daughter said.

I nodded. My stepfather is their grandfather. My natural father, whom I had only begun to mention to them that year, had a mother with a French name who died before I was born. His father was American, and gone. My father left when I was three. I visited him frequently. He was very white, patriotic, bought only American cars, and loved country music. I have not seen him since my wedding day nearly fifteen years ago. I do not think I am white to him. The funniest thing was when I finally met his father, for the first time, in Colorado. I was twenty-two. My grandfather, in his dark green work clothes, repairing an engine, had brown knuckles like burnt walnuts, a large nose in a sun-darkened face, and he looked enough like my husband's father to be a twin. They had both spent their lives working outside in harsh weather.

My skin is quite pale, my hair is blonde, and my eyes are bright blue. The girls like to comb my hair at night while we watch TV, because I sit still and don't complain. "You look like Barbie," they used to tease me. "Except your body."

"Thanks," I'd say. "Except Barbie isn't going bald from your rough little fingers."

Actually, pale blonde Barbie has lots of company in our living room. We also have Kira, who looks Asian, and Vanessa, who has dark brown skin, and Teresa, who is caramel colored. We have so many Barbies I laugh when I think of how my oldest daughter lost her first Barbie, which had been mine. My original Barbie, from 1960-something, with reddish hair and white skin and a moldy spot on her thigh that looked like a bruise. My mother had kept her for me all those years, and then Gaila took her to my husband's godmother's house, where she went while I worked. Gaila was the lightest kid there, one of the youngest. Some older kids threw Barbie into the fenced pen with her great-godfather's Doberman. No more Barbie.

My husband was never sure about those Barbies. And he's glad there's less country music. Oh, they listen to it sometimes, but they're older now. Their friends like Hanson, the blond teenyboppers, or the Spice Girls, who are calculatedly multiracial. Actually, my girls are learning about the Temptations, Aretha Franklin, and Stevie Wonder, because I always play my favorite soul oldies radio station in the kitchen while I cook.

I listen to the songs from the 1960s, '70s, and '80s that their father and I grew up with. The Jackson Five were big when I was in elementary school, and I was the only white girl in a dance group who imitated their moves. In high school, the Jacksons sang "Good Times," and Michael really worked his voice on "Let Me Show You" while my future husband and I rode around in his sister's Pinto. When I hear those, I get all teary eyed while I'm whirling around the kitchen. The girls ask me how come Michael Jackson isn't black any more.

I have to laugh. Gaila was in love with Michael Jackson when she was two. She drew pictures of him with his glove. Now she stares at him quizzically, then shrugs when I try to explain what I know. I tell her the voice singing, making me sad, is the old Michael Jackson.

I get sad, remembering. Their father doesn't live with us any more, so I'm not sure what he's listening to, but the girls tell me he plays a lot of classical music. He plays a tiny electric chess game, instead of raucous dominoes like he used to. Does all this mean he's turning white? I don't think so. Are we less black, now, as a family? I don't think so.

We're as mixed up as ever. I think because I am an artist, our house is full of all kinds of cultures. We have African and Mexican and Swiss carvings of wood in the living room. We have children of every color in the yard.

I look in the mirror, thinking about this category. Whiteness. For some reason my hair is paler since I had my last child. When my first book came out and the publisher suggested no photo on the back, I insisted on a picture. I was a white woman writing about life in a black community, and I didn't want to pull a Teena Marie. Not that she was bad. She was so good, everyone thought her first album was sung by a black woman, instead of a white woman shorter and blonder than me. My high school friends and I were all shocked by her picture on the next recording. I never wanted to surprise anyone.

My soul oldies station plays Teena Marie and the Average White Band, Scottish men who play black music. We are in the kitchen, cooking a recipe I invented by accident, the recipe my mother-in-law liked best. I only had a few things to cook with, and I needed a dish for a family reunion, so I made rice with curry and sugar and garlic, black beans and spicy sausage. I was the only white person at the reunion, as always. Everyone said the rice combination had soul. I said the combination was desperation. Friends and family requested it for years. I make the rice now.

My skin is so pale this winter that my makeup color is Ivory. My daughters picked it out at Target. I look at them playing. This is my first effort at trying to describe their color. Gaila, the oldest, is burnished gold, with mostly straight hair to her waist. She still prefers country music and less spicy food, and usually chooses blonde Barbies. Delphine, the next, is pale as almond shells, with wavier hair. She likes food and music people consider blacker, and she chooses dark Barbies. I think this is funny. My baby, Rosette, is light brown as a perfectly done pancake, her cheeks just that round, a dimple in her left one like a bubble of trapped laughter. She is my darkest child, the one who prompts questions like, "Are you babysitting?"

While I cook, her squirming butt rests on my forearm, which looks very pale against her skin. My inner arm has a permanent swath of about twenty lines, worn there from the skin being twisted under the clinging weight of three girls in a row, all that carrying when people told me I was spoiling them, babying them, and I knew I was loving them. What shade or construct is in those wrinkles, which are slightly darker grooves in the rest of the skin, I do not know.

------

[1] Copyright 1998 by Susan Straight. Reprinted by permission of The Richard Parks Agency.

A graduate of Riverside Community College, **Susan Straight** *went on to earn a scholarship to the University of Southern California and in 1984 earned her M.F.A. from the University of Massachusetts at Amherst. Her first collection of stories,* Aquaboogie *(Milkweed Editions, 1990), won the Milkweed National Fiction Prize and was named one of the best paperbacks of the year by* Publisher's Weekly. *Proving that she was not a one-shot wonder, Straight has not yet failed fans or critics in her subsequent offerings:* I Been in Sorrow's Kitchen and Licked Out All the Pots *(Anchor Books, 1993), which was selected as a "Best Book" by the* New York Times, USA Today *and* Publisher's Weekly; The Gettin Place *(Hyperion, 1996);* Blacker Than a Thousand Midnights *(Anchor Books, 1995); and* Highwire Moon *(Houghton Mifflin, 2001). A writer for* Salon, *the online magazine, Straight's essays on motherhood appear in the bestselling collection* Mothers Who Think *(Washington Square Press, 2000).*

Portrait of the author
by his son, John Henry,
about 5 at the time.

© John Henry Ignatiev

One Summer Evening

NOEL IGNATIEV

One summer evening just after high school, I was walking in downtown Philadelphia when I saw a man spread-eagled against a wall, being searched by a policeman. The man was black, the policeman white. When the policeman finished patting the man down, he bade him turn around, and when the man did so, slugged him in the gut. I ran over and said excitedly, "You can't do that. You're not supposed to hit that man." The policeman grabbed me and threw me into a police car. I spent the night in a cell in the local station house.

I was allowed to call home and the next morning my dad showed up in court. When my case was called I tried to tell what I had seen, but before I could get out more than a few words, the judge interrupted me, yelling that I had interfered with an officer. He declared me guilty of something and fined me twenty-five dollars. My dad paid the fine, and as we were leaving the court an elderly black lady walked by me and said, "God bless you."

Over forty years have passed, and I have felt blessed ever since. If I am ever called to justify the food and water I consumed on earth, I will cite that incident in my defense, and hope that it makes up for many stupid, selfish, and cowardly acts.

To be arrested for interfering with a cop beating a black man was an honor in my family. My father's job was delivering the *Philadelphia Inquirer* in the morning. His route covered a black area of West Philadelphia. From the time I turned eleven I helped him several mornings a week, and got to know many of the people we served. They frequently told me what a fine man my father was; he used to say proudly that there wasn't another white man in the city who could have served that route.

I remember only two occasions when he hit me: once for bullying my younger brother, and once for referring to someone as a "nigger." "I don't ever want to hear you say that word again," he said, as he whacked me across the back of the head.

I remember a short time later squatting in a circle of kids in the schoolyard reciting, "Eeeny, meeny, miny, mo . . . " to determine who would go first in a children's game. Before I could complete the rhyme, Tommy Knox, a black kid, said, "If you finish that I'm gonna bust you in the face." The only versions of that jingle I had heard had a tiger or a doggie as the principal character, but in a flash it struck me that there was another version and what that was. I don't know which was the better teacher, Tommy Knox or my father, who could not have loved me so much had he not loved honor more, but I am grateful to both of them.

Another time Tommy Knox and I got into a schoolyard quarrel, and I challenged him to come up to the local Y to put on the gloves and fight it out. "You know I can't go to the Y," said Tommy. I had not known, but I remember, as clearly as if it were yesterday, my anger against him immediately dissolving, to be replaced by rage at the administrators at the Y who prevented us from fighting in a ring with gloves. I must have been about ten.

At that time, in order to exclude black people, Philadelphia swimming pools called themselves private clubs and sold one-dollar "memberships" to whites only. My parents refused to patronize them, and we shared the black experience of sweltering on the streets in the summers, except for the rare occasions when we managed to open a fire hydrant. When the firemen—all white—came to shut off the valve, we would taunt them from a safe distance while our parents observed from the stoops, smiling. When the City opened its first truly public swimming pool, our family attended regularly, often the only non-black people present.

My mother was no less dedicated to racial justice than my father. Once a black high school acquaintance invited me to attend a party where I would likely be the only person who was not black. In spite of all my experience I still felt nervous, and decided not to go. I told her of my decision. "You should be ashamed of yourself," she said. Her rebuke indeed shamed me into going. Of course I had a great time.

Our home was close to the TV studio that broadcast *Bandstand*, and although I longed to go there, I didn't because it excluded black people. (At that time, *Bandstand* was a local show. The host was a man named Bob Horn (!) who was fired when it came out that he kept an apartment near the studio where he took some of the regular girls. He was replaced by Dick Clark, who was even more baby-faced then than he is now. It soon went national and became *American Bandstand*. (I thrilled later at John Waters's film *Hairspray*, which recounted the struggle to desegregate a *Bandstand*-like show in Baltimore.)

The movements of the 1960s touched me as they did millions of others. Aside from the political excitement, I recall friendships that could have been formed at no time before or after, and experiences whose significance I missed at the time but which I have since reflected upon. The person who most influenced my thinking on race was Theodore Allen.

I met Ted in 1958 and then lost touch with him. When I re-encountered him in 1966, he was developing the thesis that white supremacy, grounded in the privileges of white skin, was the Achilles' heel of American radicalism. He argued that at each turning point in U.S. history, and especially at moments when revolutionary change seemed possible, the rulers had been able to ride out the storm by appealing to the race sentiments of the white majority. The germ of the idea he got from *Black Reconstruction in America* by W. E. B. DuBois.

It made sense to me, and in 1967 I wrote a pamphlet called *The White Blindspot*, which he and I and a few others published privately.

(The title was drawn from a passage in *Black Reconstruction in America*.) It created a bit of a stir within Students for a Democratic Society and other sectors of the New Left. Among other things it introduced the term "white-skin privilege" into public discourse.

In 1968, following a wildcat strike at the Dodge Main plant in Hamtramck, Michigan, black workers and activists in Detroit joined together to create the Dodge Revolutionary Union Movement (DRUM). The movement quickly spread across Detroit as similar groups formed at other Chrysler plants, Ford, and elsewhere, and then joined together to form the League of Revolutionary Black Workers. The goal of the League was to overthrow white capitalist power, first in the Detroit auto plants and ultimately in the society as a whole. It relied on direct action and operated independently of, and often against, the official union, the United Automobile Workers. In my opinion, the League represented the highest point achieved by the movement of the 1960s.

I spent the 1970s and part of the '80s in the Chicago area working in steel mills and machine-tool factories, attempting to expand the base of the League to white workers. I cannot report any major successes, but I learned a great deal and enjoyed myself. The wave of deindustrialization that swept the country beginning in the late 1970s finally affected me; in 1984, finding myself laid off from a metalworking factory, I decided to take a step down and go to Harvard.

One of Ted's ideas was that the white race was not a biological but a social-historical category. (In 1994 he published the first of two volumes of *The Invention of the White Race*.) I had always found that an interesting notion, and so for my dissertation I chose to study how a particular group of people who had themselves been the victims of oppression very much like what Americans call racial became members of an oppressing race. The result was *How the Irish Became White*, which was published in 1995.

In the interests of survival, African Americans have always studied whiteness. There is a long tradition among them that the white race is a peculiar sort of social formation, one that depends on its members' willingness to conform to the institutions and behavior patterns that reproduce it. By the early 1990s, thanks to the work of David Roediger, Ruth Frankenburg, and others, it was becoming commonplace in the academy to speak of race, along with class and gender, as a social construct.

An old friend, John Garvey, and I had known each other for close to twenty years, had worked together on various projects, and had come to hold virtually identical views. In addition to the notion of race as a social construct, we shared another, which we owed to the West Indian Marxist, C. L. R. James: that ordinary Americans are drawn by the conditions of their lives in two opposite directions, one that mirrors and reproduces the present society of competition and exploitation, and another that points toward a new society based on freely associated activity. We believed that this internal antagonism played itself out as a civil war within the white mind, between the desire of whites to wall themselves off from black Americans and their desire to overcome the boundaries that kept them apart.

John and I decided that it was time to launch a journal to document that civil war. The result was *Race Traitor,* whose first issue appeared in the fall of 1992 with the slogan "Treason to whiteness is loyalty to humanity" on its cover. The aim was to chronicle and analyze the making, remaking, and unmaking of whiteness. My book on the Irish was the story of how people for whom whiteness had no meaning learned its rules and adapted their behavior to take advantage of them; *Race Traitor* was an attempt to run the film backwards, to explore how people who had been brought up as white might become unwhite.

If races were a product of politics, not evolution, we reasoned, then they could be dissolved by political action. Since we understood that the "white" and "black" races had not performed symmetrical functions historically, we decided not to take an even-handed approach toward them but to focus on the struggle to abolish the white race.

Race Traitor has established itself more rapidly than we anticipated. So far fourteen issues have appeared. It has been widely reviewed and commented upon; its editors frequently address popular and scholarly audiences; and interviews with them have appeared in the *New York Times* and other leading periodicals. In 1996, Routledge published an anthology of selections from the journal, also called *Race Traitor,* which won an American Book Award from the Before Columbus Foundation. The journal has a Web site, www.racetraitor.org, which the people at postfun.com set up for us on their own initiative and told us about afterward.

Thanks in part to *Race Traitor,* many people who think about race are familiar with the notion that it is a social construct and have heard of the idea that it could be dissolved; some even call themselves abolitionists. In our first issue we predicted that if it were successful, the journal would create a new audience made up of people from disparate backgrounds who shared little more than a willingness to question their membership in the white club. This has occurred, as the journal has broken out of the academy and the traditional Left. It has expanded its editorial board and brought together a core of participants beyond the two founders.

As an indication of its success in regrouping, it has published in its own name two issues on surrealism edited by people from the Surrealist Movement. *Race Traitor* may be the only small journal in America whose writers and readers range from tenured professors to prison inmates. So far, they are not the same individuals. We will be sure we have had an impact when some of the professors go to prison and some of the prison inmates are placed on university faculties. (Mumia Abu-Jamal has come closest to achieving the latter distinction by being named a commencement speaker at three colleges so far.)

Many of the articles in *Race Traitor* arrive unsolicited from people we do not know. We also receive unsolicited financial contributions, which greatly encourage us and help keep the journal going. Apart from renewal notices, we've never sent out a general appeal for funds. We send only one notice to each subscriber; our aim is not to sell magazines, but to build a movement, and we figure that people who need to be reminded repeatedly to renew their subscriptions are not ready to take part in building a movement.

That philosophy also leads me not to pass around a signup sheet at public meetings. If people express interest in working with us, I tell them to go out and do something along the lines we advocate, and then tell us about it; we will be glad to publicize their work, provide speakers and written material, and support them in any way we can.

The goal of abolishing the white race is on its face so desirable that some may find it hard to believe that it could incur any opposition other than from committed white supremacists. Of course we expected bewilderment from people who still think of race as biology. We frequently get letters accusing us of being "racists," just like the KKK, and have even been called a "hate group" by several outfits who make it their business to keep track of that sort of thing.

Our standard response is to draw an analogy with antiroyalism: to oppose monarchy does not mean killing the king; it means getting rid of crowns, thrones, royal titles, etc. Sometimes these correspondents write us back saying they appreciate the explanation, but wonder why we use such provocative language. In reply we ask, if we had expressed ourselves in conventional "antiracist" terms, would we be having this conversation about the social meaning of whiteness?

Apart from the expected opposition and bewilderment, *Race Traitor* has drawn a number of criticisms from people who consider themselves opponents of "racism." Some, usually identified with what is often called "the Left," have said that it talks too much about race and not enough about class. In my view, no reader could possibly be unaware that the editors of *Race Traitor* regard the United States as a society based on the exploitation of the working class by capital. The problem is that, for most proletarian whites, their class identity is obscured by their racial self-identification. We therefore reply that we will stop talking about race as soon as the people for whom the critics claim to speak forget that they are "white."

In a parallel charge to that made by the proponents of class, *Race Traitor* has been criticized repeatedly for neglecting gender or subordinating it to race. This charge has caused us no small concern and provoked considerable debate among us. We recognize that there are analogies and links between white supremacy and patriarchy, and that the struggle to change the world must take these into account. At the same time, the charter of *Race Traitor* is to deal with whiteness; as we wrote in reply to a correspondent, "we have no objection to calling into question 'other problematic social and historical constructions besides "race,"' *if it come fairly in the way of our business,—hunting the white whale.*"

Every group within white America has at one time or another advanced its particular and narrowly-defined interests at the expense of black people as a race. That applies to labor unionists, ethnic groups, college students, schoolteachers, taxpayers, and white women. *Race*

Traitor will not abandon its focus on whiteness, no matter how vehement the pleas and how virtuously oppressed those doing the pleading. The editors meant it when they replied to a reader, "Make no mistake about it: we intend to keep bashing the dead white males, and the live ones, and the females too, until the social construct known as 'the white race' is destroyed—not 'deconstructed' but destroyed."

I spent the spring of 2000 at the University of California at Riverside. That year 28 percent of the students were classified as "white," 40 percent "Asian," 21 percent "Hispanic," 6 percent "black," and 4 percent "other." I provoked considerable controversy and some hostility by suggesting that the school could be looked at either as a positive model of "diversity," which was the way the administration looked at it, or as a place where black students made up only half of their proportion in the California population and the remaining 94 percent consisted of whites and those waiting in the antechamber of whiteness.

My remarks were consistent with the stance of *Race Traitor,* which has been criticized for breaking society down into black and white, thereby overlooking those who are of neither African nor European descent. This criticism would have a certain validity if our project were to develop a catalogue of oppression, or to become expert on the relative misery of various groupings in the population. We are seeking neither of these things, but to abolish the white race.

The editors recognize that the white race was constructed in opposition to various peoples, including Native Americans, Chinese, Mexicans, and Filipinos, as well as Africans. At the same time, it has been periodically recomposed, absorbing groups once excluded from it or admitted only on probation (like the Irish or Italians). Much of the debate over the status of the new immigrants from Asia and "Latin" America consists of efforts to determine who will be socially white in the twenty-first century.

Strategy, not sociology, demands a bipolar model—"black" and "white"—not as ethnocultural but as sociopolitical categories. Of course it is also necessary to recognize that the outcome is not yet determined and that at any moment various peoples show aspects of intermediacy. Our goal is to prevent the whitening of the "new" immigrants and reverse the whitening of the "old."

A curious spin on this point is provided by some who claim descent from one of the European ethnic groups that have been treated as white for a century or so, but who now reject that designation in favor of "Irish," "Italian," "Jewish," etc.

One man from something calling itself the Irish Anti-Defamation League showed up at a conference at which I was supposed to speak with a leaflet attacking me as "anti-Irish." In an exchange later, he denied that Irish Americans were white, and called for affirmative action for Irish at Berkeley, on the grounds that they were underrepresented in the University of California system. I replied that that was fine with me, but I asked how he would define "Irish."

Would he count Shaquille O'Neal, Troy O'Leary, or the other millions of black people of Irish descent or with Irish surnames? In fact, I would love it if Irish, Italian, and Jewish Americans rejected their whiteness in favor of ethnic identities, but with few exceptions their claims that their history has given them an understanding of the oppression of black people are self-serving attempts to deny their complicity with white supremacy. Mostly they just want to change the name to play the game.

I frequently encounter so-called antiracist white people who fall into metaphysics at the idea of abolishing the white race. They agonize over what they call their "identity"; organize "consciousness-raising" sessions (for whites only) in which they "share their pain" and "own" (acknowledge) their whiteness. Instead of motivating them to change the world, their guilt paralyzes them. The attitude of these people—almost always from the liberal professions—contrasts with the faith of ordinary Americans that they can become something different from what they were. That faith—shown in the popularity of the film *Boys Don't Cry*—is one of the things that gives me hope for the future of this country.

When I speak publicly, I make a point of distinguishing between being antiwhite, which I am, and being unwhite, which I do not claim to have become. I know very well that (for now) I can say whatever I please in a meeting hall, but that when I walk out on the street no policeman will throw me up against a wall for it. I am aware that whatever consequences I have faced because of my unpopular stances are small potatoes compared to what an ordinary black man my age has faced from walking around in a dark skin. Yet I, too, hold out the hope that I can someday become something more than I am.

❧

My son, John Henry, who is now ten, is interested in *Race Traitor* and the whole notion of race, and has been wrestling with the relation between race and skin color. A while back he asked, "Who is white, Daddy?"

"If a person is mean to black people, that makes him white," I replied.

A few days later he brought up the subject again. "How about if a black person is mean to other black people, does that make him white?"

I remembered my father telling me that there were times he and my mother stayed up at night trying to figure out answers to my questions.

I pulled on my beard and said, "Well, John Henry, I made a mistake before. A person can only be white if he is treated as white by other whites, and a black person who is mean to other black people still won't be treated as white.

"Let me explain it another way. To be white is like knowing that whenever you go to a birthday party you're going to get the biggest piece of cake."

"What's a race traitor, then?" he asked. (I did not invent this conversation.)

"To be a race traitor is to protest as loudly when you get the biggest piece of cake as you would if you got the smallest piece," I answered.

About a week went by. "I was at my friend's house and his big sister was picking on him," reported my prince. "She's about thirteen and really big and I was scared, but I told her to stop. Is that what it means to be a race traitor?"

"Yes, it is, John Henry."

"Even though my friend isn't black?"

"That's right," I said. "Even though he isn't black."

❧

Several years ago I moved to a majority-black working-class area. I did not move there to make a statement and I do not think my presence does anything for racial justice. I moved there because it was convenient, affordable, and a pretty street. Before I moved one white friend warned me about crime. I have learned to like my neighbors, and I can now report that my most serious encounter with what society calls crime was with the neighbor who showed me how to run a jumper around one of the utility meters. I do not think that is what the friend who warned me had in mind.

Meanwhile, forty years after the summer evening I recounted at the beginning of this essay, the police still routinely hassle the black youth in my neighborhood, and occasionally kill one of them.

Noel Ignatiev *is the author of* How the Irish Became White *(Routledge, 1995),* The Lesson of the Hour: Wendell Phillips on Abolition and Strategy *(Charles H. Kerr, 2001), and co-founder and coeditor of* Race Traitor *(Routledge, 1996), which won an American Book Award in 1997. He teaches in the Department of Critical Studies at Massachusetts College of Art, and is a fellow at the W. E. B. DuBois Institute for Afro-American Research, Harvard University. He and* Race Traitor *can be reached on the Internet at www.racetraitor.org.*

Spelling Lesson

CARLTON WINFREY

JOHNNY COPELAND WAS my first white friend—or at least I think he was. We went to elementary school together in Nashville. We didn't do things together after school like my kids and their white friends do today. Johnny was my friend at school only, because we lived miles apart, physically and figuratively. You see, I'm a product of forced busing.

In first grade, I walked to school in my neighborhood, a part of town where Fisk and Tennessee State University professors lived; where Meharry doctors, dentists, and business owners built their own homes. But by second grade, everything about school had changed dramatically.

It was in the early 1970s when my siblings, our neighbors, and I became part of the great desegregation experiment. Consequently, we rode a school bus nearly an hour each way to the far corners of the county. We still came home to the same upscale black community, but we went to a rural, predominantly white school with white kids from the backwoods, some of whom lived in trailers tucked in valleys or shanties hidden in the hills of Tennessee. I was forced to sit next to, associate with, and befriend these white boys and girls. That's how I met Johnny Copeland and how he came to give me my first quick lesson on race.

We were in line that day, waiting our turn for the school's annual physical. When I took off my shirt, Johnny Copeland was so stunned, he just blurted it out.

"I didn't know you were black all over!" I will never forget how sad he was, practically in tears.

I was shocked too, but for a different reason. Of course, my parents had taught me and my siblings about the social realities of race—you must be better, smarter in order to get the same job; we're the last hired, first fired. But they had also sheltered us from many of the cruelties of race. Part of my naïveté—my "Huh?"—in response to Johnny Copeland's spontaneous utterance was because I had never before experienced a person who saw me as different in any way.

If Johnny Copeland was the first to strike a tiny nerve, there would be many others after him. (Imagine two homecoming queens, one black, one white!) Perhaps it is my memory of that racial initiation and of my parents' efforts to hold it at bay as long as possible that makes me the way I am with my children today.

I remember how my parents would spell certain words rather than say them in my presence. They were probably people's names and things about them that they didn't want us to know about and therefore repeat. Now, some thirty-plus years, a wife, and two children later, I find myself doing the same thing. The funny thing about it is my wife and I spell the words "black" and "white."

We don't do it because we use the words in some profane way. We do it, I think, because we don't want Reed, who's five, and Karli, three, to notice race as the most important thing about a person and the only thing that matters. We want them to believe that what really matters in life is the person and the relationship they have with that person.

We don't want them to preface every reference to their friends with "my white friend so-and-so" or to point to a stranger at the grocery store saying, "Look at that white lady."

So we spell "black" and "white" because, like my parents, we, too, want to shield our children as long as possible from some of the negative realities of race in America.

Of course, Reed and Karli know a black person from a white person. They even know the differences in skin tones within the same race, sad reminders of the racial realities in America that thrive generation after generation. Sort of like generation after generation spelling out words.

No matter what we do, though, inevitably Reed's and Karli's perception of race will change, much like the perception others have of them as a little black boy and little black girl.

People would "ooo" and "aahhh" over my children as babies, cooing over their curly black hair, smooth Hershey complexions, and startling eyes. As I watched these encounters, often with perfect strangers, my mind would fast-forward to the first day my sweet, innocent children will be called "niggers"; to the day they will sit alone in a school cafeteria separated by race; to the day they will endure the awkward silence that follows a racist joke told in their presence; to the day they will be followed by security officers at the mall; to the day they will be stopped by the police for being in the "wrong" neighborhood; to the day an elderly white woman will cross the street rather than pass them on the sidewalk.

What happens in those years between being adored by strangers and being feared by them? What makes a person smile and coax conversation from a little black boy and, a few years later, flee from him? What makes a person heap praise and compliments on a little black girl with thick plaits and colorful barrettes, yet despise her before too long? What happens during those years in between?

Busing forced me to meet white people who did not look like the white people on TV. It helped me understand what happens when white people and black people are not exposed to each other.

During those years of busing I learned to see the world beyond my small, nurturing, protective enclave in northwest Nashville. But perhaps most important, my experiences taught me to cultivate relationships with people from all walks of life and to understand our interaction as a two way street. This is, I believe, a critical first step toward improving race relations.

The issue of racism—race prejudice plus power—is seemingly not an issue that my generation of Americans is ready to tackle. But I still hope that my children can learn from my experiences, not so they will be accepted by the majority or even approved by the minority, but so they will grow up to be well-rounded individuals who genuinely appreciate people for who they are, not what they are.

Reed and Karli will keep having (w-h-i-t-e) friends over to play and spend the night. They will also keep learning about slavery and the centuries of oppression that continue to weigh on (b-l-a-c-k) people. While we will instill pride in their heritage and the struggle of their people, we will also teach them that throughout our history there have been and will continue to be (w-h-i-t-e) people of good will who fought the scourge of racism and oppression. Armed with this knowledge, they will be equipped to share it with people wherever they go.

In the meantime, how long can I protect Reed and Karli from, and yet educate them about, race and racism? That remains to be seen. It's a delicate balancing act, and a scary one. And I know that I am just the latest in a long line of black parents who have struggled, generation after generation, to strike that balance.

I pray that thirty years from now Reed and Karli are not spelling out words that should carry no shame or negativity. I pray that they are able to speak freely around their own children about the issue of race. I pray that for them the daily burden of being a black person or a black parent in America won't be as heavy as it was when my father was my age, or when his father was my age—as heavy as it is for me even now.

Born and raised in Nashville, Tennessee, **Carlton Winfrey** *is the night city editor for the* St. Louis Post-Dispatch.

© Joanna Eldredge Morrissey

Jasper, Texas Elegy

BERNESTINE SINGLEY

I. Prologue

I AM OBSESSED with race, not by accident, but by design. I blame my mother first, and then the rest of my community, for raising me to be this way.

It began when I was born in the middle of the night, in the middle of the year, in the middle of the twentieth century, plopped down into what passed for life beneath the heel of apartheid in the U.S. South.

I was many things that were not a cause for celebration—poor, black, female, and fatherless. Even so, I very early became a vessel into which my mother and black others poured their hopes and dreams, a small brown harbinger of the Days of Overcoming.

As the baby of our one-parent family, I was acutely aware of the thin line between, on the one hand, a safe, secure, loving home with my mother and sister and, on the other, being left an orphan. I could not imagine life without my mother. Consequently, my earliest prayer was that when my time came to die, I'd be struck dead while sitting next to her in church, thereby killing two birds with one stone: my fear of being left behind and my desire to go to heaven.

Be careful what you ask for; someone else might get it.

My obsession increased on September 15, 1963, for it was then that adult members of the Sixteenth Street Baptist Church in Birmingham, Alabama, were kneeled in prayer, and white men bombed their church and killed their children. Murdered were Denise McNair, eleven; and Addie Mae Collins, Carole Robertson, and Cynthia Wesley, at the time all fourteen years old—just like me.

Two black boys, Johnny Robinson, sixteen, and Virgil Ware, thirteen, neither in church nor in prayer, got it too that day. Grown white men killed Johnny, but it was two sixteen-year-old white boys who shot and killed Virgil. Perhaps because they did not fit into the tidy, reverential descriptive the "Four Little Girls," both Johnny and Virgil were completely dropped from acres of newsprint and miles of discussion forever after.

Anyway, two months after that, white men killed President John F. Kennedy, leaving me wary and wondering about the power of prayer.

By this time, I had already been anointed a member of the "Talented Tenth": W. E. B. DuBois's name for a mythical, educated, Negro elite he believed would lead the Negro masses in racial uplift. I loathed the concept from the first I heard of it. No matter. Time and circumstance plucked me from my meager beginnings and marked me as one of them. We were quietly but determinedly schooled in our elevated status, prepared to be the ones who would smash the lies of segregation.

Meanwhile, Ma continued toiling in two worlds: the completely segregated colored one where we lived in a public housing project, where she sent us to school and took us to church; and the completely segregated white one where she took three busses, each way, every day, to barely earn a living cleaning up behind white folks in their houses.

Each evening she returned with dispatches from her domestic psychological battlefield. During dinner, we examined her findings: tales told by food bits in a sink strainer, rumpled sheets on a bed in the wrong room, stained underwear stuffed in a briefcase, a handgun beneath a pillow, a dry cough inserted in an otherwise strained silence.

All endless intrigue in our home purposely devoid of television—"the stupid box" which we were forbidden to watch, even at a neighbor's.

Under her tutelage, we learned to pick apart the evidence and then wad it back up, the better to understand what we were up against in our escalating demands to be seen as equal, entitled, and fully human. We were experts on the relentless arrogance of white folks and their children, drenched in the rightness and mightiness of their whiteness. Food for thought, as critical for our survival, she said, as food for our bellies.

Dissecting white folks was a family pastime and we were damn good at it. Consequently, we harbored no illusions about white folks' inferiority or about their delusions of superiority.

After years of such intensive boot camp training, I itched to graduate. So, flush with patriotism, I leapt into active duty in the War for Racial Equality, presenting myself as the perfect guinea pig for the nation's brief experiment in Social Justice. In the fall of 1967, I reported to Lawrence University, an outpost in Appleton, Wisconsin, former hometown to at least two world-famous circus acts: Houdini and Joe McCarthy. In doing so, I integrated not only a college campus, but the entire Fox River Valley.

Then came Ma's final warnings.

"Don't come bringing no white boy back here," she said.

We eyed each other silently, neither one of us brave enough to be the first to look away. In my mind, I sucked my teeth and rolled my eyes. Double negatives aside, what would make her say something like that? After all, from the looks of her—blue-veined pale skin, thin lips, straight hair, sharp nose, and flat butt—white boys had clearly been all up in our family, one way or another, for generations.

Out loud I said, "Yes, ma'am, Mama."

What did she know? Too few to count had been where I was going, certainly no one we knew. Even so, she spoke then as she always did, precisely, an expert on everything, never hesitant.

"And just remember," she finished. "What you're going out there to do is more than a notion. Just keep on praying."

Ma might've been wise, but I was leaving, stepping off into the World of the White People. Intoxicated by my impending escape from the corset of Southern black life, I couldn't wait to strut my stuff among the know-nothing white folks. Her warnings were like echoes glancing off distant tunnel walls.

I should've listened.

Despite my years of preparation, it had not occurred to me that I would be under siege. Despite their invitation—backed up with a full scholarship, a work/study job, and a loan—the college had made no further plans for me. It was sink or swim.

Stranded in that sea of whiteness called college, in no time I was reaching back to snatch what comfort I could from prayer.

"Please, God," I said. "Help me get through this. Don't let them do me in."

The next spring, white men killed Dr. Martin Luther King, Jr., then Bobby Kennedy, and so on until Richard Nixon became president in 1968. There I was, nearly drained of hope and once again precariously attached to prayer.

Still, I consoled myself. "Thirty years from now, it won't be like this."

I did not doubt that my work as a Race Warrior would help wipe out racism by the end of the twentieth century. I was certain that I was, for my new white friends, their springboard to a multitude of other black friends and acquaintances. Like the canary who made it safely back out of the mines, I dreamed of flitting hither and yon, singing integration's praises.

"Thirty years from now, it won't be like this." Those nine words formed the thread from which I dangled above the trenches of race, class, and gender. Then one night in 1971, a few months shy of graduation, that thread snapped.

When it happened, I had nearly finished serving my four-year tour of duty. Feeling like a raisin in a pot of rice, I had earnestly fought the War for Racial Equality, but all prospects of an honorable discharge had vanished. I was losing anyway. With not even the C average required to graduate, I was on the verge of disgracing my family and friends, and thereby Failing the Race.

Alone in my dormitory room, I had a revelation: I didn't want to *be* white. I wanted the chance *not* to be white, and still not be invisible, the circus freak, The First, The Only.

Close on its heels, another revelation: The world was theirs and, no matter my accomplishments, I was present by invitation only, eternally subject to being found wanting and summarily ejected. Saturated with race, I had never lived a moment free of that reality.

To save myself, I shut them out and fantasized about their extinction.

White girl voices gather at the end of the hall, expanding merrily as they approach the door behind which I crouch. High-pitched squeals slip past wet towels I stuffed in the crack between the bottom of the door and the floor. Coeds saunter past, impervious to my plans for them, mocking the fragility of my barricade of closed windows and drawn blinds.

I squeeze my eyes shut and begin the countdown to their destruction. "Three . . . two . . . one . . . BOOM!"

Multiple explosions blow them apart. In the smoking rubble, I'm the only thing left standing, pristinely intact, my hands fluttering near my heart, tiptoeing among their remains. Eyes downcast, I murmur, "Oh, such nice girls . . . too soon . . . so sad. . . . Many are called . . . these were chosen. You guys, who can understand the majestic hand of God?"

For thirty days and thirty nights, a weeping lunatic, I refined my annihilation fantasies. Then, without warning, I heeded Mama's mantra: "Get up, wipe your nose, and finish what you started." I graduated.

"Thirty years from now . . ." I reminded myself while boarding the plane and fleeing Babylon.

I was halfway through law school before my true accomplishments in Wisconsin slapped me upside my head. There, in Gainesville, Florida, squared off and toe to toe with one thousand Southern white men, I had another revelation: I had broken the code of whiteness during my bleak Wisconsin years. I had become an expert in white-think and white-talk, a decorated general among Race Warriors.

A smug survivor, I set about further refining my skills. I mastered white male talk, white male power, and white male entitlement. I scored points toward a fiercely sought redemption by earning the highest A in three different law classes. I was even elected vice president of the 33,000-member University of Florida Student Government Association in the spring of 1973.

Friends and family were not surprised when I went on to graduate from Harvard Law School with a second law degree and ended up doing what the Talented Tenth does best: representing the Race.

I performed that service completely surrounded by usually hostile white people, convinced that what I was doing—juggling white-talk

and white-think with black-talk and black-think, with race representing and breathing in between—was making a difference. Good jobs,
success, money, and good living ran on the big screen up front while
daily indignities occasioned by my blackness streamed continuously in
the background. Murdered black girls, a slain president, and martyred
civil rights leaders slipped over the edge, pockets in shallow memory.

Consequently, in 1998, when news of a truck lynching blasted in
from Jasper, Texas, it caught me completely off guard. Yet, this time,
instinct born of more than thirty years on the race war's front lines kicked
in and started shutting me down. I could not afford to know the details
of one more black man's ghoulish destruction if I wished to remain sane,
going about the daily business of placing one foot before the other. So I
pressed ahead, determinedly ignorant—or trying to be. It worked until
I learned his name: James Byrd, Jr., father, son, neighbor.

Details of Byrd's dismemberment filled the air. Chunks of the saga
floated through my days. I swerved and dodged, trying to keep from
being knocked out.

Then one evening as we prepared dinner, my husband flipped on the
news. The coroner was testifying. *Byrd's torso had been found in one place;
his head and an arm a mile beyond that, ripped from his body when it
slammed into a concrete drainage ditch; his dentures further still. Seventy-five
pieces of him and his belongings, discovered on June 7, 1998, strewn along two
miles of a Texas back road.*

Sorrow descended, smothering me with despair. Mute and shuf-
fling, I dragged from one day to the next. On the seventh day, without
warning, I got up and sat down at my computer. When I rose, "Jasper,
Texas Elegy" had left itself behind.

II. Jasper, Texas Elegy

I am awake in the middle of the night, exhausted by despair. Yesterday
I was rage. In the wee hours, I am sorrow. Mama is dead and the white
folks are still ripping us apart.

A bullet in Memphis. A bomb in Birmingham. Tom on the bench.
A jury beatdown in Simi Valley. Roped like a steer, chained to a truck,
riddled with history, I am decimated by collective amnesia, drowning
in race dialogue, daily dismembered by business as usual.

On the eve of fifty, coiled like a fetus, beneath a fortress of down and flannel, I am wailing. My terror is no longer nameless and free-floating. It is clear and present, a headless, one-armed carcass bleeding down the wall, sheets of skin sheared away from flesh: *James Byrd, Jr.*

Where are all the guns when you need just one?

At 8:30 A.M., I leave home, not because I want to, but because I have to. On my own, I would cuddle up to the carcass in the corner and, with all deliberate speed, keep going crazy. But a grown woman has responsibilities, so I find something to wear that is big enough to cover my gut, ballooned by grief.

I arrive at school fifteen minutes late for my tutoring session with Cameron.* Today, while he works on reading and spelling, I struggle with comprehension.

As he feeds his pencil stub to the sharpener, I shift in my tiny chair and breathe in Mrs. Wallace's second-grade classroom in Dallas, Texas. Words and pictures cover the walls. Centuries of chalk dust float sideways through the air. Books comfort and reassure. Many years gone, I am back where I started, where everyone is black like me. We are safe.

Mrs. Wallace stands in the doorway, instructing classmates returning from a trip to the water fountain. "Come into the room quietly and drop everything and read." Beneath her calm, singsong voice, my stomach mysteriously flattens.

Cameron taps me on the shoulder and points to the schedule that we created nearly two months ago. In his meticulous script, he has written: Book time–9-9:15 A.M.; Spelling—9:15–9:30 A.M.; Drawing—9:30–9:45 A.M.; Read *Tyrone the Horrible*—9:45–10:00 A.M.; Treats—10 A.M.

A revolutionary lineup for one so small, so brown, so fragile. How long would he last, tied to the back of a pickup truck and dragged—bump, bump, bumpity bump—two miles down a country road?

We are two-thirds of the way through a spelling test when Cameron sprawls across his desk. We've hit a new word and because I have forbidden him to write each letter in perforation with the speed of molasses, he uses another stalling tactic.

Suddenly, he leans back in his chair and, with his eyes closed, says, "I think you are an old lady." He opens his eyes to see how he's doing.

---

*Not the student's or teacher's real names.

"Boy," I say, "you need to sit up in that chair and spell 'Jamaica.'"

"And I think," he continues, studying my face and ignoring half of my instructions, "that you will be very old in two days." Now he looks genuinely concerned.

I am stunned at his prescience. Since he has not yet learned the importance of lying to a woman about her looks, I know he's telling the truth. The grief that left home in my belly has crept up to my face. My throat won't work. Tears I should be swallowing squirt out of other tight places.

"Cameron," I say evenly, "we're all getting older every day. That's how life works. Anyway, don't be rude. Just spell the word. Jamaica."

Sniffing a small victory, he eyes me a bit longer, then smiles. Turning back to his sheet of paper, he intones as he writes without hesitation, "Capital J-a-m-a-i-c-a. Jamaica!"

Prodding him with peppermints, we go well past one hour. He doesn't even notice that we have skipped drawing. After an hour and a half, though, he is squirming and wiping his eyes. Finally he drops his head to his desk and pretends to be asleep. Before we call it quits for the day, I dare him to spell Jamaica one more time to convince me the first time wasn't a trick.

He's mildly indignant at first, but then spells it fast with confidence and ends with a flourish, both arms stretched above his head, TV game show style.

Even after Cameron goes back to his regular seat at the front of the classroom, I linger in our corner in the back, protected by the books and chalk dust.

I review the vocabulary words he has mastered today. *Money . . . little . . . piece . . . pennies . . . powdered . . . worth . . . candies . . . taffeta . . . material . . . finished . . . month . . . dress . . . beautiful . . . only . . . wrote . . . shoes . . . church . . . Sunday school . . . wear . . . Jamaica.*

But a grown woman has responsibilities, and I can't hide out in Mrs. Wallace's refuge all day.

My car is warm from the bright morning sun, but when I shift into first gear and pull away from the curb, sorrow descends and I am spiraling down into the deep dark again.

As my head slides below the surface, a fluttering across the schoolyard draws my eye. A tiny boy flaps his arms and makes goofy faces, weaving from laughter.

Once upon a time in 1956, James Byrd, Jr., was in the second grade. In that same year, so was I.

III. Epilogue

If the four girls at Sixteenth Street Baptist Church in Birmingham, Alabama, had not been bombed to Kingdom Come in the fall of 1963, three of them—Addie Mae, Carole, and Cynthia—would now be fifty-two, just like me. If James Byrd, Jr., had not been reassembled in pieces in a grave in Jasper, Texas, in 1998, he would be fifty-two, just like me.

From what has been reported of the hardworking, Southern black families into which they were born, it is quite likely that the four girls would have turned out a lot like me: a highly decorated member of the African American elite, seemingly destined to run circles around the white folks in whose presence we are almost always the black Only, First, or Few.

One could argue that, as the gleaming beneficiary of the Civil Rights Movement, I have no right to complain. With that in mind, I offer one last observation.

When the U.S. Presidency was handed to George W. Bush, without lifting a finger, I was, in that moment, catapulted to yet one more pinnacle of achievement, albeit not one I sought: that of having seen more of the world, having chalked up more successes, being smarter and inarguably more articulate, than the president of the United States.

This president, mind you, who was raised by a father who is a multimillionaire ex-president of the United States, himself the son of a multimillionaire United States Senator. These are the kind of white men America reveres, the kind my mother, with her sixth grade formal education, raised me to stand up to, eye to eye, toe to toe. Thanks to her, I am, like the president and his fathers, entitled, powerful, and full of myself.

So what? *Now* what?

Nearly forty years ago, when I set out to become Everybody's Version of the Perfect Negro, no one could have convinced me that these many years later white folks would still suffer from the lunacy of racism, the schizophrenia that allows them to pretend that white skin makes no difference *and* makes them superior. No one could have convinced me that forty years would not be enough time for me to shake *their* race madness from *my* head.

Perched atop a precipice of privilege, flush with resources—money, time, access, and fluency in thinking and talking black and white—I have a choice each day: to stand still and remember, or to flee and forget.

I am still standing. And I remember with a vengeance.

Bernestine Singley *is a graduate of Double Oaks Elementary School, Irwin Avenue Junior High School, J. T. Williams Junior High School, West Charlotte Senior High School, Lawrence University, the University of Florida College of Law, and Harvard Law School. She has practiced law in Boston and Dallas and, for the past twelve years, has provided management consulting services to a wide range of clients through Straightalk, the Texas-based firm she owns. She is the editor of this anthology.*

© Debi Mazar

All Souls: Civil Rights from Southie to Soweto and Back[1]

Michael Patrick MacDonald

I RECENTLY VISITED Portadown, Northern Ireland, where, on the Garvaghy Road in the Catholic neighborhood, the kids have nicknamed their isolated housing project "Soweto." The British government had officially named the barren estate "Churchill Gardens." But the Catholic kids were too conscious of their own culture and living history to call anything of theirs after an English hero. So the local Catholic residents had replaced the "Churchill Gardens" street signs with one named after an Irish martyr to British imperialism during the 1980 Hunger Strikes. However, Catholics of all ages in "The North" share a keen awareness of their lower social status, being of Irish ethnicity within what Protestant Anglo supremacists would like to call Britain. That's why most Catholics on the Garvaghy Road just go with the nickname Soweto.

317

I grew up in South Boston's lower end, the poor Irish-American enclave of Boston. Coming from "Southie," and having lived through the American experience of successful conservative and liberal plans to racially divide poor people, I had never before met so many poor and working class whites, as on the Garvaghy Road, who knew what was up.

I lived in Southie's Old Colony Housing project, which was part of a larger area found in 1994 to have had the highest concentration of white poverty in America. Seventy-three percent of the homes there were single-parent, female-headed households. Eighty-five percent of my neighbors collected welfare. I was eight years old when Old Colony became the flash point for the explosive riots in the 1970s to protest "forced busing," or school desegregation, and witnessed violence by poor whites on poor blacks, and vice versa.

As a teenager, I rebelled against the bigotry of my neighborhood and its right-wing political leaders who manipulated the constant siege of my community by the left. I began to walk among progressives, and began to learn more about the class-based left-wing bigotry toward the "white trash" of my neighborhood, my family . . . me. So-called "progressive" whites always seemed to be from the middle-class and wealthy worlds so far from the housing projects where I grew up. My neighbors were always railing against the "liberals," but during our violent revolt against busing, rocks were aimed at poor black children on yellow buses.

In Southie we were proud to be Irish. We showed it by scrawling "I.R.A." and bright shamrock graffiti faded onto the bricks of Old Colony. We showed it with the Irish flags that waved from windows open all winter to let out the stifling, dry, project heat and the cockroach fumigation. And many in my neighborhood showed it by a violent obsession with not being black.

Many Irish Americans, who often want so desperately to be Irish, aren't aware of the international class consciousness of our brothers and sisters in Northern Ireland. Most in Southie didn't want to know. In this country we're just called "white." In this country's social paradigm, to be poor and oppressed was to be black. And we were willing to go along with that, no matter how blinding our fantasy of white status. Poor? Not us. Blue collar? Maybe. But not poor.

Nor were we poor to the white liberals who always targeted our housing projects as the bastion of white privilege in America.

Drugs and violence were also black problems, yet through the 1970s and '80s drugs, crime, and violence took four of my siblings and so many neighbors like them: all white, Irish Catholic kids. Southie shared some of the highest mortality rates in Boston with Roxbury, Boston's black neighborhood. In the end, we showed our Irishness in Southie by draping the caskets of our young dead with green, white, and gold flags, and with our own shrouds of denial.

The Garvaghy Road is reported to be a stifling place, a neighborhood besieged, in this case by the right-wing Orange Order, Northern Ireland's answer to the Ku Klux Klan.

As a peace observer on the Garvaghy Road last summer, I should have been suffocating along with the Catholic residents. The Orange Order, Anglo-supremacist Protestants wearing costumes of middle-class respectability—suits, gloves, black bowler hats, and bright orange sashes—were circling the Catholic housing projects. They were threatening to once again march down the Garvaghy Road on July 12, to celebrate the seventeenth-century victory of King William of Orange, and British dominion over the Irish race. The neighborhood's six thousand Irish Catholics were hemmed in by miles of barbed wire, "guarded" by hundreds of British troops carrying heavy artillery, and constantly hovered over by noisy British surveillance helicopters.

The Garvaghy Road residents had, in the past, staged nonviolent sit-ins on the road to block the march, only to be beaten off the road by British soldiers and by the 94 percent Protestant police force, the Royal Ulster Constabulary.

Now, security forces had erected a "ring of steel," which was supposedly for the protection of the Catholic community during the marching season. In fact, it intensified the feeling of being trapped in an oppressed ghetto.

I should have been suffocating in this environment, but I wasn't, not like when I was a kid growing up in Boston.

On the Garvaghy Road I felt like I could breathe more freely than I'd ever been able to, because in Northern Ireland, poor and working-class Irish Catholics know their place within the bigger picture of oppression across the globe. On the eve of July 12, I listened in amazement while Irish faces—faces so much like those in Southie—espoused solidarity with black South Africans. Northern Irish teenagers with tough Southie scowls, wearing the same Adidas jogging suits as the kids from my neighborhood, told me how Northern Ireland's Civil Rights Movement in the 1970s sought equal access to housing and jobs, and the right of Catholics to vote in their own country. It was modeled—speeches and all—after the American Civil Rights Movement.

The Orange Order burned bonfires in the distance, throwing effigies of Irish heroes and the Virgin Mary into the fire. Anthems of Anglo-Saxon supremacy played closer to the razor wire, and the Orangemen banged their marching drums with more ferocity, while I told the Garvaghy Road kids stories from my neighborhood.

I told them about the good things: the tight-knit "village" feel of Southie, the wit and humor of people despite their oppression, the beautiful beaches nearby. Then I told them about the isolation of the neighborhood, the poverty and oppression by the left and the right, the constant suicides, overdoses, and violence of my youth, and my own dead brothers.

They were intrigued by Southie's Irishness, and one of the kids—a fourteen-year-old—asked the obvious question.

"And do youse and the blacks team up and work together?" he asked in the excited lilt of a young Irish rebel.

I didn't know how to break it to him . . .

Then I took a deep breath of "Soweto" air, and just told the truth: "No."

---

[1] *Equal Opportunity Journal, National Urban League*, Summer 2000. Reprinted with permission.

Michael Patrick MacDonald, *thirty-five, is the author of* All Souls: A Family Story from Southie *(Beacon Press, 1999). Having lost four siblings to the ravages of poverty, street crime, and the drug trade, he has worked since 1990 as an activist in Boston, developing cross-cultural coali-*

tions with common ground consciousness, to reduce crime and violence and to promote leadership development in the most impacted communities, across race. He is cofounder of Boston's successful Gun Buyback program, and has formed grassroots support groups for adult and youth survivors of violence in Boston. MacDonald is currently working on the film version of All Souls *and writing a second book.*

© Simon Griffiths

Pictures in Black and White

Hanna Griffiths

I AM SHORT. I am skinny. I have long red hair and blue eyes. I have freckles. I have braces on my top teeth and no eyebrows. I don't look like most people in my school.

I am twelve years old and am a sixth grader at Samuel M. Inman Middle School on Virginia Avenue in Atlanta, Georgia.

At my old school, Morningside Elementary, I looked like just about everyone else. I felt safe there, as if I was protected.

On my first day at Inman, it was a big change, because I was used to almost everyone being white. But here, most people are African American. Mr. Doran, our principal, says we have a ratio of about 40 percent white to 60 percent black.

That first day we stuck in little clusters. All of the Morningside Elementary kids (mostly white) stuck together, and all of the Mary Lin Elementary kids (mostly black) stuck together, on opposite sides of the room. After that first day, all our teachers told us where to sit, so all of a sudden we were mixed together. That's when I started to make friends with Skyla. She sits next to me in language arts.

She's a lot lighter brown than the other black kids are. Skyla says she is three-fourths African American. Her grandmother is white. She acts just like a normal kid. She is really into sports. She likes to skateboard and she *hates* dresses. We're a lot alike, but I've never invited her to my house. She's never invited me to her house. I'd go if I was invited. I think there is some sort of invisible barrier with us.

The first week of school, we had a sixth-grade-only dance. They had a disc jockey who played Backstreet Boys, 'N Sync, blink-182, Christina Aguilera, and even some rap. That helped people get better acquainted. Some of the black boys asked some of the white girls to dance. No one asked me to dance.

We have half lockers at Inman. I have a bottom locker. An African American boy from my homeroom has the top locker. He's always polite when I see him, but I don't even know his name.

This spring break, the Challenge Program for gifted and talented Atlanta middle school students had a ten-day trip to London, Paris, Florence, and Rome. I got to go. The Atlanta Public School System paid for most of it. (Thank *you*, Atlanta taxpayers!) I had been to Europe once before. That was to England, where my father was born. On the day we left for our school trip, we all had to wear the same color, a red shirt. It was an ocean of red shirts. But out of about sixty kids, there were only nine white kids, and just three white girls.

One white girl came from a school across town. She was the only white person from her school who went. Her name was Samantha and she talked more like an African American than a white person. Samantha blended in well with the African American kids. She could really talk the street slang. I know she is smart because I had gone against her in a city-wide debate tournament. My partner and I won, but Samantha didn't seem to be sore about it. She helped me get to know some of the African American girls. She even invited me to come sit with her black friends from her school.

There was one other white girl from my school on the trip. Her name is Anna. She can recite the entire periodic table from memory. We don't look alike at all. Anna is a lot taller than I am. She wears glasses and has dark blonde hair. A lot of the people on the trip kept thinking that Anna and I were twins and they kept mixing up our names. (Who in their right mind would name their children Hanna and Anna, especially twins?) It started to get really annoying. Anna and I decided to make sure we didn't ever act like sisters. To most of the black people on the trip, I guess all us white people looked alike.

I play on a soccer team called the Blue Devils. Our home and practice field is near the Martin Luther King, Jr., Center, but there is only one black girl on the team. Her name is Shelly and she plays just about every position, except goalie. Shelly and I are friends. Like about half the girls on the team, Shelly goes to a private school. She talks like a white person and hardly ever uses street slang.

When we play other teams, it's exciting, because we like to kick butt. I have noticed that African American teams often play rougher and tougher, but this season we are undefeated. The Caucasian parents say thing like "Great goal!" "Way to go, Blue Devils!" "Go, Hanna!" "Go, Shelly!" They praise more. The African American parents are more competitive. They shout at their kids, like our coach does: "Get down there!" "Get to the goal!" "Why didn't you make that shot?" "You got a perfect shot at the goal!" "Cross the ball!" At the end of each game, the African American parents always make a tunnel through which their children run. My team's parents won't do that. I think they're too reserved.

Henry W. Grady High is the inner-city school I will go to after Inman. It has a cool communications magnet program, which could help me in lots of different jobs later. I go over to Grady now to see the girl's soccer team play. Even though Grady is about 75 percent black, the girl's soccer team is mostly white. Everybody—lots of different colors—came to watch and scream support at the last game of the season against a powerhouse private school. Grady was defeated in double overtime. I was disappointed they lost, but I learned it didn't matter what color you are, as long as you are rooting for the same thing.

I first found out I was white when I was about two and a half. I was in a preschool and my class was run by a black teacher named Ms. Willie Ann. She's still at the preschool and I get to see her some of the time. Ms. Willie Ann helped us understand that all people are equal.

I have red hair, freckles, and white skin, and she has brown-black hair, freckles, and brown skin, but it makes no difference what our shells look like.

Hanna Griffiths is a twelve-year-old honors student who attends public school and plays soccer in Atlanta, Georgia. She is Richard's and Debbie's daughter and Ian's big sister.

© Bernestine Singley

Epilogue

DERRICK BELL

THE ESSAYS IN this volume run the gamut from heartfelt to soul wrenching. For me, after more than forty years of work in every aspect of the struggle against racism, they reinforce my decades-tardy realization that racism in all its myriad manifestations is beyond the power of law or the desire of most of our citizenry to reform.

This admission comes hard, for, like most civil rights advocates, I found little fault with the philosophical underpinnings of Gunnar Myrdal's massive midcentury study *An American Dilemma.* Myrdal argued that racism was merely an odious holdover from slavery, "a terrible and inexplicable anomaly stuck in the middle of our liberal democratic ethos."[1] While we did not think it would be easy or quick, no liberal worthy of the credential doubted that standard American policy making was adequate to the task of abolishing racism. White America, we assumed, *wanted* to abolish racism.

We were wrong.

In the United States, where property is a measure of worth, many whites with relatively little or no property of a traditional kind—money, securities, land—cling to their whiteness as a kind of property. They are reinforced in this by the law, which recognizes and protects this property right based on color the same way it recognizes and protects any other property. Professor Cheryl Harris clearly explains how it works when whiteness is valued "as treasured property . . . in a society structured on racial caste."

"In ways so embedded that it is rarely apparent," she instructs, "the set of assumptions, privileges, and benefits that accompany the status of being white have become a valuable asset that whites sought to protect. . . . Whites have come to expect and rely on these benefits, and over time these expectations have been affirmed, legitimated, and protected in law."[2]

This political advantage over blacks, though, requires that whites not identify with blacks even on matters that transcend skin color. To give continued meaning to their whiteness, poor and working-class whites identify with whites at the top of the economic pile, not with blacks with whom—save color—they have so much in common. This is why racism seems to be something that cannot be overcome and may continue to be a permanent part of the American social structure.

Many years before I developed this critique of racism in America, an old black guy responded to one of my public lectures with the shouted warning: "Professor, black folk can't get free until white folks get smart." His remark evoked some nervous laughter, and when I responded that "I would not hold my breath while waiting for their enlightenment," there was more.

Well, the good news is that there are now a host of writers and a growing number of courses and workshops designed to enlighten white people as to the real benefits and the great cost of their property in whiteness. It is a Herculean task that in substantial part is being undertaken by knowledgeable whites, including those who have shared their stories in the preceding pages.

Leonard Pitts, Jr., is right in suggesting that "Black people spend way too much time talking about race. And white people don't spend nearly enough." Far too much of race discussion focuses on blacks and the pros and cons of affirmative action, criminality, welfare dependence, and racial reparations. Many whites do not deem themselves a race but simply "normal."

It has been long in coming, but perhaps the threshold revelation is at hand. As Beverly Daniel Tatum explains in her chapter here, "Choosing to Be Black: The Ultimate White Privilege?" being white has a "racial privilege that comes with it, whether [you] want it or not." Noel Ignatiev, who suggests he coined the term *white skin privilege* more than thirty years ago, takes things a step further. He advocates that for real change in race relations to occur in American society, people who have been "brought up as white" must learn to "become unwhite."

To be sure, to get beyond race as a basis of status, the nation's whites at every level will have to wrestle with this question of whiteness. Because if blackness is not a racial code word for subordinate status, what does it really mean to be white, not as a matter of appropriate respect and pride in cultural heritage, but as a social and economic fact of life in these United States?

The old guy at my public lecture was right. Black people have been waiting a long time for whites to get enlightened about race, and although we have not been passive, even our best efforts too often translate into more property for whites and more promises for blacks. Ignatiev and Tatum point a new way for whites to speed up their own efforts to educate themselves.

In the meantime, though, we have no choice but to continue to aggressively challenge assertions of property rights based on whiteness. Indeed, resistance must remain a top priority. It is too dangerous for us to simply stand by, for in doing so, we miss the essential ingredient in the whiteness property phenomenon: it is our recognition and acceptance of white skin color as property that gives that whiteness its legitimacy. No property has value unless others recognize it, abide by its boundaries, and refrain from trespassing across its fences. Ask the American Indian.

American Indians were here first. They occupied the land, and, by long usage, it was theirs. European settlers simply refused to honor those property rights, making the lesson clear: property ownership is worthless when others refuse to respect it. We should heed the lesson, for only when we refuse to acquiesce, individually and as a group, will the property right in whiteness cease to exist.

Yes, I recognize that the property rights of American Indians were violated with guns and violent force. I recognize as well that black people do not possess great firepower. What we have is, in fact, a greater power: the power of ourselves. It is a power that comes with the recognition that our salvation—not in Heaven, but here on earth—is in our refusal to accept whiteness as a property right that trumps our entitlement to racial equality; and in our determination to no longer sacrifice our self-worth, the essence of ourselves, on the altar of whiteness. As Julianne Malveaux reminds us, "the [race card] is trumped sometimes, maybe most of the time. Not every time." When is up to us.

Forty years after Myrdal's analysis in *The New American Dilemma*, Professor Jennifer Hochschild examined what she called his "anomaly thesis" and concluded that it simply cannot explain the persistence of racial discrimination. Rather, Hochschild counters, racism is not a sore on an otherwise "fundamentally healthy liberal democratic body, but is part of what shapes and energizes the body."

Now, nearly two decades later, it is more rather than less obvious that Hochschild was right in concluding that "liberal democracy and racism in the United States are historically, even inherently, reinforcing; American society as we know it exists only because of its foundation in racially based slavery, and it thrives only because racial discrimination continues. The apparent anomaly is an actual symbiosis."[3]

And so it is that racism, which is far more complex than blatant bigotry, helps untangle the paradox of a nation built on a free market economy and its supposed antithesis, popular democracy.[4] By its very nature, capitalism enables the powerful, wealthy few to become richer and more powerful by exploiting the labor of the masses. Theoretically, in a democracy, the masses would be able to constantly challenge the wealthy and powerful by fomenting unrest and threatening revolt.

We know, of course, that this does not happen, at least not for any sustained period. Potential conflict has been more or less successfully negotiated throughout the developed world. The United States, where markets and democracy have coexisted for two hundred years, is a good example; here and elsewhere, market economies have made some material redistribution, though largely as an accommodation, primarily to stave off the demands of the less well off.

Yet, despite its status as the richest nation the world has ever known, the gap in income and wealth is greater in the United States than in most other developed nations. The reason? Social reform efforts here are easily derailed when opponents link their opposition to race, suggesting that such programs in education, housing, welfare, medical care, and drug and prison policy will help mainly undeserving blacks.

Thus, while the persons who suffer most from social neglect in America are disproportionately black, there are millions of poor, working-class, and even middle-class whites who suffer as well. By tying race to neglect, however, policy makers are able to rationalize doing little or nothing.

Restraints and restrictions on voting are another set of factors that hamstring popular democracy as a theoretical challenge to a free enterprise economy in this country. Only a few Americans were allowed to vote in the early stages of our nation's history, and even after all white males were entitled to vote, other obstacles—poll taxes, exclusion of paupers, etc.—greatly restricted the vote. Women could not vote at all until early in the twentieth century.

Despite the reforms led by civil rights advocates, the rhetoric of "one person, one vote" is undermined by powerful economic interests. Exerting disproportionate political influence, these wealthy interests are able to capture the state and federal election apparatus and use it to their advantage.

Particularly in the South, the tactics used to deny the vote to blacks have often reduced the voting power of whites as well. The Florida "chad" controversy during the 2000 presidential election is an excellent case in point. Additionally, the impact of wealth on campaigns and those who are elected is tremendous even by conservative estimates. Both the Clinton and Bush administrations prove how influential wealth is on both sides of the aisle.

I do not deny the power of the deeply held belief in upward mobility, holding that anyone, high or low, can move up the economic ladder as long as he or she is talented, hardworking, entrepreneurial, and not too unlucky. The Horatio Alger myth leads many to support policies unquestionably favoring the rich and disadvantaging the poor on the basis of "I might get rich one of these days."

In the meantime, consumerism aided by credit card debt makes it possible to acquire more things to satisfy needs that, ironically, those things cannot satisfy. Buying things as a substitute for owning real economic and political power literally consumes blacks as well as whites. Any spark of protest, once saddled with staggering debt, is extinguished before it gets started.

Undoubtedly, though, it is the ideology of racism throughout history that has convinced large numbers of less-well-off whites, in suicidal defiance of their rational economic self-interest, to identify and support whites at the top of the economic heap. Regardless of the costs to themselves, poor and working-class whites feel better about their relative plight as long as blacks remain on the bottom of society's totem pole. That is where they find their consoling sense of superiority and status vis-à-vis African Americans, Hispanic Americans, and other people of color.

How long would we search to find, for instance, the American equivalent of the impoverished Irish Catholic boys Michael Patrick MacDonald met in Northern Ireland and to whom he introduced us in his essay, "All Souls: Civil Rights from Southie to Soweto and Back"? The ones who not only identify with but also openly embrace solidarity with black South Africans *and the American Civil Rights Movement*? We would be looking for a very long time, perhaps forever.

Racism is a major reason there has never been a powerful working-class political party in the United States. Racism stymies the formation of political alliances between poor and working-class whites on the one hand and poor and working-class minorities on the other.

Poor whites supported slavery even though they were unable themselves to afford slaves and even though slavery relegated them to permanent lower-class status. It was their cherished identification with white elites that convinced poor whites to see things this way.

Slavery ended, but by then the status of "white," enhanced by the enactment of segregation laws, continued as a substitute for genuine economic well being. Racism soon became a major facilitator of the acculturation and assimilation of European immigrants during the late nineteenth and early twentieth centuries. Horribly exploited by the mine and factory owners for whom they toiled long hours under brutal conditions for subsistence wages, the shared feeling of superiority to blacks was one of the few things that united impoverished immigrants. The blackface and racially derogatory minstrel shows of that period helped immigrants acculturate and assimilate by inculcating a nationalism whose common theme was the disparagement and disadvantaging of blacks. It ensured that there would be no uniting across racial lines to resist the exploitation and deprivation that, then as now, does not respect any color line.

A blatantly racist history provides a template for current policies that are more subtle but hardly less pernicious. The ideology of whiteness continues to oppress whites as well as blacks. It is employed to make whites settle for despair in politics and anguish in the daily grind of life. Somehow, they link the fact that a majority of America's population is white and that most power is held by whites with a sense that, as whites, they are privileged and entitled to preference over people of color.

The students who broke the back of racial segregation when they risked humiliation and physical violence with their sit-ins and other nonviolent protests were manifesting the power of protecting self-worth in a righteous cause. The potential in the power that ended state-supported segregation is still there. It is up to us to unearth it.

It is understandably hard to remember given the ongoing onslaught of accusations about our shortcomings. Yet, despite the hostility to our presence we endure, the insensitivity to our pain we abide, and the inner rage we deflect—all too often onto ourselves—one thing remains true: we are worthy and the power we possess is ours to use.

If we challenge the property rights in whiteness—the very essence of racism—as our forebears challenged first slavery and then segregation, we, like they, can overcome the racial restraints of our time.

——————

[1] Gunnar Myrdal, *An American Dilemma.* Transaction Publishers (1944)."

[2] Cheryl Harris, "Whiteness as Property": *Harvard Law Review*, 106 (1993): 1707, 1713.

[3] Jennifer Hochschild, *The New American Dilemma* (Yale University Press, 1984), 5, 203.

[4] Amy L. Chua, "The Paradox of Free Market Democracy: Rethinking Development Policy": *Harv. Int'l L.J.*, 41 (2000): 287.

Derrick Bell *is a compelling voice on issues of race and class in this society. Throughout his forty-year career as a lawyer, activist, teacher, and writer, he has provoked his critics and challenged his readers with his uncompromising candor and original progressive views.*

Currently a visiting professor at New York University Law School, where he has taught since 1991, Bell is best known as the first tenured black professor at Harvard Law School, a position he gained in 1971 and relinquished in 1992 when he refused to return from a two-year unpaid leave of absence he took to protest the absence of women of color on the faculty.

Professor Bell is not a newcomer to personal protests of this character. In 1980, he left Harvard for five years to become dean of the University of Oregon Law School. He left that post in protest when the Oregon faculty refused to offer a faculty position to an Asian American woman candidate.

Bell has served as executive director of the Western Center on Law and Poverty at the University of Southern California Law School, counsel for the NAACP Legal Defense Fund, and deputy director of the Office for Civil Rights in the Department of Health, Education and Welfare.

Bell's books include Race, Racism, and American Law, *published initially in 1973, and now in its fourth edition (Aspen Publishers, 2000);* Constitutional Conflicts *(Anderson, 1997), a text intended for basic constitutional law courses; and an autobiographical work,* Confronting Authority: Reflections of an Ardent Protester *(Beacon Press, 1996), and his articles have been published in professional journals, national magazines, and newspapers.*

He is best known for the series of allegorical stories featuring his fictional heroine, Geneva Crenshaw, who appears in And We Are Not Saved *(Basic Books, 1989);* Faces at the Bottom of the Well: The Permanence of Racism *(Basic Books, 1993); and, most recently,* Afrolantica Legacies *(Third World Press, 1998).*